THE U.S. DEFENSE MOBILIZATION INFRASTRUCTURE: Problems and Priorities

Edited by
Robert L. Pfaltzgraff, Jr.
Uri Ra'anan

International Security Studies
Program The Fletcher School of
Law and Diplomacy,
Tufts University

ARCHON BOOKS
1983

© 1983 The Fletcher School of Law and Diplomacy,
Tufts University, Medford, Massachusetts 02155
All rights reserved
First published in 1983 as an Archon Book,
an imprint of The Shoe String Press, Inc.,
Hamden, Connecticut 06514
Printed in the United States of America

Library of Congress Cataloging in Publication Data

Main entry under title:

The U.S. defense mobilization infrastructure

Includes bibliographical references and index.
1. United States—Armed Forces—Mobilization—
Addresses, essays, lectures. 2. Industrial mobiliza-
tion—United States—Addresses, essays, lectures.
I. Pfaltzgraff, Robert L. II. Ra'anan, Uri.
UA913.U18   1982   355.2'8'0973   82-16381
ISBN 0-208-01984-7

THE U.S. DEFENSE MOBILIZATION INFRASTRUCTURE

Contents

About the Authors and Editors   7
Preface   9

SECTION I — What Kind of Mobilization for What Type of Conflict? (Under Attack or Protracted Twilight Conflict)

1. Mobilization in a Grand-Strategy Perspective   *William P. Wadbrook*   13
2. Mobilization for High-Level Conflict: Policy Issues   *Colin S. Gray*   33

SECTION II — Assessment of the United States Industrial and Manpower Infrastructure

3. Peacetime Industrial Preparedness for Wartime Ammunition Production (Past, Present and Future)   *Harry F. Ennis*   53
4. Strategic Assessment of National Military Mobilization in the 1980s—Manpower   *H. Rowland Ludden*   66
5. Military Recruitment and Personnel Retention—Agenda for the 1980s   *Curtis W. Tarr*   80
6. Surge Mobilization: Ground Forces   *Norman Friedman*   91
7. Civil Reserve Air Fleet   *Ralph P. Novak*   104
8. RX: The Industrial Preparedness Planning Program—Bad Medicine or Poorly Administered?   *John C. McLaurin*   112

SECTION III — The Lead-Time Required for Upgrading the Mobilization Base

9. Obsolescence, Declining Productivity, and the American Defense Mobilization Infrastructure   *Leon S. Reed*   127
10. The Mobilization Aspect of the Soviet Economy as a Factor in Preparedness for War   *Michael Checinski*   143
11. Construction Support for Mobilization: A Pacing Issue   *Edward G. Rapp*   158

SECTION IV — Current Vulnerabilities and Mobilization within the Wider Free World Context

12. Strategic and Critical Materials   *Alton D. Slay*   181

13. Oil and Western Security: The Mobilization Dilemma
    David A. Deese 189
14. C³—Damaged, Intercepted or Blocked *Lee M. Paschall* 204

SECTION V — Mobilization: Assets and Liabilities
of Interdependence

15. NATO's Nonexistent Industrial Mobilization Capability:
    Its Impact on America's Ailing Defense Industrial Base
    Thomas A. Callaghan, Jr. 219
16. The Alliance Framework: East Asia *Leonard Unger* 236

SECTION VI — Priorities for United States Mobilization

17. Mobilization Preparedness: Lessons from the Recent Past
    William K. Brehm 253
18. Government and Industry: Some Priorities for Mobilization
    E. F. Andrews 262
19. An Agenda for U.S. Mobilization Policy *Robert L.
    Pfaltzgraff, Jr.* 270

Index 289

About the Authors and Editors

1. Dr. William P. Wadbrook is International Economist in the Mobilization Plans Office of the Federal Emergency Management Agency in Washington, D.C.
2. Dr. Colin S. Gray, former Director of National Security Studies at the Hudson Institute, is President of the National Institute for Public Policy in McLean, Virginia.
3. Colonel Harry F. Ennis, USA, is former Senior Research Fellow at the National Defense University in Washington, D.C. His present assignment is Chief of Technology, Ballistic Missile Defense Program Office, Washington, D.C.
4. Dr. H. Rowland Ludden is Chief of the Mobilization Division of the Office of the Deputy Chief of Staff for Personnel of the Department of the Army.
5. Dr. Curtis W. Tarr is former Under Secretary of State for Security Assistance and Acting Deputy Under Secretary for Management; former Director of Selective Service; and former Assistant Secretary of the Air Force, Manpower and Reserve Affairs. He is now Vice-President, Management Development, of Deere & Company, Moline, Illinois.
6. Dr. Norman Friedman is on the Senior Professional Staff of the Hudson Institute.
7. LTC Ralph P. Novak, USAF, was Air Force Research Associate to the International Security Studies Program in 1980–1981. His present assignment is in the Office of the Assistant Secretary of Defense, International Security Affairs, Inter-American Region.
8. Captain John C. McLaurin, USN, has a background in patrol aviation and has been a Senior Research Fellow at the National Defense University. His present assignment is to the Navy's Long Range Planning Group.
9. Mr. Leon S. Reed is an Analyst with The Analytic Sciences Corporation (TASC). He was formerly associated with the Joint Committee on Defense Production, United States Congress, where he was responsible for defense industrial base legislation and studies.
10. Dr. Michael Checinski is Research Associate at the Russian Research Center of Harvard University, Rand Consultant, and Research Fellow of Stiftung Wissenschaft und Politik, Institute of

International Affairs, Ebenhausen, West Germany.
11. Colonel Edward G. Rapp, USA, is Special Assistant for Mobilization in the Office of the Chief of Engineers, Department of the Army.
12. General Alton D. Slay, USAF (Ret.) is former Commander, Air Force Systems Command, Andrews Air Force Base. He is President of Slay Enterprises, Inc., in Washington, D.C.
13. Dr. David A. Deese received his Ph.D. degree from The Fletcher School of Law and Diplomacy in November, 1977. He is Assistant Professor in the Department of Political Science at Boston College, Research Associate at the Kennedy School of Government of Harvard University, and Visiting Research Scientist at the Energy Laboratory at the Massachusetts Institute of Technology.
14. General Lee M. Paschall, USAF (Ret.) is former Director, Defense Communications Agency, Washington, D.C., and is President and Chief Executive Officer of the American Satellite Company.
15. Dr. Thomas A. Callaghan, Jr., is associated with the Center for Strategic and International Studies, Georgetown University, and President of Ex-Im Tech, Inc.
16. Professor Leonard Unger is a former United States Ambassador and is Professor of Diplomacy at The Fletcher School of Law and Diplomacy.
17. Mr. William K. Brehm is a former Assistant Secretary of Defense and also a former Assistant Secretary of the Army. He is now the Chairman of the Board, Systems Research and Applications Corporation, Arlington, Virginia.
18. Mr. E. F. Andrews is former National President of the National Association of Purchasing Management, former Chairman of the Critical Material Committee of the American Iron and Steel Institute. He is now Vice President for Materials and Services, Allegheny International, Pittsburgh, Pennsylvania.

Dr. Robert L. Pfaltzgraff, Jr., is Professor of International Politics at The Fletcher School of Law and Diplomacy, and President of the Institute for Foreign Policy Analysis in Cambridge, Massachusetts and Washington, D.C.

Professor Uri Ra'anan is Professor of International Politics and Chairman of the International Security Studies Program at The Fletcher School of Law and Diplomacy.

Preface

Among the national security issues confronting the United States in the 1980s is the adequacy of its industrial infrastructure in light of existing and planned programs of defense. Closely related is the question of the availability of needed human resources as part of our defense mobilization capability. The present volume represents an outgrowth of the Tenth Annual Conference of the International Security Studies Program of The Fletcher School of Law and Diplomacy, Tufts University. As in the case of preceding conferences, the purpose of this meeting was to provide a forum for discussion among persons representing diverse perspectives. The participants in this conference included representatives of the academic-policy community, the armed services, the United States Government and the corporate community. It was particularly fortuitous that the Industrial College of the Armed Forces at Fort McNair was engaged in a parallel examination of problems confronting the United States in its industrial mobilization capabilities. The organizers of the Tenth Annual Conference of the International Security Studies Program drew upon expertise available as a result of the work of the Industrial College of the Armed Forces. It was possible also to benefit from a variety of other ongoing studies addressed to issues of direct importance to defense mobilization in the United States. These included problems of access to, and the stockpiling of, vitally important energy and nonfuel minerals; the development of adequate and secure command, control and communications; and the development of the necessary means for the transport of various types of military capabilities.

This volume contains chapters designed both to assess alternative mobilization needs in light of historic experience and to take account of alternative hypothesized future conflicts. An effort is made to examine in depth the important issues of military recruitment and personnel retention. Although the principal focus of the volume is the U.S. mobilization base, the several contributors examine such issues in a broader global context. The Soviet mobilization base is compared and contrasted with that of the United States. The question of an extended mobilization base, including especially allies in Western Europe and the Western Pacific, is examined. Other chapters consider the pressing problems associated with the lead time both for the upgrading of the mobilization base itself and for the production of new capabilities. A final chapter offers a substantive agenda for U.S. mobilization policy.

In the preparation of this volume, the editors wish to express thanks to the Program's Administrative Assistant, Charlotte C. Wise, for her contribution as well as for her organization of the conference itself, and to Captain John Midgley for his help in the editorial work.

> Robert L. Pfaltzgraff, Jr.
> Uri Ra'anan
>
> July, 1982
> Medford, Massachusetts

Section I

What Kind of Mobilization
for What Type of Conflict?
(Under Attack or Protracted Twilight Conflict)

1

Mobilization in a Grand-Strategy Perspective

William P. Wadbrook

The Strategic Problem of Mobilization

Studies of mobilization resources availabilities, and of mobilization procedural adequacy, have enjoyed noticeably increased prominence of late. Less wholeheartedly addressed, however, has been the great question of what is to be accomplished strategically with the whole mobilization concept. The answer to this question, of course, radically affects all resource and procedure calculations.

In trying to evaluate the place of mobilization within the overall strategic stance of the United States, we face a vast network of hypothetical causations and feedbacks on many planes. In such a maze, both analyses and their conclusions seem entirely subject to the choice of which issues are stressed. Truly relevant data is also extremely scarce. Yet even such difficulties cannot justify postponing an examination of the central issue of mobilization—its place in U.S. defense policy and purpose. Let us therefore try to trace and prune the branches of a mobilization decision tree, in order to identify and weigh the strategic postures and contingencies that would make mobilization both feasible and relevant. Until this teleological effort is made, detailed questions of resources, capacities and procedures must be left almost entirely aside.

For these purposes, mobilization should initially be defined broadly, to encompass all contingency-driven resource reallocations. Within this wide field, however, the main issue areas surely concern politicomilitary hostilities rather than, say, economic or natural contingencies. Dual-use mobilization-preparedness measures only make real sense if such measures for politico-military contingencies can be independently justified. Furthermore, our analytical focus must be on resource reallocations that go well beyond simple redeployments of existing military forces. Thus, concern centers on nonmilitary resource reallocations for essentially military contingencies.

Within the mobilization field thus circumscribed, however, the core issues are narrower still, being conditioned by the scope and speed of the reallocations. This mobilization "tempo" determines the time-profiles both of what is needed and of what becomes available; that is, it determines the entire shape and nature of the effort. Give us fifty years, indeed, and we will accomplish almost anything you care to specify—but we will not call this exercise "mobilization."

Mobilization, then, is here visualized as the swift, broad, real time reallocation of nonmilitary resources to meet a politico-military challenge. National mobilization policy therefore in practice consists of pre-crisis measures to improve the tempo of such crisis-period reallocations, whether or not these preparedness measures can also serve other purposes. Until this kind of policy is adequately justified at the strategic level, questions of detail (i.e., questions of ways and means) are premature and in fact worse than useless.

Mobilization has here been visualized as resource reallocations provoked by, and designed to meet, politico-military contingencies. In what immediately follows, we will consider what is implicit in "meeting" a contingency, what contingencies are most relevant, and what basic elements contribute most to the tempo by which such contingencies are met. Mobilization preparedness would then correctly consist of taking advance measures to improve the critical elements of mobilization tempo.

Three general types of response to a politico-military contingency are conceivable: doing just enough to restore the status quo ante; consciously attempting to over-respond (in hopes, for example, of building up a "legacy" of postcrisis military dominance); or consciously attempting to do less than enough (i.e., to make a demonstration only). Of these three response modes, clearly the ability to do enough to meet and neutralize any relevant threat is the minimum critical threshold, below which it is not worthwhile to operate. Consciously doing too little, as a demonstration or deterrent, can be effective only if the requisite follow-through capability is also visible and in place. And this follow-through capability must be present for essentially all relevant contingencies, if only because one class of contingency can modulate into another, so that it is impossible to determine in real time what the ultimate nature of any given crisis will be.

In general, therefore, the minimum worthwhile in-place mobilization capability is the ability to do enough to reverse any relevant contingency. The strategic issues of mobilization policy thus seem to center on the ability to meet any relevant politico-military contingency. What are these contingencies, in which nonmilitary resource reallocation has a feasible and effective role?

Grand-Strategy Perspective

A large class of contingencies can be called "non-central." They do not involve the most vital national interests, and they do not require an immediate response paced exactly to the adversary's tempo of escalation. Such a crisis can degenerate into a central contingency only if the chips committed or threatened on either side begin to exceed that which is strictly nonvital. Almost by definition, therefore, a noncentral contingency would afford the United States time for an adequate mobilization, no matter what the pre-existing baseline of preparedness. To deter any degeneration to a central threat, of course, a central-contingency mobilization capability must be available throughout.

A noncentral challenge, in other words, is to be deterred and contained, not by an in-place mobilization capability tailored to the noncentral threat itself, but by an overarching ability to handle any relevant central contingency. A mobilization capability limited to the noncentral level would be both costly in peacetime and inadequate in hostilities: it thus falls well below the minimum needed effort. Neither is it economically worthwhile to maintain such an elaborately prepared, in-place, noncentral mobilization capability by itself; the net extra cost of crash mobilizations during minor crises is more than repaid by the manifold economic advantages of not maintaining a semiwartime stance in time of peace.

Among the possible central contingencies, the most meaningful analytical breakdown for our purposes is into short and long crises. A short crisis does not, by its nature, permit extensive nonmilitary resource reallocations. Even manpower mobilization would have negligible direct effect on a military crisis of under, say, four months. Industrial mobilization would have no impact for much longer periods.

The notion of a short politico-military crisis suggests the possible use of nuclear weapons. It seems to be the present consensus that a nuclear exchange at the tactical level would be both militarily and politically disadvantageous to the West, given our defensive posture and our vast transoceanic supply lines. This is not the sort of problem that a mobilization capability, as visualized here, can alleviate.

A strategic nuclear exchange, on the other hand, would seem to make both civil-defense mobilization and strategic-force mobilization relevant. It would not be hard to improve our virtually nonexistent civil-defense arrangements, but it would be difficult indeed, given our social-economic-political structure, to make our civil-defense capability even approximately adequate to the threat. Until technology or social psychology can show us a realistic way of achieving the minimum critical capability in this area, the present "do nothing" posture may be the most rational.

Strategic-force mobilization, on the other hand, whether offensive or defensive, seems almost a contradiction in terms, given the very great preponderance of long lead time elements in such systems. In terms of marginal cost, too, it would seem that any strategic system that is available for mobilization ought also to be consistently operational in full readiness state. The capital-intensity of strategic systems makes their "mobilization" almost entirely a matter of simple redeployment.

But even if a degree of civil-defense and strategic-force mobilization is possible, the overall meaning of nuclear war, for the West at least, is mutual cultural suicide. The threat to commit suicide, whether or not we expect to take the adversary with us, is not an ideal strategic posture. This consideration, too, makes mobilization preparedness for a short nuclear contingency seem unrealistic. Whether nuclear or not, then, a short crisis affords almost no real scope for mobilization as here conceptualized.

It is a protracted central crisis alone, therefore, that makes mobilization truly relevant. This is also the contingency for which the present Administration appears to base its planning. Among the protracted-crisis contingencies, the most favorable for U.S. mobilization might be one in which political tensions remained high for months (or rather, for years), without precipitating actual armed conflict. What is not at all clear in such a scenario, of course, is why the adversary would persist in rousing and exercising the United States in the very field in which he has most reason to fear it, and then sit back without follow-through, to watch it rearm. After his notorious sacrifices in many other fields of competition, the adversary is not now likely to permit the United States to surpass him militarily as well. Perhaps we are here dreaming the classic American preparedness dream of a Pearl Harbor; i.e., of an optimally scaled, optimally timed catastrophe. We are likely to be handed neither such a pat catastrophe, nor a deep but slow (and essentially deceptive) crisis.

If we insist upon a replay of the World War I and World War II mobilization tempos, however, we might consider the ploy of trading space (territory) for time. But an extrapolation of the experience of two World Wars is, after all, discouraging on this score as well: a third "Blitzkrieg" in Europe would probably have its high water mark, not at the Marne River or at the English Channel, but at the Atlantic Coast. The situation is surely no better in other regions of the world.

It is hardly sagacious to begin planning on the assumption that important territory will have to be abandoned in order to gain time for mobilization. Alone, the abandonment of territory would not gain enough time: a fighting abandonment is needed. Such a policy will hardly be supported in Europe, either in the retreat stage or in the recovery stage. To reduce Europe to a glacis is to lose Europe politically, without a fight. Nor is it even certain today that the American people themselves have the fiber to sacrifice for mobilization in the face of a discouraging series of latter-day Dunkirks, Norways, and Malayas.

A possible variant of the space-for-time strategy involves the reorientation of U.S. strategic emphasis away from Europe and toward, say, Latin America. A new "NATO" could be created, based on the resources and industry of Brazil, Mexico, and the several other burgeoning economies of Central and South America. Once again (and all other considerations aside), this amounts to a strategic write-off of Europe—this time an overt one.

If both of these "loss of Europe" variants contain absurdities, it seems at least equally absurd to plan on abandoning (with or without a fight) any non-European territory that could be considered to be a central interest of the United States. Non-European central interests are apt to be those that relate to the resource import dependency of the U.S. economy. The only remaining possibility for a protracted conflict over vital interests, then, is literally to struggle for a long time on the vital territory itself; that is, to stabilize the military operations somewhere in, say, Europe or Eastern Europe, and then to mobilize resources to support this stabilized battle-line.

This investigation has, thus far, focused on the tempo of nonmilitary resource reallocation to meet, stabilize and reverse, ultimately, a protracted central politico-military threat. All other forms of "mobilization" have been discarded as irrelevant, or infeasible, or mere verbal confusions (such as confounding redeployment with mobilization).

The Triad of Mobilization Tempo

What are the chief ingredients of a successful stabilization cum mobilization strategy? They seem to fall under the headings of timely reaction to warning, holding out with in-being forces, and gearing up the allocated mobilization effort proper. Let us place each of these elements in its grand-strategy environment, and consider its contribution to mobilization tempo.

WARNING AND RESPONSE

Mobilization tempo is fundamentally affected by perceptions of, and reactions to, warning. Due to the progressive deterioration of the world military balance, strategic warning today relies more and more on the assessment of intentions, rather than of capabilities. It is thus a harder signal to acquire convincingly, especially where both sides may simply be stumbling into hostilities. Let us here assume the "best case," viz., that a warning signal does objectively exist, that the signal-gathering apparatus has not been desensitized by well-known politico-bureaucratic processes, and that the signal is a politically avowable one, publicly usable to galvanize action.

In the crepuscular atmosphere of peacetime, what will be the reaction to such a signal? Speculating on this question involves looking at the historical record and at the underlying social, economic and political system of the West. To paraphrase a remark of Norman Friedman, the state of a nation's institutions is a measure of its mobilization capacity. Let us consider some aspects of these institutions in the United States within the context of the best-case mobilization contingency, a slowly building crisis.

Western societies include commercial power centers which thrive on their adaptiveness. Any strong thrust applied from without to such a decentralized system tends to become self-amplifying through the adaptive reactions of the commercial competitors. Thus the very threat signal that calls forth government mobilization-preparedness policies is at the same time also calling forth commercial adaptive strategies, which eventually create long-horizoned business commitments fully conformed to the threat environment and prepared to profit by it. For example, the same apparent Soviet growth crunch that seems ominously destabilizing to many students of geopolitics is also a source of lucrative private sales opportunities.

Such vested commercial interests may, through their channels of influence, discourage or offset mobilization-preparedness policies. At the strategic level, then, an essential preparedness measure would be to prevent the vesting of such interests, perhaps through a publicly canvassed code of strategic-economic behavior for business. Such a code is conceivable only against a background of heightened public understanding of the role of mobilization (assuming that the case for such a role can indeed be made).

Unless such a new understanding can be achieved, it would, in general, seem that the truly realistic scenarios for mobilization must be exclusively those in which the great firms have cogent and obvious reason to conclude that mobilization is in their own immediate net interests, as they themselves see and measure those interests. This is not likely ever to be the case; short of some critical threshold of national weakness, the outside threat will be too unclear to produce the necessary short-run-oriented commercial consensus. After this threshold of disadvantage is exceeded, the military risk in mobilizing at all will be only too obvious.

In a similar way, our general cultural acceptance of rapid institutional change also works against Western mobilization reactiveness. Amidst bewildering change, it is all but impossible to keep national interests in any consensual focus. Our cultural penchant is to minimize future threats, and to adapt to present catastrophes, all in the name of business as usual. In a period of twilight conflict, therefore, an all-important mobilization-preparedness measure would be to articulate clearly for the public the permanent basic interests of the nation as well as the threats thereto, and to explain realistically the role of mobilization so far as it may be an appropriate response to those threats.

It is also quite possible that the American multinational firms, possessing as they do a self-justifying ideology as an emerging non-national world order, have diluted the attention and loyalty of U.S. elite groups which once were the stabilizing banner-bearers of opinion around which competing group interests could coalesce into a recognizable national interest. In general, the track record of business in putting any kind of collective goal ahead of business as usual is (perhaps understandably) not good. In the specific field of mobilization preparedness, the historical record (except in the cases of certain "defense industries") is even more dismal. The rise of the multinational firm would seem to have worsened these prospects still further. And beyond these purely commercial frictions, the various kinds of international interdependence also, in effect, require the "permission" of our allies and trade partners for certain types of mobilization.

Our present social-political arrangements are further clogs to mobilization efforts. A very large segment of our population today expects that, in effect, any spare societal resources will be devoted to social equalization rather than to such efforts as mobilization preparedness. A great many livelihoods, and a great many political and bureaucratic careers, are now dependent on such distribution-oriented resource flows. Thus brought to the fore, the distribution question has long predominated in the United States over the questions of production of resources or their defense. In a classic spiral, this distribution struggle has weakened our willingness to defend the worldwide inputs used to produce the very wealth and leisure that have, in turn, largely fostered the distribution debate.

As we thus progressively lose our cheap and easy access to resources, our oligopolistic domestic economic system tends rather to adapt to and profit by the resulting shortages than to overcome them—often abetted in this by our government. As our real living standards decay, the distribution question is further exacerbated—it is far harder to distribute losses than gains. In this situation, the obvious strategy for an adversary is to nibble at our worldwide resource tentacles and watch the fun. It need hardly be asked whether this scenario is not already in progress.

Mobilization-preparedness efforts must therefore be framed in such a way as to break into this vicious circle of weakness without appearing to drain off yet more of society's hotly disputed resources. Preparedness measures thus need very careful public justification, in order to maximize their net contribution to our unity and strength.

Again, the people who must bear the brunt of any mobilization efforts and sacrifices are no longer so certain that the overall system they would thus support is fully theirs. Inflation and the recent scarcity-driven tilt toward property incomes are further widening the gap between the affluent few and the struggling many. The hard-pressed "middle class" is alienated by multiplying signs of social decay. To all appearances, respect for institutions and mutual trust are only just beginning a precarious recovery from almost unprecedented lows. There is no longer a natural seeming deference for the classes from which the mobilization "czars" have always come. It would be difficult to say what image the word "Congressman" evokes today.

Mobilization preparations must therefore involve clear public discussion, understanding and participation, lending mobilization a pro bono publico aura. Up to now, by contrast, perhaps our most serious mobilization-preparedness measure has been the preservation of property records, aimed at a postnuclear resurrection of the ancient socioeconomic landmarks.

In a period of twilight conflict, as Walter Laqueur has put it, "creeping crises produce no great tensions and generate no great passions; there is always the hope that the threat may suddenly go away." At present, indeed, Western politicians seem so inhibited by their respective domestic socio-economic structures that NATO commanders can not really count on sufficient warning to recall active-duty soldiers from leave, let alone as part of any precrisis mobilization efforts. Yet, if the West were directly attacked tonight, could we say, in the hypothetical retrospect of tomorrow, that it had been "out of the blue"?

In this situation, it has been argued, mobilization-preparedness measures might provide politicians with a graduated series of escalations known in advance to all concerned, and thus giving a feeling of plan and consensus, and not of arbitrariness and discontinuity. At the same time, of course, this function of escalation may be equally well understood by the adversary, and lead him to see such a mobilization style as a "cop-out" alternative to fighting. Henry Kissinger has argued plausibly that ending a confrontation requires rapid, brutal escalation, conveying implacability rather than an image of nicely calculated and graduated steps.

In sum, there is much to suggest doubt as to the speed of our national reaction to strategic warning. Yet a successful mobilization tempo will reflect the inequality: political reaction time plus mobilization gear-up time must be less than unreinforced hold-out time.

GEARING UP FOR REALLOCATION

Let us turn then from the problems of warning (or, perhaps more expressively, of the will to mobilize) to the second element of the mobilization "triad": the actual ability to gear up military power through the reallocation of nonmilitary resources.

If there presently existed emergency resource-reallocation patterns that could effectively protect the United States from sabotage or terrorism, or from conventional attack, or from chemical, biological or selective nuclear attack, or from economic warfare, and if the United States were thereby enabled to pursue a successful central military-industrial mobilization, then an essential role would certainly also fall to the various kinds of civil-defense mobilization steps.

It seems doubtful, however, that what we may call "traditional" civil-defense measures can both protect the United States against these types of contingency and also permit the carrying out of a central mobilization. The same negative conclusion would seem to hold a fortiori for the less traditional notion of crisis relocation of people—quite apart from its inherent unworkability in this country.

Eliminating such doubts about civil-defense capabilities would be extremely costly in itself, and in all probability prohibitively so if economic and military mobilization preparations were attempted simultaneously.

Beyond all this, however, lies the probability that U.S. central military-industrial mobilization efforts would prove too little and too late, even if the continental United States were never disturbed in any way by the adversary. It is to this more basic proposition that we now turn. In our economic system, mobilization will change not only the resource allocations themselves, but also the very allocative institutions and the entire allocative philosophy and rationale. Yet the market allocative mechanism which we must harness, or even partially abandon, during mobilization lies close to the heart of our whole national ideology. To the eye of this ideology, we are in mobilization by definition shifting to a less efficient, even a less effective, mechanism.

Our normal institutions of finance and trade (such as insurance, capital markets, fine-tuning speculative markets and the like), which are in peacetime basic sources of our efficiency and wealth, require confidence and continuity or they can swiftly collapse. Considerations such as these put another huge psychological and ideological damper on radical institutional and allocated changes.

Thus, mobilization puts the West in the position of making a very difficult and delicate institutional shift, in addition to all the obvious human and resource shifts. The adversary does not face this difficulty to any comparable degree. Perhaps it might seem to follow that the West could compensate for this asymmetry by keeping its mobilization, specific logistics, plans and institutions in excellent fighting trim. But, as we know, more or less the reverse is the truth.

The second-best, second-class status of mobilization in Western societies is nowhere better illustrated than in the character of their mobilization-preparedness arrangements. The standby nature of these arrangements seems to rob them of a sense of continuity, of legitimacy, or even of serious purpose. This in turn leads to their tolerance of questionable concepts, their underutilization, and their suspected political misuse. In an unfashionable, backwater function, both quantity and quality of resources and personnel become problems. Jobs choose people; an unreal, no-win function eventually repels success-oriented people.

The need to justify bureaucratic positions (as well as peacetime billets for the officer cadres of a shrunken military establishment) supports a tendency to emphasize time-consuming managerial process over product. An overelaborated, overrationalized planning mentality develops. In hopes of eliciting meaningful decisions from uninterested policymakers, more and more "precise" parameters and calculations are sought for the famous "policy options." Every conceivable factor is weighed up and mixed in; the status and trends of the rest of the world, and even the policies and initiatives of the adversary, are treated as givens. U.S. interests and policies come insensibly to be treated as residuals. A purely reactive and passive planning posture results.

This absence of realism and initiative, coupled with the almost total lack of top-management continuity in government, fosters safe and fashionable ways of thinking among the lesser bureaucrats; it seems hardly worthwhile to make a nuisance of oneself over the least likely hypothetical scenarios. Anodyne assumptions are made about biological and chemical war, warning times, foreign-trade reliability, communications and medical viability, agricultural contamination, crisis social behavior, and the imperfections of decision-makers.

The basic list of military mobilization requirements is "massaged" and "finessed" in pursuit of acceptable budgetary requests. Whole staffs devote themselves to "managing" the perception of threat rather than the response to it. In the politically enforced absence of credible planning assumptions, authoritative ones are sought—and accepted—instead.

Paperwork, an administrative apparatus, comes to be mistaken for real-life strategy; the administrative allocation system substitutes for the intellectual model of what allocations to make; order-precedence arrangements play the role of such criteria. Powerful agencies, based on "interest group state" constituencies and jealous of jurisdictional "turf," create pervasive difficulties of so-called "coordination," which in turn are patched over with further paper accommodations involving hypothetical real-time crisis "adjudications." The Congress and the Administration find themselves sponsoring sprawling studies of their own "policies," in the hope of discovering (rather than determining) what they are.

Once "determined" by such processes, mobilization policies turn out to be largely concerned with the least important (but most bureaucratically interesting) items of preparedness: massive manuals of formalized procedures in response to planning "scenarios" which themselves tend to reflect, not reality, but rather the desire to exercise those same procedures. What is called "planning" is often merely scripting for exercises. A vision arises of a "mobilized" Washington racing to its filing cabinets and telephones to exchange volumes of half-understood preprogrammed directives.

At the first sign of real crisis, of course, this twilight zone allocative apparatus will doubtless be pushed aside in favor of the usual trial and error by corporate czars. In the meantime, this apparatus is nominally managing real-life mobilization preparations. In doing so, it is faced with the further handicap of an unfamiliar, semilegitimate, and almost unworkable rationale. The pecuniary, tastedriven, short-term commercial calculations of peacetime must be replaced by the costing of real budgetary measures in vague social-opportunity terms, and by estimating probabilistic benefits in the form of a public good (defense), all within an overarching strategic-gaming framework which is itself ultimately incapable of being rationalized. Even if the planning logics were adequate, the requisite fine-grained industrial data is almost entirely lacking or proprietary. An essential mobilization-preparedness measure would therefore be the achievement of the public consensus needed for putting our mobilization institutions back on the real-world map, and for developing an accepted overall crisis resource-allocation rationale. This cannot be regarded as an easy task.

Even given such a shift of bureaucratic attitudes and thinking, however, the pecuniary basis of the wider U.S. economic system would of course remain intact. With today's sensitivity to inflation, to taxes, and to the erosion of real competition, an attempt to mobilize based primarily on pecuniary incentives would soon founder (even with price controls) on massive hedging, bartering, black-marketeering, debt repudiation, and tax default, to say nothing of panic buying and speculation.

The discretionary costs and economic rents endemic to oligarchy, and the "hidden economy" syndrome engendered by our tax system, in themselves promise to undo price controls and distort the mobilization process, while also dimming the prospects for postcrisis economic reconstitution. As was noted earlier, Western financial and trading institutions might tend to discourage any mobilization decision in the first instance. They could also clog the mobilization process itself, by their tendency to magnify and spread initial shocks from any kind of discontinuity, hostile or defensive. For similar reasons, they of course also multiply the dangers of economic warfare.

Gear-up problems are, in fact, rooted more deeply than in our governmental or market-based allocation arrangements. Some segments of broader American society appear either to have no usable skills in the best of circumstances, or to be caught up in various forms of anomie, hedonism, drug abuse, and other societal aberrations, or else to be alienated from (or simply alien to) U.S. ideals and institutions. This situation has implication, not only for national will and morale, but also for manpower mobilization as well. Idleness, crime, nonproductive activities, and social order, social welfare and therapeutic callings will continue, even in crises, to absorb noticeable fractions of our working-age contingents, and even, if we are not careful, of our Armed Forces.

From a purely manpower standpoint, indeed, it is extremely doubtful, given social conditions and attitudes in the United States today, whether sufficient effective additional fighting units could be formed within any useful period of time, except possibly under a threat so grave and imminent as to make it too late to contemplate military mobilization at all. This is not the place to recite the long litany of social problems which have led to a general questioning of the economic and political shape and direction of the nation; to lack of faith in institutions, in groups, and in each other as individuals; to growing impotence of national institutions to define, act and lead; and to the visible corruption and contamination of many prominent sectors of society.

Only time will tell whether the current Administration's policies represent a genuine across-the-board resurgence of America, a reactionary worsening of the basic structural problems of society, or mere reactive sound and fury with no real effect on long-term trends. Decadence tends to produce problems so deep-seated that only ignorance has the courage to face them. Until America's resurgence is attained, we remain a pecuniary, hedonistic, fragmented society. Roman statesman Marcus Cato well expressed the problem of reallocation in such a society: "It is hard to save a city where a fish sells for more than an ox."

It may well be that U.S. society is essentially wired for only two mobilization gears: dead stop and desperation speed. In modern, interdependent economic systems, where the power to disrupt often confers more leverage than the power to produce, disproportionate importance falls to the alienated and discontented who must exist in every stratified society. In such a society of strata, of course, it is mathematically impossible to equalize the burdens of mobilization in both the absolute and the relative senses. Alienation and discontent doubtless played a part in the German lack of mobilization early in World War II, and in the U.S. lack of mobilization for Vietnam.

Public familiarity with and acceptance of the mobilization concept could both ease the shift of political gears into the mobilization mode, and also at the same time reduce the sense of social fragility that could lead to such reactions as the spontaneous crisis withdrawal of target-area populations. If this kind of confidence cannot be achieved, the question arises whether the degree of threat that is necessary to arouse a U.S. mobilization response would not also be sufficient to disperse U.S. mobilization resources.

Such social considerations are crucial. There is, after all, nothing at all new or paradoxical in the often cited situation of the West, whose greater Gross National Product (GNP) produces less power (i.e., less strength actually brought to bear on interests), when compared to that of its adversary. As we measure GNP today, top-heavy with service industries, social services, and service-riddled manufacturing sectors, the same pseudoparadox could have been applied to Rome vis-a-vis the barbarians. Above a certain threshold of sheer resource availability, it is the social wiring that becomes decisive for Net National Power. In our own case, certainly, it is institutions and attitudes that will determine our ability to mobilize, as the pseudoparadox itself makes plain: resource availability is clearly not our critical constraint. Instead, it is the defects in our social wiring, and indeed even our very peacetime virtues (such as democracy and competition), that become ambiguous in the twilight conflict.

Despite all this, we seldom give the social wiring its due weight in our discussions, and where we do so, it is often to make complacent and unsophisticated comparisons with our adversaries. Thus, the "flexibility" of our allocation institutions is often contrasted, for example, with the apparently cumbersome rigidity of the adversary's institutions. This recurrent theme seems to be in large measure a mere shibboleth, backed only by dogmatic assertion and anecdotal evidence. We tend to mythicize the energizing potential of our own decentralized system, and to debunk that of the adversary's centralized one, as if the United States did not display, even in twilight peace, the common human foibles of all modern bureaucratic societies, such as off-the-top perks, turf-building waste, fast-buck horizons, and entrenched and lazy management. It is a hopeful sign that recent studies, such as those of Jacques Gansler and the Air Force Systems Command under General Alton Slay, seem to have abandoned this wishful dogma.

In fact, the adversary, semimobilized even in the twilight conflict period, wired and posed for full mobilization without violent institutional and philosophical shifts, and in control of the tempo of mobilization (that is, of the very shape of mobilization) through his posture of initiative and attack, is in a position not only to overwhelm us on the initial battlefields, but also to outpeak us militarily in the intermediate run of up to a year, if not longer. This latter consideration, which does not always receive the prominence in our thinking that it deserves, puts a new light on notions like "protracted crisis," "strategic warning," or even "twilight conflict." Time, at least intermediate runs of time, is after all not on our side, and not ours to play with strategically.

In this light, it is obvious that policy analysts must make explicit assumptions as to the mobilization impacts of our economic institutions, social structure, and national will and morale in general. These are not esoteric problems, little understood though they may be. They have already decisively affected several past conflict situations, and surely they are the key to the West's pseudoparadoxical weakness of today. These social-polity elements affect both the entire calculation of the costs and the entire estimation of the benefits of mobilization. Without clear, explicit and consistent assumptions in this area, planning becomes a matter of varying and incompatible fairy tales, and "coordinated" planning (whether among agencies or among allies) stumbles over the tacitly differing planning bases.

The fact seems to be that, in a long list of key areas, the United States today will tolerate far less effort and sacrifice than one, two, or three score years ago. The heroic assumption that all will be well, if we but think it well, could be a sign that planners at all levels are content, more or less consciously, to make unrealistic, unreconcilable plans. Planning scenarios that begin, for example, with the point at which mobilization is decided upon, ipso facto embody a long series of tacit "best case" assumptions about the whole strategic place of mobilization.

To paraphrase Professor George Sabine, intelligent policy-making must think of psychological and ideological factors in broadly the way it looks at material factors. It has to recognize their existence, to understand how they work, to realize that they can never be safely ignored, and to see that there is no sense in trying to argue them out of existence on the ground that they seem to be unreasonable or stupid.

In today's interdependent world, in sum, mobilization decisions tend more and more to require the effective permission of a number of key resource-holders. The influence of our own public, in terms of feasible austerity, productivity, market behavior, military manpower, and potential harbor for terrorists, saboteurs and spies, is quite clear. Similarly, the multinational firms hold key materials and transportation assets, as well as technical skills and capacities that can drastically affect mobilization and reconstitution efforts. Our allies and trade partners, noncontiguous, nonsubjected, and with interests intermingled with those of the great international firms, affect strategic imports (including energy), D-day support requirements, and today even weapons system production.

Despite all this, much of the attention devoted to assessing the attitudes and reactions of these key resource-holders (where it has not in fact amounted to nil) has been trifling and amateurish. A mobilization policy that ignores (or "finesses") these calculations is not serious, and will not be taken seriously by public, business, or allies.

We have here suggested that a strategy of offshore battlefield stabilization is the main option that makes mobilization both feasible and relevant to a central contingency. We have then recited some of the considerations that throw doubt on our reaction time and on our reallocation time in such a contingency. Until these two phases are completed, of course, our threatened interests must be defended by forces in-being. Let us then turn briefly to a consideration of this last leg of the mobilization triad, the capability of our unreinforced deployments to contain a central attack.

HOLDING OUT

Facing "outside" lines of communication, our central conventional-war strategy may take any of several paths. First, we may trade territory for the time in which to mobilize "Fortress America." Such a strategy, as we have seen, seems to entail either the military or the political loss of Europe. Alternatively, we might opt for an expeditionary war, involving massive resupply efforts before the battlefield could be stabilized. This approach suits much military thinking that has long been traditional (and indeed institutionalized in the worst sense) in the United States, envisioning broad defensive fronts, with emphasis on massive logistical frameworks, and considerable forces diverted to line-of-communication garrison and patrol.

The result of this mindset is evident in a comparison of NATO and Warsaw Pact "tooth-to-tail" ratios. Indeed, even some possible NATO "reinforcement" configurations seem likely to add more tail than tooth at the very peak of crisis.

One great obstacle to the credibility of this kind of expeditionary strategic posture is the plain fact that our allies do not want to provide the battlefield for such an extended and extensive war. Europe has yet to assimilate the notion that neither major prospective belligerent has any overriding interest in Europe's surviving the short-war alternative. Another serious obstacle to expeditionary warfare is the extreme vulnerability of traditional logistical facilities to H-hour targeting.

Prepositioned logistics are subject to an even greater vulnerability discount than pipeline logistics, since any real reliance on this concept for repelling a major attack would involve truly astronomical amounts of prepositioned material. The political risks of such inanimate hostages would also be correspondingly increased; we may recall our recent difficulties in using certain European facilities during a crisis outside of the NATO region.

Yet another battlefield-stabilizing option is to "go nuclear." At present, as noted above, it seems that theater nuclear war favors the adversary on several counts, quite apart from its unpalatability to our allies in its path. This imbalance will probably not be redressed by any eventual implementation of recently agreed changes in our theater nuclear stance. Presumably, in any case, it is precisely the progressive abandonment of the old concept of theater nuclear weapons as a kind of "half-crazed" prelude to Mutual Assured Destruction, that has resurrected the mobilization concept in the first instance. After all, if MAD is not madness, we have far less need of mobilization.

In a final "hold-out" option, we could field a fully-forward-deployed intratheater force with organic logistics matching the adversary's, and with appropriately remodelled organization and tactics, capable without significant reinforcement of absorbing and stabilizing a major central attack. Though the West at present lacks such a force, perhaps some fusion of the Army and the Marine rapid-deployment concepts will yet produce a truly viable structure.

Such a deployment would provide a sensible and believable role for mobilization in the sense discussed here. Immediate, military-deployment mobilization would project the battlefield-stabilizing formations. Intermediate, classic mobilization would sustain the essential force regeneration after the initial battlefield has been stabilized. Long-term, industrial mobilization would then fall in place for the longer haul.

Although, for many of the same reasons that affect our warning perceptions and our gearing-up tempo, the West has not been socially able to afford such a deployment, the synergism between a logistically believable hold-out concept and the resulting public acceptance of the role of mobilization could generate the needed support. Credible battlefield stabilization plus serious gear-up plans could in their turn encourage hardier reactions by political leaders to strategic warning. The ultimate result would of course be an all-round improvement of mobilization tempo.

Mobilization-Preparedness Policy

Presently, none of our elements of mobilization tempo is really credible. Yet a nation or an alliance with pretensions to world influence and interests simply must have in its repertory at least one central war which it has a chance of both winning—and bringing about.

What then is the easiest, cheapest, most direct fix for our situation? Can we not conclude, as just suggested, that, while classic gear-up mobilization has many potential roles within a sound strategic posture, our present posture is itself a loser? Can we not conclude that, while such mobilization will enhance a well-conceived strategy, it cannot by itself create one? Indeed, is it not thinkable that a mobilization capability alone, in the absence of certain more direct strategic fixes, would in fact be a highly expensive (and distinctly non-Punic) white elephant?

It seems, in sum, that our hold-out capacity is so limited relative to our reaction and gear-up capabilities, and relative to the adversary's preparations, that we really cannot *get to* the classic mobilization war in which we feel we might have an advantage. The adversary, after all, can outpeak us militarily in any intermediate race, be it a phoney-war force-augmentation phase, or a postclash force-regeneration phase.

In dynamic terms, everything in the adversary's posture of permanent semimobilization seems to indicate his respect for our putative mobilization potential, and his determination to strain every nerve to cut us off from that potential—to ensure the occurrence of a different war. This notion raises the question whether, if we did have an industrial-mobilization capability in being, it would not merely be deterring a war the adversary is already sufficiently averse to. What then is the marginal cost of achieving any marginal impact on this aversion, after netting out the effects of the adversary's countermoves? If the adversary is clearly averse to a mobilization war, will our moves to attain a mobilization capability not provoke him into countermoves to shorten his steamroller time as we shorten our gear-up time? Brezhnev had in fact announced in so many words that such a course would be a "hopeless" undertaking for us; Andropov apparently agrees.

Yet, the adversary's economic-social-demographic problems could ultimately make such a prolonged and intensive countermobilization untenable for him over time. The very promise of successful deterrence in our mobilization preparations could thus actually provoke war, much as deterrent resource sanctions pushed Japan into war with the West, or as Germany's pre-World War I naval catch-up was regarded almost as a casus belli by Britain.

We must therefore weigh with extreme care whether mobilization preparedness, and if so which form of mobilization preparedness, can most effectively cut into this delicate web of feedbacks. We may already have "steered" the adversary into a posture of Blitzkrieg preparedness; we must avoid "levering" him into the Blitzkrieg itself. This latter effect might occur if he sees, by our own discontinuous preparations, that he has indeed given us some kind of signal, perceived by us as warning.

It must also be borne in mind, finally, that, if we were today miraculously handed an instantaneous mobilization capability, it might add very little, at the margin, to deterring a central war, as long as our adversary can still beat us to the initial military peak.

In sum, most elements of our mobilization potential so lack credibility that we must move very warily in trying to restore them—in order to retain allied and public-opinion adherence, in order to forestall adversary countermoves, and in order to avoid mobilization-preparedness measures so inappropriate and hence unbelievable as to appear to be mere "cop-out" alternatives to fighting. We must also take care to avoid being stampeded into wasteful measures by industrial and military interests and attitudes. In essence, the credibility of our mobilization preparedness must be derived from the credibility of our whole strategic posture—and not vice versa.

Our entire discussion can be recapitulated as follows: the core strategic issues of mobilization center around the swift reallocation of nonmilitary resources to meet a central politico-military contingency, essentially by supporting a battlefield-stabilization strategy. The three chief elements of this mobilization tempo do not presently encourage us to hope for such a meaningful and successful role for mobilization. So feeble, indeed, are these elements that a determined attempt to mend them could in itself be strategically destabilizing. The cost-effective, direct, and stable way to restore a meaningful mobilization capability is to improve the in-being "hold-out," or battlefield-stabilizing element of mobilization tempo, in support of which nonmilitary mobilization can find a credible role.

A credible role for mobilization can in turn produce the degree of political understanding and support that is critical for a worthwhile mobilization-preparedness effort. Short of some considerable degree of such support, competition for minuscule resources among the myriad complementary preparedness measures will forever stymie efforts to implement a more than merely verbal mobilization policy.

What is to be done, then, at the practical level of the present? The writer believes mobilization-preparedness policy faces two immediate desiderata: a battlefield fix, and getting the message out.

Literally backing into a mobilization capability through an initial emphasis on in-being forces—paradoxical at first view—has upon close scrutiny emerged as our most direct and strategically stable option. The build-up of in-being forces should not, however, merely pour new funding wine into the old doctrinal wineskins, as seems likely to happen in any present-day military-procurement boom. On the contrary, the major emphasis should be on creating something new: a truly credible central battlefield-stabilizing force. This new-model holding force must not be wedded to traditional notions of massive logistical structures and resupply pipelines. It must instead become literally capable of breaking a major attack without significant reinforcement, and without cumbrous logistic apparatus.

In the attempt to cut back our H-hour casualty list of logistics-heavy formations and facilities, we could well devote some special effort to developing a "breakthrough" technological fix for the initial battlefield: relatively easily and cheaply forward-deployable systems that could offset some of the preparedness averseness of our social structure, and face the adversary with a sudden strategic fait accompli without the destabilizing effects of an overt preparedness race. Given our traditional technological prowess, and given the inherent advantages of the defense for system emplacement and target acquisition, it should be possible to devise weapons which would turn the adversary's very initiative and mobility into net disadvantages. And perhaps something more than mere technology is wanted here: Ralph Ajello once tossed out the idea that a symposium among military commanders, scientists, and the creators of *Stars Wars* and Disney World might well prove a fruitful source of tactical imagination.

New formations, shaped around logistically trivial battlefield-stabilizing emplacements, and a full use, at least within Europe, of NATO reserve potential should completely eliminate any military-manpower mobilization bottleneck for the West. In such ways as these, we may be able to reverse radically the peacetime tendencies of our western military establishments to stress personnel over procurement, and procurement over readiness.

The second great desideratum of mobilization policy today is to "get the message out." This means authoritative articulation and public acceptance of a clear role for mobilization that is truly strategically integrated and hence fully credible. Force regeneration in support of a stabilized central battlefield, as developed above, can be such a role.

It will certainly have been noted that public articulation and acceptance of the mobilization concept is a recurrent theme of this whole discussion. The problem of acceptance may be viewed as a Catch-22 proposition: mobilization can't get the resources to make it feasible without previous public understanding of its feasibility. Or it may be seen in terms of a "1937 syndrome": in 1941 you get fired for not having done what you would have been fired in 1937 for suggesting. However it is formulated, the need for popular, political, and business acceptance and support is crucial and obvious; only a threshold of support and resources can harmonize the demands of competing mobilization-preparedness measures that are in fact complementary and hence individually worthless.

Behind the authoritative articulation of policy must stand a credible policy apparatus, shaped more as a decision forum than as a planning cloister. Such a decision forum must have visible responsibility, and possess the power to decide the old in-being–versus–mobilization questions and to mandate the necessary planning and budgetary interfaces, from the ground up, to exploit the complementarities between these two rivals for support.

When these and a number of second order preparedness issues have been authoritatively clarified, most of the present cacophony of opposing considerations will find their harmony within the main policy thrust, and the relatively few remaining hard-core policy issues can be traded off on a rational basis.

Such a positive and fully integrated and articulated strategic posture can provide the entire West with clearly agreed common planning assumptions, and can be systematically fleshed out with such subsidiary elements as: planning concepts (e.g., "critically," "capacity"), data, information and calculation systems, management cadres and procedures, legislative authorities and legitimating familiarization, allocable plans, balanced incentive/control systems, and exercise feedbacks.

Until such a posture is developed and promulgated, those of us who have followed the fortunes of preparedness through an epoch of unreasonable unpopularity are apt to be ambivalent about a possibly dawning era of equally unreasonable fashionability. All too often, as we are all aware, policy buzzwords can sweep across the bureaucracies when there is in fact no rational policy, but only empty slogans. Too much about our stance in adjacent arenas of policy, and indeed about our whole society, counsels caution.

In the writer's view, our first preparedness concern should be to adjust the mobilization triad by radically reducing the logistic requirements of the initial central battlefield. Among the many far-from-rhetorical questions still seeking resolution, this new modeling of military logistical concepts seems most central today.

2

Mobilization for High-Level Conflict: Policy Issues

Colin S. Gray

Future Wars: The Conceit of Scenario Writers

The general staffs of Europe prior to August 1914 assumed a short war—and were, without exception, in error.[1] In 1939, Germany assumed a short war and Britain and France assumed a long war[2]—only Britain was (half) correct, courtesy of a twenty mile wide moat. November 1940 was not unlike (late) November 1914; neither Britain nor Germany had any plausible theory of victory. If there is any moral to be drawn from the military history of the twentieth century, it is that "the best and the brightest" have tended "to get it wrong."

Defense programs in democracies in peacetime have to be defended, year after year in front of legislative oversight committees which require the provision of "plausible scenarios." The bizarre is easily ridiculed. But, the historical fact remains that very few of the "outbreak scenarios" of the major wars of recent centuries could have been predicted in detail by strategic experts. Indeed, some of the pertinent sequences of events were so abstruse that no scenario writer would dared to have predicted them.[3] Would an American think tank analyst today dare to invent drunken Russian (and French) officials, a German leader signing a blank check and then going on vacation, military officials unobtainable for advice, and so forth?—of course not. But all of these occurred in July 1914.

The dilemma of the defense planner in 1981 is not strikingly dissimilar from that of the defense planner of 1913 or 1938—future major war could be long or short. An important difference between today and those earlier occasions is that this time the potential belligerents do not endorse a single "dominant scenario" for the guidance of their general war planning. Somewhat belatedly, and still uncertainly, the United

States recently has come to join the Soviet Union in the belief that general war could be protracted.[4]

In World War II, because Hitler and his advisers knew that Germany could not win a long war, they planned only for a short one. Defense planners tend to be the first victims of their own "dominant scenarios." Scenario writers, and readers, seem to find it all too easy to forget that a scenario, if well designed, is a heuristic device—no more and perhaps no less. In its scenario writing for high-level conflict, the U.S. Government, and in particular the Joint Chiefs of Staff, has been guilty of drafting *preferred* scenarios, almost regardless of known Soviet military "style" and likely Soviet-perceived interests. It may be appropriate to teach hatred of the enemy to the sharp end of the American armed forces, but the thinking end of those forces has to be taught to understand and respect the enemy on his own terms. As Winston Churchill once said, "It is sometimes necessary to take the enemy into consideration."

As in 1914 and 1939, the defense planners of the 1980s have at hand a military machine whose potential they do not understand very well. None of the super and great powers have road-tested their military posture and doctrine against a first-class adversary since 1945. This lack of evidence does not pertain only to nuclear weapons; it also applies to conventional chemical weapons. It is possible, if not particularly plausible, that tactical-offensive movement on the battlefield in the mid to late 1980s will prove to be as costly and unproductive as was movement beyond the established trench-lines from late 1914 to 1918. It is not difficult to imagine a situation wherein both sides, in the 1980s, like their puzzled predecessors in late November 1914, have exhausted both munitions and ideas.

Mobilization in Defense Planning and Defense Policy

Soviet General Staff officials, looking at the U.S. economy, should have no difficulty understanding that there is enormous "slack" in terms of capacity which could be utlized for defense production purposes. Those Soviet planners should have few problems recalling the prodigious breadth and depth of defense production achieved by the United States in World War II[5]—or, possibly of greater relevance, the response of U.S. high-technology industry to the security shock of the North Korean invasion of June 25, 1950. The structure of the United States economy has altered detrimentally from the viewpoint of defense mobilization since 1950–53, but Soviet planners are likely still to be impressed by the fact that the United States' gross national product is roughly double that of the Soviet Union.

The American defense problem today is not so much physical capacity, rather it is strategic comprehension and political will. U.S. weapons procurement seems to be under the shadow of a de facto "ten year rule."[6] In the United States today, nothing in the defense area appears to be urgent. Weapons acquisition is paced less by technical problems than by local political and legal issues. Presidential Directive (PD) 59, of July 1980, which is an authoritative policy document on "nuclear weapons employment policy," could not be implemented in the absence of a survivable land-based ICBM force; yet the survivability of the U.S. land-based ICBM force is hostage to the play of domestic politics. The MX is being acquired on a peacetime, "business as usual," timetable.[7] "Business as usual" is so pervasive an assumption that it is close to impossible to question the representatives of defense industry with respect to weapons acquisition schedules geared to an alternative assumption. President Reagan's foreign policy has yet to be matched with directives for weapons acquisition reflecting a sense of urgency—let alone a willingness to challenge legislation of the Environmental Protection Agency for national security reasons.

Studies conducted by Hudson Institute over the past few years with reference to defense mobilization cast severe doubt upon official peacetime estimates of mobilization lead time.[8] The United States, traditionally, has been the country that could solve engineering-type problems. Today, U.S. officials tend to ask defense industry how rapidly it could expand production of ships, tanks, missiles and so forth, and they receive depressing answers because the parameters of the inquiry are peacetime, "business as usual," procedures. Virtually none of the currently available lead time estimates for weapons production is to be trusted. Representatives of defense industry tend to answer questions on mobilization by means simply of extrapolating current standards, procedures and constraints. If one suggests a willingness to compromise on usual peacetime practices (with respect to quality of materials, training of workers, dedication of tooling, etc.), then the lead time estimates for weapons production contract by orders of magnitude.[9]

Anyone who is strongly skeptical concerning the optimistic thesis that runs through the above paragraph is recommended to look closely at U.S. defense mobilization in the period 1940–44. The U.S. economy does have a different structure today, and it cannot be doubted that at the end of the Great Depression there was a great deal of slack in the U.S. economy. Nonetheless, the point here is that the U.S. economy, in that period, solved problems as they arose, a practice which was not appreciated well in advance in this country. (In fact, German estimates of American defense production capacity proved to be more accurate than were American estimates.)

The United States has two long suits which simply sidestep most of the now traditional arguments about the credibility of deterrence. In Soviet eyes, the United States is recognized as the technological leader—the one country capable of technological breakthrough in the arms competition. Soviet leaders do not need to be reminded of the fact that the United States, traditionally, has been strongly motivated to substitute military technology for American lives,[10] and that an American industrial structure currently oriented towards the production of consumer durables could be converted relatively easily to the production of defense items. The willingness of the United States to entertain casualty lists in multiples of ten million is, properly, subject to considerable question, but the ability of U.S. industry to produce the material sinews of war is subject, in Soviet eyes at least, to no such degree of skepticism.

It should follow from the above that U.S. defense mobilization should be an integral part of U.S. defense policy. U.S. defense mobilization, in response to peacetime challenges, threatens to change the future balance of military power. Paul Bracken has defined mobilization "as the rapid assembly, production or deployment of a superior force of arms."[11]

There is no doubt but that high-level conflict in the future could erupt so rapidly out of a peacetime situation that defense mobilization would be a totally irrelevant concept. However, central wars "out of the blue" are exceedingly improbable. Although history may well surprise us, there are more plausible scenarios to which defense mobilization would be relevant than there are scenarios to which it would not.

It is important to stress that defense mobilization could provide major benefits for pre-, and even intra-war deterrence. A policy of defense mobilization, if actually implemented, does not commit a U.S. President to any course of action in particular—defense mobilization provides military muscle "down the road," to be used in whatever fashion is deemed to be expedient. A United States that were to opt for a defense mobilization response to Soviet foreign-policy moves in the early 1980s would not be a United States investing solely in bigger and better ways of doing those things that currently are underway in military research and development. A truly vast influx of funds would very likely have an explosively effective impact upon programs that otherwise would have remained on the drawing boards for twenty years or more.[12]

The virtue of U.S. defense mobilization for deterrence is that not merely does it point to an area of obvious American strength, it also opens the door to Soviet anxieties concerning the technological breakthroughs that might be accomplished. A mobilization component in U.S. defense policy bears the promise that even if the United States should be defeated, regionally, in the near term, the long-term consequence will be the activation of the most mighty defense-production system the world has yet seen.

Over the past ten years the United States has sought to advertise "strategic offsets" for loss in relative strategic muscle. Both National Security Decision Memorandum (NSDM) 242 of January 17, 1974,[13] and Presidential Directive (PD) 59 of July 25, 1980,[14] sought to assert a "countervailing strategy," to deny victory to the enemy, in lieu of overwhelming U.S. military power.[15] Unfortunately, Soviet victory-denial is fully compatible with U.S. defeat, and cannot serve as an adequate pre-eminent guide to U.S. strategic planning. Defense mobilization should provide a satisfactory halfway house for those unhappy with the defeat implications of current U.S. strategy, yet unwilling to endorse a U.S. defense build-up on a massive scale.

Limited, Selective, and Partial Mobilization

Over the past few years some officials, and others, have suggested that the United States should adopt a flexible, or limited, defense mobilization policy.[16] Instead of defense mobilization being geared to one or two major "thresholds" of public alarm, U.S. defense industry should be tasked and directed to respond on an analog of the familiar *Def Con.* system. This idea has everything to recommend it save practicality. This author is not convinced that American strategic culture can accommodate the idea of a "limited mobilization."[17] The Korean mobilization saw U.S. Total Obligational Authority for defense leap from $14–16 billion to $50 billion as a result of weeks of debate. This three-to-four fold expansion in defense authorization was justified explicitly with reference to the strong probability of the near-term outbreak of general East-West war. The Reagan increases in Total Obligational Authority (TOA) for FY 1982—which come (net) roughly to $26 billion—do not comprise a mobilization response to perceived external danger. The scale of the proposed Reagan defense budgets reflects orders of magnitude that show less alarm, by implication, than did the U.S. defense budgets of the early 1950s.

Democracies tend to rearm only in response to widespread perception of a clear and present danger. Unfortunately, by the time a danger is clear and present, one is unlikely to have available many months, let alone years, for a mobilization policy to produce much in the way of completed defense materiel or combat-ready soldiers prior to the onset of hostilities. On the one hand, the United States is able to effect a noteworthy increase in its peacetime defense efforts, as at present, though the increase is still bounded by previous political assumptions. Reagan's defense program reflects the belief that war with the Soviet Union is very unlikely over the next few years. On the other hand, the United States can mobilize for war, as it has done three times in this century already. In other words, the United States can increase its defense effort by 10–15%, or by 200–300% (plus), but it is not obvious that anything in between is culturally feasible.

For a democracy to increase its defense effort in peacetime by 50%

or 100% over a short space of time, its leaders have to paint so black a picture of foreign menace that the 50–100% range would likely be judged to be inappropriately modest. Very little political leadership would be needed to persuade a democracy to expand its defense effort by 200–300% or more. Public alarm would demand full-scale mobilization. To ask a mobilization response of a democracy the danger must be self-evident. Among the many lessons of the Vietnam experience was the political fact that Americans tend to believe that if a war is not worth winning it cannot be worth fighting. An apparently half-hearted, or limited, mobilization could well face a similar political difficulty.[18] Half-measures of mobilization may be sensible to the analyst or policy-maker who is genuinely uncertain as to just how dangerous the times are, but they will lack political support. They will be seen to be either too little or too much.

However, the judgment in this section is not at all insensitive to the case for selectivity in mobilization planning. The United States may wish to augment particular kinds of military capability—for example, and perhaps most persuasively in the case of anticipated truly high-level conflict, with respect to active homeland defense. The argument advanced in this section does not lead to the conclusion that the United States can implement only one type of defense mobilization. Such a claim would be as absurd as would be the claim that the United States can fight only one kind of war. Types of defense mobilization can be as varied as can the types of wars to which they are intended to be relevant.

Some High-Level Conflicts

The case for mobilization planning is identical to the case for a robust, so-called (pejoratively) warfighting posture. Such a posture both enhances the quality of deterrence effect in the minds of potential enemies (who anticipate that they will not fare well should war occur), and provides vitally needed denial capability if armed conflict breaks out. The Soviet Union anticipates a protracted political struggle for influence, globally, with the United States—a process that carries with it, endemically, the risk of more or less acute superpower crisis; and Soviet military science is sensibly ambivalent on the issue of whether East-West war would be short or long. Moreover, defense mobilization speaks to the strength of a whole society—it is the kind of concept that Soviet leaders understand and approve.[19]

The basic question is "what is the value of defense mobilization (industrial and military manpower) in the context of future 'high-level' conflict?" The answer is as follows: defense mobilization capability:

— may help deter acute crises and wars; or,

— could make the difference between success and failures in crisis confrontation and war.

For the better part of thirty years commentators and strategic theorists in the West have assumed that general East-West war would be short. This assumption has flowed over from being merely a prediction to enjoying the status of a statement of objective (U.S./NATO) reality—because Western military forces were, and remain, designed to be able to wage only very short wars. For example, "spasm" nuclear war has been a physical reality because U.S. strategic forces lack endurance—while command, control, communications and intelligence (C^3I) assets would be unlikely to survive the first day of central nuclear combat.[20]

It is argued here that a serious policy of defense mobilization is worth having whether or not high-level conflict is short. Probably the strongest argument for mobilization planning pertains to its possible deterrence value.[21] In other words, advocates of defense mobilization should not have to design plausible scenarios of protracted central conflict in order to make their case.[22] Even if Soviet General Staff and U.S. JCS planners really believe that World War III will last only for a week or two (at most)—they cannot be certain in that belief.

In the remainder of this section five cases are identified and outlined which illustrate the relevance of mobilization planning for high-level conflict.

CASE (1) MOBILIZATION IN "PEACETIME"

The most likely trigger of a U.S. general-war–relevant defense mobilization program is not a theater (or central) war that grinds to a military halt fairly rapidly, but rather "a crisis too far." Democracies, historically, have chosen to rearm not when war actually broke, but when they crossed a critical threshold of belief that war was in sight. The American condition today is not unlike that of the British in late 1938: there is intense suspicion of, and hostility towards, a foreign country; there remain some residual hopes that armed conflict can be avoided (hopes influenced, in this context, by the qualitative change in weaponry since late 1938);[23] yet there is a fairly strong expectation that Soviet-American relations are going to deteriorate further before they will improve. Soviet foreign policy produced a dimension of the 1980 U.S. Presidential election wherein both candidates were running against Moscow. The downward defense budgetary trend of the 1970s has been reversed in a noteworthy way, but the U.S. Government has yet to be catalyzed into a "war is in sight" defense program.

Soviet leaders should understand that democracies do not prepare for defense in a rational manner. The United States' defense effort is propelled according to guidance from a transmission that basically has only two forward speeds, bottom and top.[24] In 1981 the United States is in "bottom plus." If the Soviet Union, over the next year or so, behaves in a manner that most Americans (sensibly or otherwise) define as aggressive, it is likely to find that the United States will not add 5% or 10% to its FY 1982 TOA figure, instead it may expand TOA by orders of magnitude. In short, the Soviet Union may drive Americans from their current position of believing that war is a distant possibility, to the position of believing that war could well occur at any time.

Should the Soviet Union miscalculate the temper of the American body politic and launch "a crisis too far," a policy of defense mobilization almost certainly would be more supportive of Western interests, long term, than would an attempt at near-term military action. Mobilization, as a part of U.S. foreign and defense policy,[25] should greatly alter any Soviet calculation of cost-benefit with respect to an individual crisis. There is a strong element of uncertainty here. However, Soviet leaders should worry that the United States already is at the end of its "business as usual" defense program options.

Defense mobilization, as a deterrent, will not dissuade Soviet leaders from taking actions that they deem essential to preserve the integrity of their empire. But such a threat should be very persuasive in conditions where Soviet leaders are considering policy moves for positive gain (e.g., is renewed Soviet acquisition of a very restive Yugoslavia worth a tripling of the U.S. defense budget?)—in other words, with respect to discretionary behavior.

A problem with this case of defense mobilization, as with the others, is that the credible promise of a great deal more military capability tomorrow logically could increase the adversary's incentive to fight today. This may not be a problem, if his distaste for (nuclear) war is sufficiently high—almost regardless of the assayed state of the multilevel military balance—but it is well to prepare defense mobilization plans in such a way that production of short term "cover" is surged in tandem with the development of longer term programs.[26]

CASE (2) WAR BY MISCALCULATION OR ACCIDENT

Soviet writers are prone to assert that the military character of a war will be determined by its political purposes. However, general East-West war might occur not because politicians on either side had decided upon a "day of decision," but rather because local military circumstances evaded central control. No very great skill in scenario design is required to draft a script for a Soviet imperial policing operation in East-Central Europe which "spills over" the Warsaw Pact/NATO demarcation line. A general war in Europe might begin to unfold for reasons of the dynamics of an acute crisis that the Soviet Union initially defined in very restricted political terms.

Such an emerging East-West war might rapidly be halted by a de facto armistice because this would be a war which, presumably, no one intended or desired, and also more likely than not, this would be a war for which neither side was well prepared. Defense mobilization in the West could follow the brief period of active hostilities as NATO countries reacted to the evidence that war really could occur. The shock of actual hostilities need not, of course, promote a NATO-wide policy response of defense mobilization. The policy response might take the form of increased interest in political neutrality, or stronger insistence upon arms control.

Nonetheless, notwithstanding the several ways in which an unplanned East-West military crisis could evolve, cessation of immediate combat and the launching of mobilization is among them.

CASE (3) PROTRACTED, AND PERHAPS INTERMITTENT, THEATER WAR

War plans in action have been known to surprise their authors. It is unlikely, but not impossible, that both sides to an East-West war in Europe might quite rapidly find themselves in positions analogous to those of the Great Powers in November 1914. In the 1980s, as in 1914, the Soviet Union/Imperial Germany might register very considerable initial success, but be unable to consummate a definitive military victory in the very near term. However, Soviet leaders and their military advisers may believe that victory is possible—if only sufficient additional military power can be mobilized and applied.

On the NATO side in the 1980s, as in 1914 for France, Belgium and Britain, defeat might be avoided, but the military-political status quo would be unacceptable because of the large amount of West German (and Danish and possibly Dutch) territory that would have been lost. NATO could not accept the de facto armistice line and survive as an alliance; that line could not serve as the basis for negotiations over war termination; and NATO governments (some of them at least) might well be encouraged—not to say surprised—by the effectiveness of NATO arms and the political fortitude displayed, to the effect that a crash mobilization program would be judged to be essential either should the campaign be renewed, or, preferably, as a means of exerting leverage on the Soviet Union to return to her starting line. "Mobilization war" to use Paul Bracken's suggestive phrase, purchases time for political temporizing on both sides.[27]

It is fairly commonplace to assert that war in Europe would be short and decisive. Instead, as outlined here, it might be short and indecisive, but with the ever-present possibility of being renewed. All that is advanced here is the possibility that the detailed Soviet preplanned offensive comes unraveled at a very early stage. It is implausible to deny the possibility that a war in Europe could degenerate through unprecedented (and perhaps unexpected) losses and the difficulty of movement into confusion and mutual paralysis. This possibility rests upon recognition of such factors as the unusual vulnerability of the Soviet armed forces to C^3 degradation: the strangeness of the terrain (notwithstanding map familiarity); the unprecedented fear of constantly running "nuclear (and CW) scared;" the absence of real combat experience with anything even approximating that encountered in the high-technology European battle area; the disruptive effect of a vast quantity of civilian refugee traffic; and last but not least—the possibility that NATO forces (or, at least, some NATO forces) may fight very effectively indeed.

If November 1914 is a possibility as a pertinent model, NATO and the Soviet Union would, in theory, have the options of digging in and mobilizing; searching for some face-saving peace formula; expanding the war at, or to, sea, in Scandinavia, the Middle East, the Persian Gulf and the Far East; or escalating to central nuclear employment. These are not mutually exclusive options. One need not be unduly imaginative to anticipate that many NATO governments would far prefer to conduct "a war by arms race," in the event of a military stalemate in Europe, than to expand, escalate, or even renew locally the actual combat.

CASE (4) PROTRACTED CENTRAL WAR

The U.S. Government recently has endorsed the relevance of the idea of a protracted central nuclear campaign. Instead of war by a rapid sequence of Single Integrated Operational Plan (SIOP)-level spasms, it is envisaged that a general war including—but not limited to—central nuclear systems might last for as long as six months (or perhaps longer). The implicit conflict scenarios are ones wherein: following very modestly sized (and carefully directed) opening salvos, homeland to homeland, both sides recoil in horror (and mutual deterrence) and prefer to wage surrogate or phoney war by defense mobilization; both sides launch large countermilitary strikes, while exercising great care to avoid unwanted collateral damage, and thereafter conduct what in the early 1950s was called "broken-backed" war, supplementing surviving forces from a substantially undamaged war-supporting industry; or, the central (and other) war is continuous, but is conducted in very slow motion.

A central nuclear war may prove to be a mobilization scenario, but that may not be a very useful perspective to adopt for such a conflict. U.S. defense technicians recently have come to be attentive to the problems of the endurance of strategic forces and C^3I assets, but this technical fascination has yet to be matched with a very plausible policy story.[28] Proponents of protracted (nuclear) campaigns in the United States today are not asserting, by and large, that a country like the United States can absorb a great deal of damage and remain a formidable adversary. Instead, they are saying, implicitly, that the superpowers could wage a protracted central war if they chose to exercise great, and reciprocated, targeting restraint. In other words, today's American argument is more about the functioning of intra-war deterrence than it is about the resilience of large countries.

Soviet "style" in central nuclear targeting, as best that "style" can be appreciated, is not noticeably friendly to the protracted war thesis. The Soviet General Staff, apparently, places great reliance upon preemption ("going first in the last resort"), and is totally unfriendly to many of the scholarly conceits of American strategic theorists.[29]

Although Western defense mobilization, both of an industrial and of a manpower character, can be a most potent threat to change the balance of ready military power dramatically tomorrow, it does bear the danger of serving as an alibi for inactivity. A generic problem in all defense mobilization scenarios is the need to explain just why it is that the Soviet Union chooses to be deterred by the prospect of much more Western military power tomorrow, rather than seeking a military solution today (when, by definition, Soviet prospects of military success are at their highest).

A not implausible answer to the problem identified above is that the Soviet Union, albeit self-assessed to be in a superior relative military condition today, as opposed to tomorrow, still would shrink from inviting the full horror of central nuclear war.[30] Over most political issues, at most times, this judgment almost certainly is correct. However, the subject here is not most issues or most times, rather is it the one occasion in thirty or forty years when the Soviet Union would risk triggering a true U.S. defense mobilization response. A Soviet Union willing to catalyze, or seriously risk catalyzing, a U.S. mobilization response in a central war context, is not likely to be a Soviet Union willing easily to be deterred from pressing its case explosively. Above all else, it is difficult to argue that the Soviet Union would be willing to proceed militarily to the point of a central war exchange—and then observe a tacit armistice while the United States effected a crash program of rearmament in strategic forces and homeland defense.

CASE (5) DEFENSE MOBILIZATION AS THE KNIGHT'S MOVE

This case differs from case (1) only in that it would be triggered not by an acute crisis, or series of crises, but by an overt limited military move by the U.S.S.R. Herman Kahn favors the example of a Soviet seizure of West Berlin, in response to which the United States declares war—to change the legal context and to declare unequivocally that "this is unfinished business"—and triples (or more) U.S. defense expenditures.[31] Particular scenarios may be challenged as to their plausibility, but the general argument is clear enough. In addition to the constrained military moves NATO has on its agenda as response options in the event of inimical, though apparently limited, Soviet policy actions, one should add defense mobilization possibilities.

Mobilization Planning and Force Structure Design

Given that defense mobilization bears the promise of providing impressive amounts of military capability tomorrow, theorists and policy-planners of mobilization must balance near-term risks against longer term benefits. If the United States were to decide to proceed rapidly with a program of defense mobilization, there would be a need for short-term cover as well as for long-term theories of competitive success. The United States faces two, near-structural, problems in planning mobilization for high-level conflict. First, it is important to note a difference between American and Soviet "national style" in mobilization.[32] Soviet style calls largely for a manpower mobilization, i.e., reservists would be called up, provided with stored equipment and, after little delay, sent to the front. American style, understandable in a country traditionally protected by ocean distances, is to organize both industrial mobilization and military manpower mobilization. The United States, unlike the Soviet Union, has neither millions of recently trained reservists, nor vast vehicle parks and equipment stores.

Second, deterring though U.S. defense mobilization is in prospect, it should not be forgotten that the Soviet Union is a society already semi-mobilized for war.[33] Although the United States, given adequate supplies of raw materials and energy, could outproduce the Soviet Union virtually across the board of military, or militarily utilizable equipment, the Soviet Union—by and large—has warm production lines and the United States does not.

The certainty of war today may be so adequately deterring a prospect that Soviet leaders would prefer to accept the risks of a markedly deteriorating military balance—as the West mobilizes manpower and materiel resources—as the price to be paid for avoiding war. The underlying subject here is not the deterrence of a Soviet Union that is bent upon conducting its foreign affairs in a peacetime, "business as usual" spirit. Instead, this study has considered defense mobilization as an alternative to the initiation, or resumption, of military action, up to and including the level of central nuclear systems employment.

With few exceptions, the Soviet Union of these scenarios is a Soviet

Union that may well be on the brink of being, quite literally, beyond deterrence. That should not be assumed, but it is well to remember that the Soviet Union of the 1980s is very unlikely to be willing to offer replays of the essential scripts of the East-West crises of the 1940s, 1950s, and 1960s.[34] In the 1980s, the Soviet Union has achieved "useful advantage," to employ John Erickson's term,[35] in many dimensions of military power, and should not be expected easily to acquiesce in a Western mobilization response to local or central crises. If the United States cannot surge ready military capability (that is "good enough") in the short term, it is as likely as not that the Soviet Union will not permit the longer term programs to achieve maturity.

Detailed discussion of the force structure design that should guide mobilization has to be the subject of a separate study. However, it is useful to itemize some of the important questions that should be asked of defense programs considered for the implementation of mobilization.[36]

1. *How great a threat does the program pose, in Soviet eyes?* Earth-penetrating reentry vehicles are very expensive in payload, but matched with declaratory threats to Soviet political and military command bunkers, may pose "the ultimate threat" in Soviet eyes.
2. *How much leverage does the program offer in the military competition?* Most potential BMD systems can be countered, evaded, thwarted cleverly, or saturated, but at what cost and with what degree of confidence?
3. *How capital intensive is the mobilization program?* A manpower intensive mobilization (e.g. 1914), as with the Soviet program, cannot be sustained: hence, the traditional truth that "mobilization means war."[37]
4. *How durable are the weapons emphasized in the mobilization program?* Surge production of unreliable weapons without a large inventory of spare parts would look like an intention to fight in the near term.
5. *How great a dislocation will the defense mobilization program cause for the economy as a whole?* Great Britain shifted to a genuine, centrally planned, "total war economy" in 1939-40—"for the duration." Nazi Germany slowly, and incompletely, effected such a shift over the years 1942-44.[38] If, for example, the Soviet Union were to seize West Berlin or Iran, and the United States were to respond by mobilization and not by direct and immediate military action, for how long would American society tolerate a "war economy" in peacetime?
6. *How are the "teeth" and the "tail" of military capability to be phased into the inventory?* U.S. and NATO forces, in normal times, tend to be "teeth light" and "tail heavy." However, in a mobiliza-

tion program one might prefer to surge teeth at the expense, initially, of support, repair and replacement—if only to maximize the "up front" combat threat and to hedge against the possibility that war might occur tomorrow rather than next month.

7. *Does the program have any salutary shock value for Soviet military assessment?* Is there anything the United States can deploy, or (preferably) reassign, which would effect—in the likely Soviet view—a major near-term favorable discontinuity in U.S. military capability? Somewhat heretically, perhaps, this chapter sees mobilization not only in terms of machines and men, but also in terms of strategic and tactical ideas. A useful upward discontinuity in NATO's deterrence clout might be effected were the Alliance to advertise, and redeploy for, a basically offensive (or, at the least, counteroffensive), as opposed to defensive, strategy.[39] The opportunities for the rapid effecting of "deterrence discontinuity" are even more evident at the central war level than they are in respect to theater conflict.[40]

8. *Does a proposed weapon (or, more generally, defense) program lend itself to benign misassessment by the Soviet Union?* Because of the endemic danger of Soviet forceful interdiction of the Western mobilization process, it would be very desirable if that process could be designed in such a way that Soviet assessors were prone to be misled (on the high side, of course) as to the state of actual Western combat capability. For example, the world at large could be told that the United States was producing SLCMs just as rapidly as two or three shifts in the relevant plants could produce them (and their warheads and guidance). Also, the United States could announce and offer a few appropriate photographs—that SLCMs were being deployed very widely indeed on U.S. naval vessels (of all kinds). Provided that *Aviation Week* could be persuaded to do its patriotic duty, Soviet naval intelligence would be likely greatly to overestimate the pace and scale of the actual deployment achieved.

Conclusions

One should not be doctrinaire about the value of mobilization planning. Just because one can invent a scenario that provides no time for defense mobilization, it does not follow that mobilization, ergo, can play no important part in U.S. national security policy. This study, while generically very friendly to the idea that defense mobilization may play a vital role as a policy response to high level conflict, either actual or anticipated, has also sought to be attentive to the traditional criticisms of mobilization policy. The case for a defense mobilization component of U.S. national security policy would seem, virtually, to make itself. Provided defense mobilization is not seen as a panacea, its role as a policy tool can only be beneficial. American policy-makers should be reminded constantly of the fact that no matter how problematical are their promises of particular strategic action policy responses, the Soviet Union has no difficulty whatsoever believing in the productive capacity of American defense industry.

NOTES

I am very grateful to Keith Payne of the National Institute of Public Policy for his assistance with this study.

1. See L.L. Farrar, Jr., *The Short-War Illusion: German Policy, Strategy and Domestic Affairs*, August–December 1914 (Santa Barbara, Cal.: ABC-Clio, 1973), particularly p. 4.

2. The best study of France in this period remains Richard Challener, *The French Theory of The Nation in Arms, 1866-1939* (New York: Russell and Russell, 1965).

3. See A.J.P. Taylor, *How Wars Begin* (New York: Atheneum, 1979).

4. In Presidential Directive (PD)-59 of July 25, 1980.

5. For a brilliant overview of the economic dimension of World War II, see Alan S. Milward, *War, Economy and Society, 1939-1945* (Berkeley, Cal.: University of California Press, 1977).

6. On August 15, 1919, the United Kingdom adopted, as a defense planning principle, the assumption that major conflict would not occur for ten years. This "ten-year rule" endured until 1932. For the historical context, see Norman H. Gibbs, *Grand Strategy: Volume I: Rearmament Policy* (London: Her Majesty's Stationary Office, 1973).

7. For the strategy case for MX/MPS, see Colin S. Gray, *Strategy and the MX* (Washington, D.C.: The Heritage Foundation, 1980).

8. These studies have been conducted by Frank Armbruster, Norman Friedman, William Schneider, Jr., and John Thomas.

9. This, at least, has been the recent experience with studies conducted by Hudson Institute.

10. See James H. Toner, "American Society and the American Way of War: Korea and Beyond," *Parameters*, Vol. XI, No. 1 (March 1981), pp. 79-90; and Colin S. Gray, "National Style in Strategy: The American Example," *International Security*, V. 6, No. 2 (Fall 1981), pp. 21-47.

11. Paul Bracken, "Mobilization in the Nuclear Age," *International Security*, Vol. 3, No. 3 (Winter 1978/1979), p. 74. The adjective "superior" is not necessary for the definition.

12. Defense mobilization for high-level conflict today would free funds for a crash program in directed-energy weapons research. Even on a "business as usual" basis, this category of research and development is expected to produce a useful, first-generation, BMD weapon (space-based) by the mid-1990s. A "Manhattan Project"-style program in the weaponization of directed energy possiblities could well have military consequences surprising both to Washington and Moscow.

13. See Lynn E. Davis, *Limited Nuclear Options: Deterrence and the New American Doctrine*, Adelphi Paper No. 121 (London: International Institute for Strategic Studies—IISS—Winter 1975/76).

14. See Colin S. Gray, "Presidential Directive 59: Flawed but Useful," *Parameters*, Vol. XI, No. 1 (March 1981), pp. 29-37.

15. See Harold Brown, *Department of Defense Annual Report, Fiscal Year 1982* (Washington, D.C.: U.S. Government Printing Office), January 19, 1981, pp. 38-45.

16. See Richard B. Foster and Francis P. Hoeber, "Limited Mobilization: A Strategy for Preparedness and Deterrence in the Eighties," *Orbis*, Vol. 24, No. 3 (Fall 1980), particularly pp. 449-50.

17. However, Foster and Hoeber do envisage a "limited mobilization" on the scale of a doubling or tripling of the current U.S. defense effort. Ibid., pp. 452, 456.

18. This is not to argue that a limited mobilization necessarily is politically infeasible domestically, only that such an effort, in the future has to be geared to an explicit, and easily understandable threat and theory of victory. As Ronald Reagan has said, intervention in Vietnam was a "noble cause"—that cause needed, but never acquired, a matching theory of victory.

19. The stability of domestic society was one of Stalin's "permanently operating factors" and is as relevant today as it was when Stalin first elevated it to the level of doctrinal concern.

20. Regardless of the contemporary fashion in U.S. strategic nuclear doctrine, in the late 1970s the United States lacked survivable command, control, communications and intelligence (C^3I), and hence, almost certainly would have been driven to conduct a central war, had it occurred, in a spasm mode.

21. This argument is handled particularly persuasively in Bracken, "Mobilization in the Nuclear Age," Op. Cit.

22. Foster and Hoeber (in "Limited Mobilization"), rest their case for a very muscular program of "limited mobilization" on current (in)security conditions and trends.

23. However, too much should not be made of the uniqueness of the "nuclear dread" element. The Western democracies, in 1938-39, feared devastating air attack (including the use of poison gas).

24. Which is why I am politically skeptical both of Paul Bracken's arguments for "partial" mobilization, and of Richard Foster and Francis Hoeber's arguments for "limited mobilization."

25. Richard Foster certainly is correct in saying that mobilization should be an established line-item in the U.S. defense budget. "Limited Mobilization," Op. Cit., p. 451.

26. See Bracken, "Mobilization in the Nuclear Age," Op. Cit., pp. 80, 92. Fully cognizant though he is of the problem of possible Soviet preemption, Bracken does not treat this problem as seriously as he should. The same judgment applies to Foster and Hoeber, "Limited Mobilization," p. 453.

27. Bracken, "Mobilization in the Nuclear Age," Op. Cit., pp. 79-81.

28. Hudson Institute has worked on a design of "protracted nuclear campaigns."

29. See my study (conducted for the U.S. Defense Nuclear Agency) *Nuclear Strategy and National Style*, (July 1981). An excellent discussion is provided in Robert Bathurst, "Two Languages of War," in Derek Leebaert, ed., *Soviet Military Thinking* (London: Allen and Unwin, 1981), pp. 42-75. There is a totality to the Soviet view of conflict which is far removed from the narrowly military fascination so evident in the United States. In Bathurst's words, "[t]he Soviet language of war does not begin where the American does, with a breach of legality, or end where it does with a military defeat. It begins

with the exacerbation of class warfare (which emerges often as the warfare of political parties) and ends with nothing less than the transformation of society. The last Soviet battle does not take place when the missiles have ceased to fly, but when the revolutionary executions against the wall have stopped." p. 47.

30. See Foster and Hoeber, "Limited Mobilization," Op. Cit., p. 453.

31. Bracken (and Kahn) argues that the United States could afford a trillion dollar defense program by the mid-1980s. Ibid., p. 86.

32. Paul Bracken ("Mobilization in the Nuclear Age") believes that the great changes in the Soviet (and American) economy since the early 1950s have eroded, and possibly invalidated, this distinction. I am not convinced. See Norman Friedman and Colin S. Gray, *U.S.-USSR Mobilization Policies, Volume I, Net Assessment*, HI-2738-RR (Croton-on-Hudson, New York: Hudson Institute, November 30, 1977). Also see Norman Friedman, "The Soviet Mobilization Base," *Air Force Magazine*, Vol. 62, No. 3 (March 1979), pp. 65-71.

33. Which is not to deny that Soviet industry could considerably expand its production of defense goods. See Bracken, "Mobilization in the Nuclear Age," Op. Cit., pp. 82-91. However it is well to note that the defense procurement burden (alone) on Soviet GNP for the 1980-1989 period may well be as high as 17% (as opposed to the CIA estimate of 5%)—if Professor Steven Rosefielde of the University of North Carolina is correct (in a forthcoming book).

34. See Colin S. Gray, "Strategic Forces, General Purpose Forces, and Crisis Management," *The Annals* (November 1981), pp. 67-77.

35. John Erickson, "The Soviet Military System: Doctrine, Technology, and 'Style'," in Erickson and E.J. Feuchtwanger, eds., *Soviet Military Power and Performance* (Hamden, Conn.: Archon, 1979), p. 28.

36. These questions were identified in an outstanding paper by Norman Friedman. *Weapon Systems for Mobilization War*, HI-2203/2-DP (Croton-on-Hudson, New York: Hudson Institute, March 31, 1975), pp. 2-7.

37. For example, on November 23, 1912, the Russian Prime Minister, Kokovtzov, observed to a conference of the Czar's advisers that "no matter what we chose to call the projected measures [a "partial mobilization" was under consideration], a mobilization remained a mobilization, to be countered by our adversaries with actual war." Quoted in L.C.F. Turner, "The Russian Mobilization of 1914," in Paul M. Kennedy, ed., *The War Plans of the Great Powers, 1880-1914* (London: Allen and Unwin, 1979), p. 255.

39. For some relevant ideas, see Edward N. Luttwak, "The Operational Level of War," *International Security*, Vol. 5, No. 3 (Winter 1980/81), pp. 61-79.

40. See Colin S. Gray, "Nuclear Strategy: The Case for a Theory of Victory," *International Security*, Vol. 4, No. 1 (Summer 1979), pp. 54-87.

Section II

Assessment of the United States
Industrial and Manpower Infrastructure

3

Peacetime Industrial Preparedness for Wartime Ammunition Production (Past, Present and Future)

Harry F. Ennis

Introduction

Ammunition is essential to modern warfare. A shortage of ammunition has mandated revisions in operational plans in the past and might well have more severe effects in the future. Such shortages in wartime can derive from a number of sources. Prewar economic and political priorities may have obscured the wartime needs. Insufficient initial stockage at the outset of the war certainly springs to mind as a primary cause of shortages of supplies. Failures or inadequacies in the transportation and distribution systems could create localized shortages of wartime commodities. Enemy and accidental actions might produce the same result. In a protracted engagement, the lack of an adequate industrial capability to compensate for insufficient levels of initial stockage and to replenish consumption and combat losses could cause critical shortages to develop. It is to this latter potential cause that this chapter is addressed.

Ammunition will be used as an example of a wartime commodity which is clearly dependent upon the existence of a sound industrial base for long-term supplies. However, the experience with ammunition supply and consumption provides a useful analogue in dealing with other members of the military commodity family which are inextricably bound to the industrial sector of the economy. Like large-caliber ammunition, there are other items of military materiel which have no direct commercial counterpart. Examples include: land combat vehicles; large-caliber and automatic weapons; and to an extent, combat aircraft and naval vessels. These commodities are commercial anomalies but, for the most part, find their source in the commercial sector. Therefore, in an open market economy, extraordinary measures must be taken to insure that the capability exists to manufacture these specialized items of military hardware.

Since munitions manufacturing capabilities cannot be created instantaneously when they are needed most, at the outbreak of war, attention must be given to providing for production capabilities which can be activated in a reasonable time to meet national defense needs when required. The purpose of this study is to present the results of a selective investigation into the current status of the industrial base for representative ammunition production, to analyze its sufficiency to meet our potential national security needs, and to offer some suggestions for improvement of our industrial preparedness posture.

A brief look into our nation's history will highlight the importance of industrial preparedness and suggest future actions from the hard-won experiences of the past. The present status of the industrial base for the production of selected ammunition items will be examined. The broad philosophical implications for preparedness will have meaning to all of the Armed Services. This chapter will suggest some practical solutions to the difficult dilemma of providing concurrently for near-term readiness and intermediate-range sustainability.

The Past

The difficulty of estimating accurately the requirements for future wars and making necessary peacetime preparations is as old as antiquity. Vegetius, the fourth century Roman military advisor to the Emperor Valentinian wrote:

> An exact calculation must therefore be made before the commencement of the war as to the number of troops and the expenses incident thereto, so that the provinces may in plenty of time furnish the forage, corn, and all other kinds of provisions of them.[1]

This quotation captures the essence of mobilization; the conversion of a nation at peace to a nation at war. The inability to predict the intensity or duration of future wars argues persuasively that inventories of war reserve stocks, in and of themselves, cannot sustain combat indefinitely. The mix must be found between war reserve stocks and replenishment capabilities which will meet the broad-range needs of our national security. In the past, materiel mobilization, rather than manpower mobilization, dictated the speed with which an effective fighting force could be deployed. In looking back we see that each of our wars presented an opportunity to learn how better to provide for our national security. Some of the lessons were learned early and well, and some we were destined to repeat.

Along with the many national traditions established during our early formative years, the lack of interest in things martial between wars seems to have been born before the American Revolution. The capability which existed for powder manufacture in the Colonies during the French and Indian War had been permitted to atrophy. Both the physical plants and the manufacturing expertise had passed from the scene by 1775.[2] George Washington's army, besieging the British in Boston, suffered severe shortages of gunpowder (which equated to ammunition firepower potential in those simpler technological days). In Washington's letters one finds the anguished report:

> Our advanced works and theirs are within musket-shot. We daily undergo a cannonade, which has done no injury to our works, and very little hurt to our men. These insults we are compelled to submit to for want of powder, being obliged, except for now and then giving them a shot, to reserve what we have for closer work than cannon-distance.[3]

The Revolutionary War taught the nation its first lessons in materiel mobilization. Successful conduct of war is inextricably bound to the availability of warfighting supplies and equipment. Without prior planning and action, mobilization of the necessary resources cannot take place after the war begins without suffering attendant inefficiency and waste.

As our needs expanded from gunpowder and muskets to repeating weapons and breach-loading cannons, the size and the appetite of our armies grew. The early response to the industrial need was answered with the creation of government arsenals and armories to supplement private manufacturers, with the faint hope of their being able to take over the entire manufacturing job for the Armed Forces. The American Civil War clearly demonstrated that only a marriage of U.S. Government and the burgeoning private industrial sector could hope to meet the munitions needs of modern warfare.

The First World War taught the importance of a single mobilization authority and of Allied cooperation on a scale unprecedented up to that time. Especially noteworthy was the materiel support furnished the American Expeditionary Force (AEF) by our French and British Allies. It became abundantly clear that we could quickly provide the uniformed manpower, but not the military hardware, from a peacetime standing start. These inadequacies were addressed in the interwar years through organizational and educational reforms. However, despite early post-war interest, the deterioration of the defense industrial base was well advanced by the mid-1930s. The U.S. involvement in World War II was preceded by a period in which our industrial machinery was activated to support the war in Europe almost two years before the United States was drawn into the war. Financial resources were lavished on the industrial base as war approached and the prodigous industrial output of the "Arsenal of Democracy" provided the lion's share of munitions throughout the war. Since World War II, the United States has had to learn how to support and fight in wars for which there is no declaration of national emergency. In many ways this environment tries the industrial ingenuity of the country more severely than does an all-out declared emergency.

From this brief recitation it is clear that our responses to national emergencies throughout history have had to be flexible enough to respond to a broad spectrum of conflict. National security has been tested against scenarios ranging from intermittent Indian Wars and a three-month war with Spain to global war of immense proportions. Through it all there has emerged a consistent thread of features, common enough to each of our experiences to be cited reasonably collectively as lessons learned. They are presented here in summary form.

(1) In wartime, manpower can be mobilized more quickly than the materiel resources needed for troop support.
(2) Wars are of uncertain duration.
(3) Preparatory actions must be taken in peacetime to insure responsiveness of the industrial sector and to avoid waste in wartime.
(4) The mobilization process must have a centralized focal point at the national level.

Preparedness is preferable to unpreparedness in mobilizing for national security; to hold otherwise would be to defy logic. The question is how best to achieve the level of preparedness desired. Provisions must be made for manpower and materiel stockpiles. Additionally, in deference to the possibility of protracted war, industrial readiness must get its share of national attention.

The Present

The posture of the present industrial base for defense production appears to be driven by the belief that future wars will be very intense and of short duration. Clearly, the earliest phase of any future conflict, or the entire conflict if it be short enough, will have to be supported by forces in being and supplies on hand. Recent debate regarding the probable duration of a war has produced an interpretation known as the "short war scenario."[4] This concept holds that a short intense war will be fought which will end quickly or escalate to the use of tactical or selected strategic nuclear weapons. Under these conditions, the settlement would occur before any effect could be felt from the existence of an industrial capacity which could be turned to support of the war effort. Therefore, industrial staying power, especially for ammunition production, has been deemphasized.

The production of ammunition is highly capital intensive. Since virtually no commercial market for military ammunition exists and since ammunition production capital is inherently under-utilized in peacetime, potential producers are reluctant to make the large capital investments necessary to insure that a wartime capability exists. Because of these factors, the ammunition production base is composed of three interrelated elements: (1) twenty-eight governmentally owned factories (fifteen ammunition plants and one arsenal, presently active); (2) one hundred sixty-five governmentally owned plant equipment packages (PEP's);[5] and (3) nearly one thousand agreements with private industry to augment the Government's production capability.

The condition of the ammunition base ranges from very efficient, well maintained, modernized active lines; through neglected real property and unuseable PEP's; to ineffective mobilization agreements with private industry. The plant modernization program and the construction of the first new ammunition plant in this country in twenty-five years[6] are direct and positive responses to the substandard condition of the base evident during the Vietnam war. These measures contribute to the well being of the active production facilities. However, the inactive portion of the base is being neglected and is showing signs of serious deterioration. It is estimated that approximately $40 million in backlogged maintenance projects exist at our ammunition plants and that only about one-third (31%) of the ammunition plant equipment packages (PEP's) is useable without extensive repair. The condition of the mobilization agreements is no less deficient. Planning agreements are not contracts; therefore neither the Government nor the planned producer is bound by their provisions. Contractors prepare them in a perfunctory manner and the Government, at its convenience, ignores them.

With the base and its condition having been reviewed, it is appropriate next to examine how these conditions are manifested in the ability of the base to respond to increases in the rate of production of certain ammunition items currently being manufactured. Three ammunition items have been selected as examples: (1) The 155mm high-explosive artillery projectile, M483, improved conventional munition (ICM)—workhorse of the Division Artillery; (2) The 105mm hypervelocity antitank cartridge, M735; and, (3) The Air Force 30mm aircraft ammunition (GAU-8).

The artillery round (M483) is presently being assembled at two locations. The load, assemble, and package (LAP) operation is the pacing activity in the production of this round; that is, the component manufacturers are able to stay ahead of the final assembly facilities.

Each of the two government owned plants is presently capable of producing a maximum 42,000 completed rounds per month. The disparity between maximum production and wartime needs is dramatic. The combined U.S. Army and U.S. Marine Corps requirement for the M483 is 448,000 rounds per month or more than five times the present maximum capability.[7] Part of the recognized deficit in the base for the production of this round will be redressed when the new plant in Mississippi comes on line in 1983. The Mississippi plant will be capable of loading 120,000 rounds per month. However, even this enhanced capacity will meet less than half of the expected mobilization requirement.

In the case of the tank round (M735) a two-tier production capacity problem exists. The metal parts components are the pacing items and a combined capability of 21,000 of these components per month is represented in the factories of two commercial manufacturers. The LAP facility has a maximum assembly capability of 40,000 per month if sufficient components could be provided. Even at this rate, however, the production of the end item would fall far short of the mobilization requirement of 162,400 rounds per month for the Army and the Marine Corps.[8]

The Army's production base plan for both of these items of ammunition shows an M-day action (i.e., action to be taken upon the declaration of mobilization) of developing the facilities to fill the void with an estimated lead time of thirteen months. There is little hope of building, in peacetime, the facilities needed to support the full mobilization requirements; however, improvements can be made in the present responsiveness of the base. Suggested improvements are discussed below.

The Air Force procures the GAU-8 ammunition at a peak peacetime rate of approximately eleven million rounds per year from two qualified commercial vendors. To encourage private capital investment and to enhance competition, each manufacturer has been permitted by the Air Force to acquire active production facilities capable of producing 60% of the peacetime requirement. A provision is included in the production contract to indemnify the producers for unrecovered capital investment losses if they were incurred as a result of the production of GAU-8 ammunition. This innovative contracting procedure permits an immediate expansion capability of 20% since only 100% of the current or peacetime procurement is distributed between the two competing producers. Thus, the ability to expand production rapidly is built into current procurement contracts. Although 20% would be a modest expansion if a full-scale war were to be supported, this technique represents a tangible first step toward what has come to be known as "surge contracting." Surge contracting differs fundamentally from surge planning in that it carries contractual responsibility for performance. Extension of the surge contracting techniques pioneered in the GAU-8 procurement will contribute significantly to industrial preparedness.

It appears from the brief review of the sample of ammunition items that current production needs can be adequately met by the industrial capacity dedicated to that purpose. However, the ability to surge in peacetime or to produce at significantly higher rates quickly under mobilization conditions is subject to serious question. Since industrial responsiveness can substitute for on-hand inventory, a cost benefit will be shown in the tradeoff between investments in industrial preparedness improvements and the cost of end item stockpiles otherwise required to sustain a war during a buildup in production.

A Cost Benefit Analysis

The preponderance of current literature recognizes the inadequacies of the munitions industrial sector to expand quickly to wartime, or significantly higher peacetime, production rates. Unfortunately, most of these analyses conclude that the solution to the problem lies in the infusion of additional financial resources into the Army budget to facilitate corrective action. This portion of the study will suggest finding an economical tradeoff between satisfying needs of present-day readiness and long-term sustainability within currently available resources.

Perceived requirements for military materiel dictate the size and responsiveness of the industrial base. Past national experience has shown this perception to be markedly different in periods of wartime and peacetime.

When a war is going on, the nature of the conflict prescribes the combat demands; e.g., combat intensity, attrition, and, of course, the duration of the conflict. These combat demands translate into a demand on national resources. Resources are allocated and the logistical system (including the industrial base) converts the resources into warfighting supplies and equipment. The materiel output of the logistical system contributes to the movement (or nonmovement in the case of defense) of the forward edge of the battle area (FEBA) on the conventional battlefield. If the supplies have proved to be inadequate, combat demands rise, greater demand is placed on the logistical system, and output is increased accordingly, or vice versa. In short, in wartime, combat requirements determine resource allocation.

In peacetime, actual combat demand is noticeable by its absence. No yardstick exists for measuring the effectiveness of the resource input stream. Consequently, reductions in the peacetime allocation of resources to the logistical base are not immediately perceived as adversely affecting combat capability. Operational plans often overlook logistical shortcomings. Therefore, it appears that in peacetime, resource allocation is the independent variable upon which warfighting ability depends.

Unfortunately, this peacetime view is susceptible to being transformed abruptly into a wartime reality by world events. In the late 1930s when the nation was dedicating approximately 1% of its gross national product to national defense, it would have been difficult to comprehend the resources required to bring World War II to a successful conclusion. During the peak years of 1943-1945, upwards of 40% of the national wealth was dedicated to the war effort.[9] How, then, can a logistical planner anticipate future demands accurately, and judiciously allocate peacetime resources to provide the necessary warfighting capability should war come? A cost benefit analytical methodology applicable to the solution of this difficult planning dilemma, together with some preliminary analytical results, is offered for thoughtful consideration.

In November 1978, a study was released by the Department of the Army entitled the *Ammunition Production Base Leadtime Study*.[10] This excellent work was performed by Kaiser Engineers in association with Stetter Associates, Inc., under contract with the office of the Project Manager, Munitions Production Base Modernization and Expansion. The Leadtime Study investigated the present condition of the base for the production of representative items of ammunition. Then, through the application of a critical path methodology (CPM), the study identified and analyzed production bottlenecks and suggested cost-effective improvements to enhance the responsiveness of the base. Critical path analysis is particularly well suited to this application since it assists in identifying the path through the maze which contains the time-constraining activities. That is, if the overall completion time of a project is to be compressed, improvements along the critical path must be found. The study proceeded as follows:

(1) A standard critical path network was created and is shown schematically in Figure 1.

Figure 1—The Standard Network

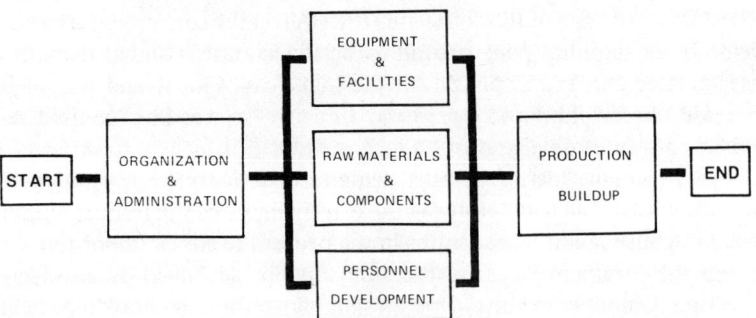

(2) Deficiencies in the present base which would constrain individual production lines from reaching prescribed mobilization production rates were then identified. The goal was to identify improvements which would reduce industrial response time by four months. A representation of the result of this step in the methodology is shown in Figure 2. For a hypothetical monthly mobilization production rate of 90,000 end items per month, the current maximum production capability of components and end items are shown during the period of production buildup after M-day. The component and end item production deficiencies which constrain the particular plant from attaining the target rate in the early periods of production buildup describe the critical path through the network.

Figure 2—Ammunition Production in Thousands Per Month

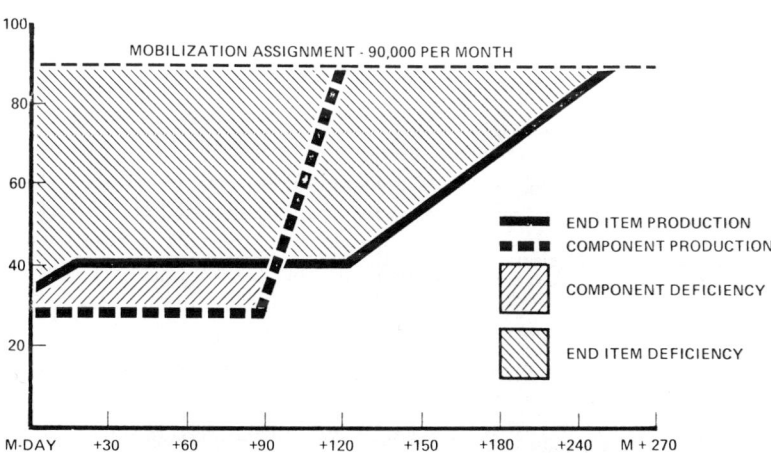

(3) With the critical path thus identified, improvements were suggested. Examples of beneficial pre-M-day improvements include: increasing raw material and component inventories; installation of industrial plant equipment; development of training, start-up, and inspection procedures. By simulating the application of the suggested improvements to the network, the critical path was theoretically shortened.

During this process, pre-M-day costs were recorded for both the present and improved condition of the industrial facility to serve as a basis of comparison. The results were tabulated for each production line examined. One such tabulation is provided illustratively as Figure 3.[11] This illustration is of improvements which could be applied to the production of the M483, 155mm artillery projectile. It will be noted that the costs (negative savings) of the improvement investments total nearly $9 million. When these costs are subtracted from the possible savings through reductions of pre-M-day stockpiles of $78 million, a net saving of over $69 million is estimated. By applying similar analyses to the other selected items of ammunition, the Leadtime Study concluded that $81 million in net savings could be realized for the total investment in improvements of $35 million (a better than two to one return on investment) for the items investigated.[12]

Figure 3

INVESTMENTS AND SAVINGS
PROJECTILE, 155MM HE, ICM, M483
AMMUNITION PRODUCTION BASE LEADTIME STUDY

ITEM	LINE CONDITION	QUANTITY	COST ($1,000)	IMPROVEMENT INVESTMENT ($1,000)	NET SAVINGS ($1,000)
END ITEM LAP	CURRENT	247,050	113,127	-	-
	IMPROVED	114,180	52,284	583	-
	SAVINGS	132,870	60,843	(583)	60,260
SHELL MPTS	CURRENT	24,150	3,427	-	-
	IMPROVED	37,475	5,318	2,494	-
	SAVINGS	(13,325)	(1,891)	(2,494)	(4,386)
M42/M46 GRENADE BODY	CURRENT	7,294,080	8,352	-	-
	IMPROVED	7,498,560	8,586	386	-
	SAVINGS	(204,480)	(234)	(386)	(620)
FUZE M223	CURRENT	27,315,227	11,390	-	-
	IMPROVED	15,818,400	6,596	1,398	-
	SAVINGS	11,496,827	4,794	(1,398)	3,396
FUZE MPTS M577	CURRENT	407,550	24,506	-	-
	IMPROVED	164,717	9,904	4,034	-
	SAVINGS	242,833	14,602	(4,034)	10,568
TOTAL	CURRENT	-	160,802	-	-
	IMPROVED	-	82,688	2,895	-
	SAVINGS	-	78,114	(8,895)	69,219

Despite these examples of rather compelling evidence, it remains extremely difficult to convince policy-makers that it is more prudent and more cost effective to invest in inactive production capability than it is to invest in additional units of hardware for inventory.

From the Seventies Into the Eighties

As the United States withdrew from the trauma of the war in Vietnam, national consciousness lapsed into its traditional peacetime state. In this, yet another interwar era in U.S. history, interest in mobilization and industrial preparedness began to wane. The national focal point for mobilization matters, the Office of Emergency Preparedness, was abolished in 1973, leaving the effort without effective centralized leadership and without a voice on the National Security Council. The curriculum of the Industrial College of the Armed Forces shifted from mobilization to the broader subjects of human relations and executive skills. Fortunately, the emphasis on materiel acquisition and mobilization is being revived in the curriculum offerings.[13]

This general decline in interest is evident notwithstanding the very recent appearance (late 1980 and throughout 1981) of four in-depth studies of the defense industrial base:
- The House Armed Services Committee Industrial Base Panel report, "The Ailing Defense Industrial Base: Unready for Crisis," 31 December 1980.
- A Defense Science Board Task Force report on industrial responsiveness, 21 November 1980.
- An Air Force Systems Command statement on defense industrial base issues, 13 November 1980.
- A book, *The Defense Industry*, by J.S. Gansler, M.I.T. Press, October 1980.
- A plan, "The Department of Defense Master Plan for Mobilization," 1981.

These studies and the positive notes represented by the enlightened Leadtime Study and surge contracting techniques provide ample hope for future improvements in the responsiveness of the industrial base.

The Future

The future of peacetime industrial preparedness for wartime ammunition production depends upon the initiatives taken in response to the lessons of the past and the careful analysis of the present condition of the base.

The record indicates that wars have been of uncertain duration and nations prepared to fight only short wars were tragically embarrassed when the wars did not end quickly. Earlier wars have also demonstrated the fact that mobilization of materiel has proved to be far more difficult and time consuming than the mobilization of manpower. Modern wars revealed the close and incontrovertible relationship between the Government and private industry. Centralized leadership and control of the gearing up for war has repeatedly proved its worth in the past. Since wars tend to be of uncertain duration, requirements for stockpiling of materiel cannot be accurately estimated. Therefore, complete reliance can never be placed on having a big enough stockpile to obviate the need for a follow-on production capability. Finally, the study of our past wartime mobilization experiences indicated that to be effective, mobilization actions must be taken before M-day to avoid waste and reduce risk.

The review of the current industrial capability for production of munitions suggests certain imperatives for future action. The absence of a centralized programmatical and budgetary authority begs for the re-establishment of a mobilization focal point on the National Security Council. As the urgency of the ammunition requirements to support the Vietnam War recedes further from the national memory, no less pressing is the need to modernize the nation's aging ammunition manufacturing base. The current modernization of the base should be continued to completion. The present deteriorating condition of the inactive portion of the government owned production facilities demands attention and funding support. Government access to the industrial potential inherent in the private sector of the nation's economy is emasculated by the ineffective mobilization planning mechanism, which has been perpetuated from an earlier age and has no relation to present-day needs or perceptions. The production planning schedules must be replaced with surge contracting which carries contractual obligation and provides the wherewithal to expand production quickly when needed. Near-term readiness and long-term sustainability need not be mutually exclusive propositions. Cost effective marginal investments in sustainability complement near-term readiness and may indeed enhance it. What is to be concluded?

The preoccupation of the United States with budgetary constraints and short-war scenarios seems to have caused an imbalance to occur in national defense considerations in favor of short-term requirements. The ability to expand significantly the production of ammunition and other materiel is dependent on the viability of the government owned manufacturing base and on mobilization agreements with private industry. Since these two elements have been shown to be woefully inadequate to the task, it may be reasonably concluded that mobilization planning and industrial preparedness for U.S. Army ammunition production are not sufficiently flexible to meet a wide variety of possible peacetime and wartime contingencies.

If war does come again to the United States and it be protracted, there will be little consolation in the knowledge that the nation was well prepared to fight a short war. It would be sad indeed to reflect on this period in the nation's history and realize that more could have been done, but was not done, to assure a sustained warfighting capability. Rather than relearning the lessons the United States learned in Korea or Imperial Germany learned in the First World War, United States leadership must take advantage of this period of peace and take positive actions to assure preparedness to fight America's next war. These include:

(1) reestablish a national centralized mobilization authority;
(2) preserve the present defense industrial base through continued modernization efforts and maintenance of the inactive manufacturing capability; and,
(3) combine mobilization planning with current production of defense materiel through expanded use of "surge contracting" techniques.

The Reagan Administration has demonstrated its support of the defense of the nation in the President's budget submitted to the Congress. If approved, it is incumbent upon the Defense Department to apply the increased appropriations wisely to the problems that need to be solved. If the suggested improvements in industrial preparedness be made, U.S. defense industry can once again realize its potential as a critically important strategic (and deterrence) national resource.

NOTES

1. Flavius Renatus Vegetius, "The Military Institutions of the Romans," trans. John Clarke in *Roots of Strategy*, ed. Thomas R. Phillips (Harrisburg, Pa.: The Military Service Publishing Company, 1940), p. 128.
2. Orlando W. Stephenson, "The Supply of Gunpowder in 1776," *The American Historical Review*, V. 30, (January 1925), p. 271.
3. George Washington, *The Writings of George Washington*, ed. Jared Sparks, III (Boston: Russell, Odiorne and Metcalf; and Hilliard, Gray, and Co., 1834), p. 122.
4. Examples can be found in: U.S. Congress, Joint Committee on Defense Production, *Defense Industrial Base: Industrial Preparedness and Nuclear War Survival. Hearings before the Joint Committee on Defense Production, Part I*, 94th Cong., 2d sess., 1976, p. 1; U.S. Congress, Joint Committee on Defense Production, *Civil Preparedness Review, Part I, Emergency Preparedness and Industrial Mobilization. Report by the Joint Committee on Defense Production*, 95th Cong., 1st sess., 1977, pp. 77-79; and more recently, General Sir John Hackett, *The Third World War* (New York: Macmillan Publishing Co., Inc., 1978), pp. 315-316.
5. Vincent J. Gorman, "Munitions Production Base and Plant Equipment Package: Modernization Program Overview," presented to American Defense Preparedness Association Symposium on Industrial Base Planning (Alexandria, Va.: Washington Field Office, Project Manager, Munitions Production Base Modernization and Expansion, (24-25 April 1979), pp. 29-31.
6. American Defense Preparedness Association, "Mississippi Army Ammunition Plant," *National Defense*, V. 62 (March-April 1978), p. 479.
7. U.S. Department of Defense, *Production Base Plan/Analysis for FY 1981)*, (Rock Island, Illinois: U.S. Army Armament Materiel Readiness Command), schedule number 3647, p. 1.
8. Ibid., U.S. schedule number 2657, p. 1.
9. U.S. Department of Defense, *National Budget Estimates for FY 1980*, (Washington, D.C.: Office of the Assistant Secretary of Defense (Comptroller), n.d.), p. 16.
10. U.S. Department of the Army, *Ammunition Production Base Leadtime Study*, (Dover, N.J.: Project Manager, Munitions Production Base Modernization and Expansion, November 1978).
11. Ibid., V. I, Part I, Table 1-1.
12. Ibid., Executive Summary Table 2-2.
13. James E. Dalton, Maj. Gen., U.S.A.F., "What Kind of Mobilization for What Type of Conflict? ('Under Attack' or Protracted 'Twilight Conflict')". Opening address, Tenth Annual Conference, International Security Studies Program, The Fletcher School of Law and Diplomacy, Tufts University, Cambridge, Massachusetts, 4 May 1981.

4

Strategic Assessment of National Military Mobilization in the 1980s—Manpower

H. Rowland Ludden*

Introduction

An assessment of the manpower element of national military mobilization in the 1980s requires examination of three different types of manpower: 1) pretrained military manpower available at mobilization, 2) nonprior military service manpower to be trained after mobilization, and 3) civilian manpower in the military departments. Although all of the military Services have some elements in common in the manpower area, they also have significant differences among them. However, the Army has the most serious problem of all the Services, at least quantitatively. This assessment will examine the situation in the Army alone, and will not attempt to address the special aspects of Air Force, Navy or Marine Corps mobilization manpower.

Several types or levels of mobilization must be considered in military planning. These range from the President's authority under U.S. law to mobilize up to 100,000 members from all Services of the Selected Reserve (primarily units) for up to ninety days, through a partial mobilization of up to one million ready reserves from all Services for not more than two years when the President declares a national emergency, to full mobilization of the authorized force structure and reserves of all Services when Congress authorizes or declares war or a national emergency. A step beyond full mobilization would be total mobilization in which all the resources of the nation were called upon and additional military units were established beyond the currently authorized force structure. The actions required and the problems of these various types of mobilization are rather different. However, this analysis will be limited to consideration of full mobilization, the type of mobilization that would probably occur initially in response to a crisis involving actual conflict or the prospect of conflict between NATO and the Warsaw Pact.

---

* The views and opinions contained in this chapter are those of the author and should not be construed as an official Department of the Army or Department of Defense position, policy or decision.

Strategic Assessment

Army Manpower Today

Before examining the military mobilization manpower situation in detail, it will be helpful to take a brief look at where the Army is today and, in gross numbers, where it has been since inception of the all volunteer force. Figure 1 shows the manpower picture from 1974 through 1980 for the Army National Guard, the U.S. Army Reserve, the Active Army, the Army's civilian work force, and the Individual Ready Reserve (IRR), a pool of trained manpower needed to fill active and reserve units to wartime strength and meet casualty replacement requirements until newly trained draftees are available.

Figure 1

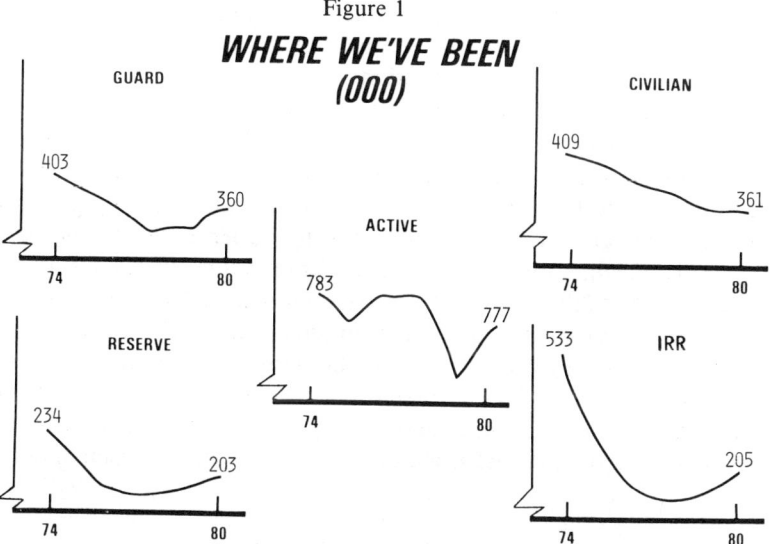

WHERE WE'VE BEEN (000)

After steady decline in both the Guard and Reserve, Fiscal Year 1979 saw a reversal in that downtrend. Although admittedly modest, that reversal continued in FY 1980, and is an encouraging sign. With additional resources programmed for FY 1981, continued improvement in both components is anticipated. This improvement is badly needed— the end FY 1980 strengths shown here are still short of the desired FY 1980 peacetime objective in the Guard (400.0) by 40,000 and in the Reserve (260.0) by 57,000, and against our wartime requirements by even more substantial numbers.

The Active Army recouped the recruiting shortfall experiences in FY 1979, and met the budgeted peacetime end strength for FY 1980. With Congressional support for additional resources and incentives, a near-term improvement is anticipated in the high school graduate content, despite a diminishing population and increased competition in that market.

Innovative, forward-looking adjustments are needed to offset unacceptable low levels of civilian manning. This is a major challenge. The Reagan Administration's decision to request additional civilians in FY 1981 and FY 1982 was a most welcome sign after six years of declining strength. The 382,000 requested for FY 1982 is a 21,000 increase over the FY 1980 level, but still some 40,000 below the Army's objective level.

Similarly, the overall availability of pretrained manpower is sharply limited; despite some recent increase in numbers, the Army remains approximately 250,000 below its wartime requirements. The risk inherent in that shortfall will be examined in detail later.

How did this bleak manpower picture come about?

The Active Army recruiting decline, which peaked in 1979, resulted primarily from a one-third reduction in recruiting resources, together with a combination of factors which included loss of the GI Bill, lowered unemployment among youth, and reduced attractiveness of enlistment/reenlistment options. Reduction of recruiting resources also diverted the Army from the high school market into the easier non-high school market at the expense of recruits possessing higher levels of education and skills. Further, there is an inverse relationship between the state of the economy and the Army's ability to recruit. Figure 2 depicts the Army experience in recruiting high school graduates (HSDG). These accessions of recruits are charted against the Army's recruiting resources. Projections through 1982 are based on assumptions of the effect on recruiting of pay raises, modifications of the Veteran's Education Assistance Program (VEAP), and a shorter (two year) enlistment option.

Figure 2

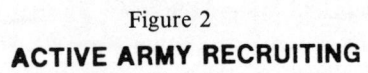

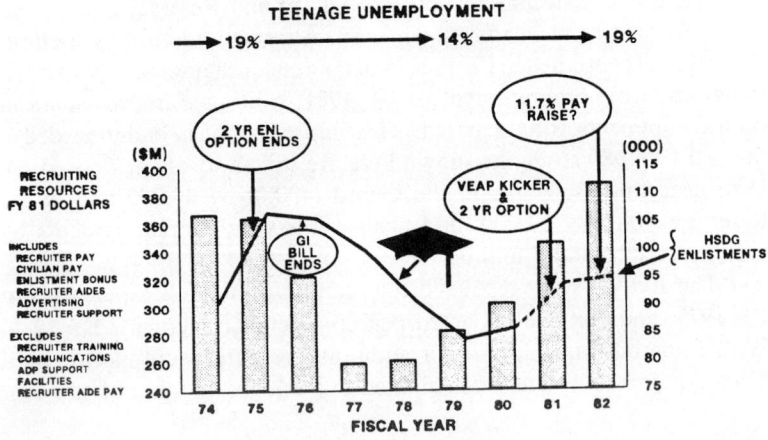

The decline in the reserve component strength of the Army National Guard and the U.S. Army Reserve can be tied to the loss of volunteers who were motivated by the threat of the draft for active service. The Army and the Office of the Secretary of Defense did not react soon enough with recruitment and retention incentives to offset the loss of draft motivated volunteers. The decline in both the Army National Guard and reserve strength continued over several years until it was halted in FY 1979 when incentives initiated in FY 1977 began to take hold. Some of those initial incentives were provided by Congress based on the Army's legislative program. Subsequently, initiatives have been expanded, and new ones added, and it is clear that strength improvement in the ARNG and USAR—both in terms of recruiting and retention progress—can be continued only if the initiatives in the Army budget and program are continued. Additional incentives may be required to accelerate planned growth or to accommodate unique skill problems.

Civilian strength levels have become a major manning challenge for the Army. Although federal civilian employment levels declined by one percent between 1974–1980, Army civilian levels were reduced by 11% in the same period. Despite the fact that the equivalent of more than a division of soldiers is diverted daily from military units to perform tasks previously done by civilians, reductions continued, due to hiring freezes and other management constraints.

The Individual Ready Reserve (IRR) portion of the Army's pretrained manpower has become a major challenge in manning the force. During the late 1960s and early 1970s the IRR was very large; in fact, it was larger than mobilization requirements justified. This was because the Active Army was much larger than it has been in recent years, and many of the soldiers had entered the Army through the draft. As soldiers finished their tours of active duty they were transferred to the reserves to fulfill the remainder of their six year military service obligation (MSO). Since the Army was large and draftees had only a two year active duty tour, large numbers of individuals entered the IRR and remained there for another four years. However, with the termination of the draft in 1973 and a reduction of the size of the Army after the end of the fighting in Vietnam, the flow of soldiers into the IRR declined drastically. In the All Volunteer Army first term active duty tours were either three or four years, so individuals transferring to the reserves at the end of their first term of active duty had less time remaining on their MSOs and stayed in the IRR for a shorter period. In addition, increased efforts to retain soldiers in the Army through vigorous reenlistment programs succeeded. This built a strong corps of noncommissioned officers (NCO) in the Active Army but still further reduced the flow of individuals into the IRR. The result was a drastic drop in IRR strength from nearly a million at its peak to less than 200,000 in the late 1970s.

Various actions have reversed that decline, and the IRR today has slightly over 200,000 members.

Pretrained Military Manpower

The Army must have enough pretrained manpower available to fill the 24 division force to full wartime levels at mobilization and to sustain it under warfighting conditions until trained draftees are available. Because of shortages in the Active Army, the Army National Guard and Army Reserve units and low strength levels of the Individual Ready Reserve and the Standby Reserve, the Army has a trained manpower shortfall of approximately 250,000.

The following analysis shows how that shortfall is determined.

Figure 3 illustrates the time-passed *trained military manpower structure* requirements (in thousands) for the Army's current 24 division force from mobilization, or M-day, to M+210. Starting at the left bottom of the chart, the peacetime active component structure increases at M-day to bring the active Army to its full wartime level. To this must be added the reserve component unit structure of the Army National Guard and the Army Reserve at wartime levels. The *structure* requirement is expanded by next adding the increase in nondeploying units and

Figure 3

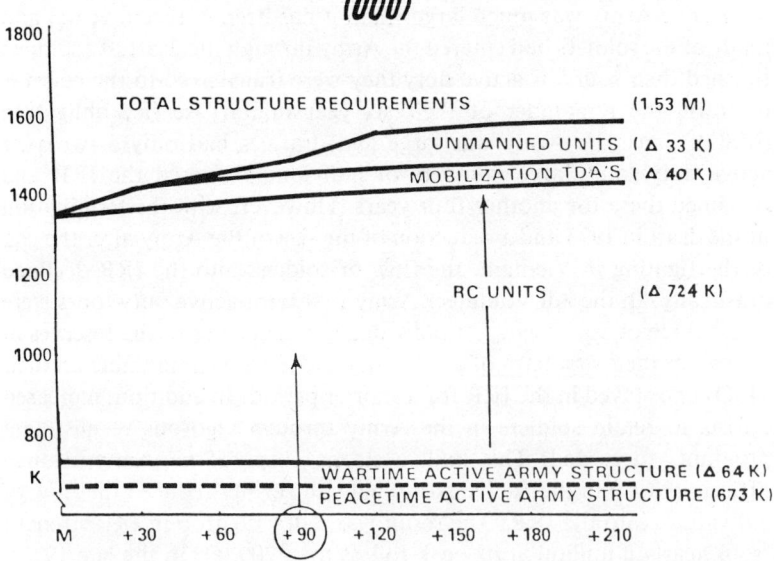

STRUCTURE REQUIREMENTS FOR TRAINED MANPOWER (FY 80)

organizations (exclusive of civilians who will be addressed separately) that are needed to support the larger, mobilized force on active duty. This includes expanded garrisons, base operations support, ammunition handlers, maintenance and so on. Finally, to reach the total structure, we must include requirements for currently unmanned support units that are needed for warfighting but can neither be manned nor equipped in peacetime because of resource constraints. These are called COMPO 4 units, the fourth military component of the total Army. (The Active Army, the Army National Guard and the U.S. Army Reserve are COMPOs 1, 2 and 3 respectively.)

In order to determine the total trained military manpower requirement (Figure 4), we must include (1) an overhead account, i.e., transients and students—but not trainees, and (2) the estimated net casualty replacements that would be needed to sustain the force under warfighting conditions. These estimates are based on current plans for the worst case situation of a NATO-Warsaw Pact war.

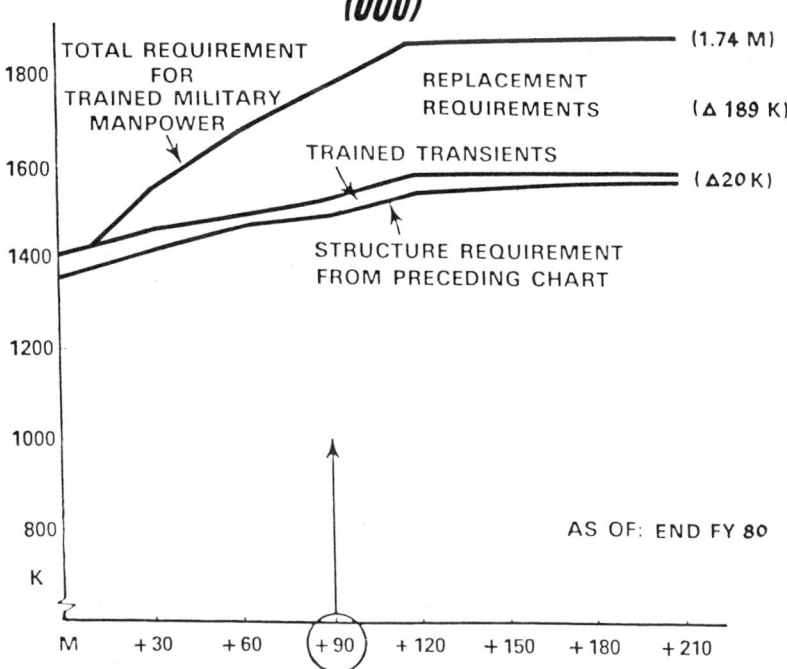

Figure 4

Moving to the Army's *supply of trained manpower* to meet these requirements, Figure 5 shows a breakout of sources of manpower on a time-phased basis. The active component strength starts at actual operating strength plus the transients, students, and "holdee" account and increases slightly due to the output of trainees from the training base after M-day. Reserve component unit, Individual Ready Reserve, and Standby Reserve (a small pool of trained personnel not as readily available as the IRR) strengths are calculated using the estimated show rates of 95%, 70% and 50%, respectively. Added to these sources are 40,000 retirees who would be recalled for duty in the United States. In 1981 the number of retirees to be recalled will increase to approximately 80,000. The wedge of volunteers starting at M+100 represents newly trained, post–M-day volunteers.

Figure 5

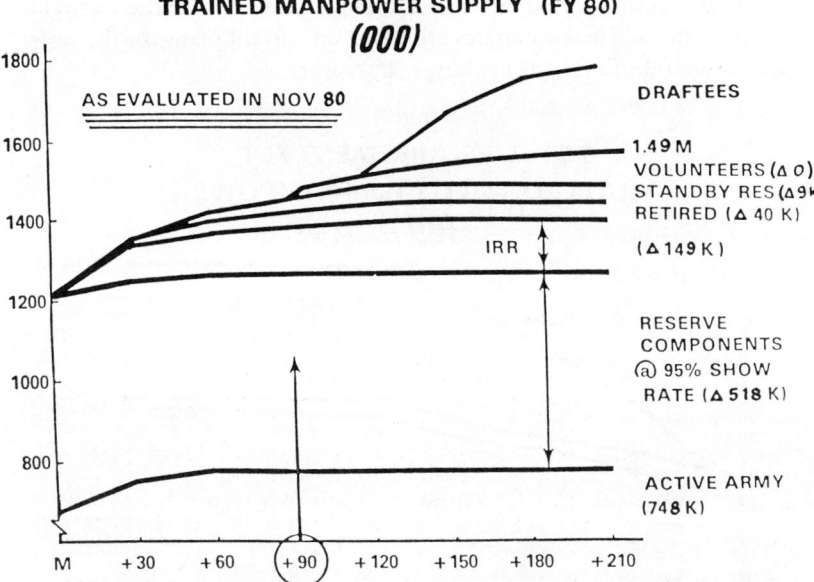

The sharp slope starting just before M+120 reflects the arrival in units of the first trained draftees. This is based on the current condition of peacetime registration which will provide draftees for induction by M+13. After one hundred days for training (eighty-four days are required by law before deployment), processing and transportation, trained draftees would become available at M+113 to sustain the fighting force.

Prior to the resumption of peacetime registration, inductions could not have started until M+85. Under those conditions, the first trained draftees would not have been ready for employment until M+185, or some seventy-two days later than our present capability. If peacetime registration were to be stopped, it is uncertain how rapidly a registration

Strategic Assessment

system could be reestablished in an emergency. However long that took, several weeks or several months, it would cost the Army critical time in providing trained draftees to sustain the force.

During PROUD SPIRIT/MOBEX 80, a major mobilization exercise in 1980, the Selective Service System (SSS) tested its procedures and systems for emergency resumption of inductions. In this test, SSS conducted a lottery whose results were certified by the National Bureau of Standards; ran the induction computer programs that generate induction orders; sent out induction orders via Western Union mailgrams to 700 SSS reservists across the country, and transmitted a live induction computer tape to the Military Enlistment Processing Command (MEPCOM) which told them who had been ordered to report to each Armed Forces' Examining and Entrance Station (AFEES). This realtime test showed that, with peacetime registration, the first draftees can in fact be provided to the AFEES at $M+13$, and the military training bases can be kept filled to capacity thereafter.

Figure 6 compares the total requirement with the total supply and

Figure 6

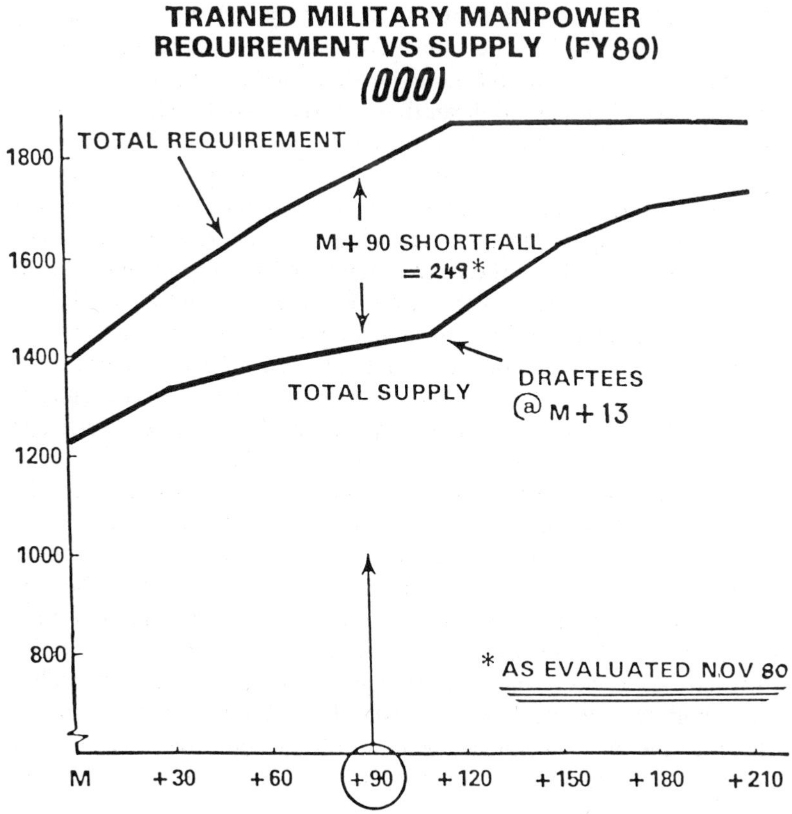

TRAINED MILITARY MANPOWER REQUIREMENT VS SUPPLY (FY80)
(000)

M + 90 SHORTFALL = 249*

TOTAL REQUIREMENT

TOTAL SUPPLY

DRAFTEES @ M+13

* AS EVALUATED NOV 80

emphasizes the serious shortfall in trained military manpower. The shortfall at M + 90 is 249,000, 14.3% of the total requirements, and reaches a high of 254,000 at M + 120 under current registration procedures. (These shortfalls are largely, but not completely, caused by the need to replace combat casualties so as to sustain the deployed force in the combat theater.) It consists primarily of personnel in critical combat and medical skills. The seriousness of these critical skill shortfalls is shown by the Army's most recent calculations. Balancing all sources of supply against all requirements and using end-FY 1980 actual data, the M + 90 fill for selected career management fields is shown as follows:

Infantry	56%
Armor	60%
Artillery	87%
Combat Engineer	57%
Medical Corpsman	82%

With these shortfalls, units based in Europe, and those deploying to Europe soon after mobilization, will have to fight at less than their wartime required strength; active and reserve units planned for later deployment and the continental U.S. training and support base may have to provide trained personnel for casualty replacements and for priority units. There would be severe shortages of critical combat and medical skills. This would mean that the Army would fight while short of trained people for more than six months, and there could be no early expansion of the force beyond the current 24 division force structure.

What is being done to correct this situation? Many initiatives have been taken during the last few years. Enlistment and retention incentives have been provided for the Active Army and the reserve units in the Army National Guard and the Army Reserve. Pay and compensation have been increased. Various enlistment options have been tested and/or implemented to attract more people into the Active Army and the reserve units. Various programs have been developed to improve the quality of life for soldiers and their families. By increasing the personnel strength of active and reserve units, the shortfalls are reduced.

A large number of statutory, management and program changes have been made to increase the strength of the IRR and its counterpart in the National Guard, the Inactive National Guard (ING). Congress established a six year military service obligation (MSO) for females and for enlistees 26 years of age and older. (Prior to these changes, both categories had only incurred an obligation for the length of their active duty term of service.) The Congress has authorized and funded reenlistment bonuses for the IRR and ING. In addition to these statutory changes, the Army's management actions include: termination of a policy of automatically transferring individuals from the IRR to the

Standby Reserve at the end of the fifth year of their MSO; transferring soldiers who do not complete their full enlistment tour into the IRR, instead of discharging them, if they are determined to have potential usefulness under mobilization conditions; and eliminating the time spent in the delayed entry program (DEP), prior to starting training, from counting toward the six year MSO. As a byproduct of Active Army and reserve unit enlistment options requiring shorter periods of service with more of the total MSO spent in the IRR, the strength of the IRR is increased. Under guidance from the Office of the Secretary of Defense, the Army conducted a test of direct enlistment in the IRR without incentives. The results of this test were mixed, at best, but it provided a slight increase in IRR strength. If the program were funded and extended nationwide, it could provide a modest increase in IRR membership.

The Army has established a program for the recall of retired personnel in an emergency. In fiscal 1981, over 40,000 retirees could be ordered to active duty quickly for service in the continental United States. This number increased to 80,000 by the end of 1981 and will rise to a planned 120,000 by 1986. These experienced individuals can valuably assist the expansion and efficient operation of the support and training base within the United States. However, even though these retirees are counted as part of the trained manpower supply, their recall would not immediately permit the release of younger personnel for deployment or other duties, and they are not a source of young officers and enlisted personnel to meet the critical shortages in combat and field medical skills.

The Army is currently analyzing data to determine the desirability and feasibility of establishing a program to encourage veteran volunteers at the time of mobilization. Because these veterans are trained and experienced, they would probably require a shorter period of training and conditioning than would non-prior service draftees. Thus, they could help reduce the trained military manpower shortfall more rapidly in an emergency.

Even if all of the programmed initiatives are funded and fully successful, the trained military manpower shortfall at $M + 90$ will still exceed 100,000 at the end of FY 86. There is no short term solution to this problem. If the risk associated with this shortfall is unacceptable, there appear to be only two alternatives to eliminate it: increased incentives, which might eliminate the shortfall in a few years, or a peacetime draft designed to meet reserve unit or IRR requirements.

Postmobilization Training of Military Manpower

In the preceding analysis of pretrained military manpower, the calculation of the supply of trained military manpower included, after $M + 100$, people who were in training on M-day and those who had started training after mobilization, including trained draftees who would become available starting at M + 113. To complete the picture of the Army's mobilization and warfighting military manpower capability, it is necessary to take a brief look at the sources of manpower available for postmobilization training and the capability of the Army to train such people.

In peacetime, the Army's training base consists of various Active Army units and installations plus some reserve training units on duty for short training periods. During mobilization, this capacity is expanded rapidly by the mobilization of reserve training divisions and brigades and the opening of additional installations. If this total training capability is increased to the maximum in an emergency, the training unit structure can accept 133,000 new trainees by M + 30, an additional 150,000 new trainees by M + 60 and 50,000 more by M + 90.

Several categories of people would be available to start training almost immediately after M-day. These include individuals in the delayed entry program (DEP) who are awaiting training for entrance into the Active Army, reservists awaiting training, volunteers after M-day, and members of the IRR who would be retrained in critical shortage skills from their existing, less critical support skills. These categories of trainees would use over 50,000 of the 133,000 trainee capability by M + 30, and about 80,000 draftees would fill the remainder of that capacity. During the second month after mobilization, the bulk of the new trainees would be draftees along with a number of volunteers. (The number of volunteers would of course depend on the "popularity" of the war based on public attitudes and perceptions of the nature of the threat to the United States.) Trained military manpower would start to flow to Army units one hundred days after individuals entered the service for training.

According to the planned surge capability of the mobilized training base to accept 133,000 new trainees between M-day and M + 30, approximately that number of newly trained military personnel, less perhaps 5% for attrition during training, would be available to sustain the Army by M + 130. However, the reserve training units are significantly short of people; training bases do not have all the facilities needed to handle that number of new trainees; there is insufficient major equipment, such as tanks, available to train that number of people, and there are inadequate supplies of clothing and personal equipment for that number of new trainees. Major financial expenditures will be required, some of which are included in present programming actions, and additional qualified personnel must be identified to permit the training base to operate at such a maximum surge rate. The Army is examining the ability of retirees to provide the additional manpower. But at the present time, the training base could actually operate at only approximately two-thirds of its hypothetical maximum rate.

An additional factor complicates the training situation, and actually the whole warfighting capability. The time-phased training output requirements by skill are calculated on the basis of meeting the total military manpower requirements. These requirements, as previously indicated, are based on the full, wartime structure requirements of the 24 division Army, and assume that equipment is available to maintain that full force structure. However, it is no secret that the Army is short of many major equipment items. With expected high battlefield attrition of such items as tanks, helicopters, and armored personnel carriers, and the inability of U.S. industry to replace them rapidly, there would be little purpose in training large numbers of people in the skills to use such equipment, if it would not be available for them to operate. The Army is developing a methodology to determine the optimum distribution of equipment and people considering anticipated battlefield attrition. Until that methodology is developed, tested and proven, the Army cannot determine precisely how many people should be trained in specific skills by certain times.

Army Civilian Personnel

Significant civilian personnel issues further complicate the Army's mobilization manpower situation. Army civilian manpower is a critical component of the total Army. It is essential to the maintenance of force readiness, and is the one resource that can be utilized selectively and in a timely manner as new missions, readiness and force modernization needs dictate. It can be an invaluable resource to help accomplish force structure changes, relieve manning shortfalls, improve military training, assist the modernization process, and provide a basis for mobilization and sustainability. However, past arbitrary contraints on the amount and type of civilian manpower has tended to reduce its potential in solving Army readiness problems. The Army's civilian manpower program has been reduced by over 55,000 spaces since FY 1974. This represents an 11% drawdown while documented workloads have increased significantly.

Approximately 96% of Army civilians are employed in direct support of Army missions; only 13,700 perform management headquarters functions. Workload has increased because Army weapons development and procurement have greatly increased. The number and types of weapons supported by the civilian workforce have increased and are still rising. Equipment maintenance workloads and backlogs have grown. Training has become more demanding and complex. Army facilities are aging and in need of increased repair. Because of these conditions, military manpower in excess of a division's strength—

25,000 to 28,000 daily average—has to be diverted to do civilian jobs.

The current civilian strength for military functions is 359,000 which is more than 50,000 below peacetime needs. In addition, it must be emphasized that the requirement for civilian manpower rises to 534,000 upon mobilization to provide the necessary support for the larger force on active duty. Even with emergency hiring authority, and under favorable labor market conditions, considerable difficulty is expected in meeting the shortfall, especially in certain skills that pose recruitment problems even during peacetime. Under mobilization the demand for these skills becomes even more critical. The most critical of these are skills in fields such as engineering, medicine, accounting, data processing, electrical/electronic equipment repair and automotive repair.

With the increasing sophistication of modern weaponry, greater reliance has been placed on civilian technicians and contractor personnel to operate and maintain equipment. Although extensive research indicates there has been no real problem with retaining these key civilian employees in overseas areas during mobilization and hostilities, no legal authority exists for retaining such employees against their wishes. To close this potential loophole and obtain a legal basis for ensuring reliability in the future, a legislative proposal would give overseas commanders the authority to retain key civilian employees under conditions of hostility. The Department of Defense is working with the Services and the Joint Chiefs of Staff to develop a number of options which will help this situation.

Conclusions

This brief analysis has highlighted the major aspects of the Army's mobilization manpower situation. There are both pluses and minuses. On the plus side, the most significant improvement has been the reinstitution of Selective Service registration which will permit inductions to begin rapidly in an emergency and provide trained draftees to sustain the force much earlier than would be the case without peacetime registration. However, the Army's mobilization training base cannot now be manned, equipped and supplied to permit it to train the optimum number of non-prior service personnel in the early months of a major emergency. It is hoped that the resources to solve this problem will be forthcoming in the near future.

Another plus is the apparent willingness of the Reagan Administration to support increased peacetime civilian strength for the Army. A move toward justifiable civilian end strengths over the next few years would significantly improve the readiness of the Army to perform its missions in national defense.

However, even if this does come to pass, it will not solve the problem of rapid expansion of the civilian workforce at mobilization, nor does it provide a means for retaining necessary civilian skills in a warfighting zone in a future emergency. These problems must be the object of much additional planning and imaginative innovation.

The key remaining minus is the fact that the Army is dangerously short of the pretrained military manpower needed to fill and sustain the force during the early months of a major conflict until trained draftees become available. There is no apparent near term solution to this problem. The country must either accept the substantial risk involved or make a choice of alternatives: either substantially increase incentives for the all volunteer Army or institute some sort of peacetime conscription.

5

Military Recruitment and Personnel Retention—Agenda for the 1980s

Curtis W. Tarr

The weekend of February 21-22, 1970 brought to many Americans, discouraged by an ugly war in Vietnam, a gratifying promise. It was then that the Gates Commission, composed of respected American leaders, confirmed to President Nixon that the nation could maintain its armed forces in peacetime with volunteers. The Commission, led by former Secretary of Defense Thomas Gates, judged that if the nation provided adequate financial incentives it would attract enough recruits to maintain armed forces of 2.5 million and that these people would be capable of using the sophisticated weapons of modern warfare. The members of the Commission believed that superior individuals would enlist for longer periods of service than the two years required under the draft, thus reducing the size and expense of the training establishment in what would become a lean, professional military force. Finally, the Commission concluded that the armed forces would reflect a cross-section of American youth, and that they would not be heavily dependent upon blacks or women to fill their ranks.

Now, after eight years of experience with volunteerism, the American people clearly have doubts. A variety of popular literature has focused attention upon the inadequacy of the armed forces[1] and has issued warnings about the nation's military preparedness and the need to replace volunteerism with conscription.[2] These and other judgments center upon two critical problems of the armed forces today: recruitment, the most publicized, and retention, perhaps the most serious deterrent to readiness. Many critics argue that those recruited for service do not have the potential to be trained for demanding jobs, that they lack the motivation to persevere, and that they do not reenlist in sufficient numbers; thus the armed forces cannot meet the requirements placed upon them. Some argue the reason for these difficulties is that military pay and benefits have fallen compared to civilian salaries. Others believe that regardless of pay, volunteerism will not provide the forces we require.

While public alarm has increased, military leaders have voiced their fears as well. General David Jones, former Chairman of the Joint Chiefs of Staff, has observed that the greatest problem facing the armed forces today is manpower. His peers agree. The Chief of Staff of the Army, General Edward C. Meyer, complains that manpower shortages have caused the U.S. Army to become a "hollow" force, not prepared for an emergency. The former Chief of Naval Operations, Admiral T.B. Hayward, judges that the Navy has no needs greater than for more people, better prepared for the jobs they are given.[3] General Lew Allen, Jr., former Chief of Staff of the Air Force, reported "an alarming deficiency" among volunteers for the armed forces. Speaking out from retirement, General William C. Westmoreland, Army Chief of Staff from 1968 to 1972, was more forceful when he wrote that volunteerism is not meeting America's manpower requirements.[4] The following examination of the All-Volunteer Force considers the problems of recruitment and retention, and will allow some insights into the future of military manpower programs.

Recruiting an Active Force

In judging recruitment for an active force, usual considerations include the number of accessions compared to objectives, the qualifications of recruits, and the composition of the forces between males and females, white and minority persons.

ACCESSIONS.

Experience in Fiscal Year 1981 through February has encouraged the proponents of volunteerism. The armed forces recruited 138,000 young people, meeting their objectives, and exceeding slightly their prior-service accession goals, meaning that the force was a bit older and more experienced than expected.[5] Recruitment has not always been so successful. The Department of Defense attracted desired numbers of youths in 1980, 1976, and 1975, but fell below its planned acquisitions in the other years of the All-Volunteer Force, by 2% to 9%.[6] During this time, the armed forces have declined in size, from 2.3 million in 1973 to 2.045 million in 1980.[7]

QUALIFICATIONS OF RECRUITS.

Armed forces personnel specialists believe that high school graduates succeed in training and service better that do those who drop out. Applying this criterion, recruitment has produced good personnel through February 1981. On the 104,000 young men joining the armed forces without prior military experience during this period, 74% had been graduated from high school, and 90% of the young women had done so. The Army figure was 70%.[8] Only in 1978 did the Army do better, when 74% of its recruits had a high school diploma; by 1980, the figure had dropped to 54%.[9] These figures compare with 80% of American youth who complete high school.

The Marine Corps, with similar recruiting problems, had insisted upon higher qualifications. Only half of the Marine recruits had completed high school in 1974 and leaders of the Corps decided upon more stringent standards, regardless of the number of young people recruited. Thereafter they attracted higher numbers of high school graduates. In 1980, 78% of the Marine recruits had completed high school; in the first months of 1981, 71% of the males and 100% of the females had received a diploma.[10]

Despite the improvement in high school graduation, recent Army recruits did not score well on the Armed Forces Qualification Test (AFQT). Candidates who take the examination are rated in one of five categories. Those in category V (the lowest 10% of the population), are not eligible for military service. A recruit in category IV has the reading ability, at best, of a fifth grade student in elementary school.

In the first quarter of 1981, 19% of all recruits have been in category IV, with Army recruits highest among the services at 32%. This is an improvement over 1980, when the services learned that the AFQT had been calibrated incorrectly, allowing the armed forces to accept many more category IV recruits than intended. Thus after gaining accurate data, the Army learned that it had accepted half of its recruits in this category through February 1980.[11] The services, since the All-Volunteer Force began in 1973, have attracted fewer recruits in categories I and II, and many more in category III. Congress now has enacted legislation that limits the number of category IV recruits to 25% for 1981 and 20% for each service by 1983.[12]

During the Vietnamese War, the Department of Defense inaugurated "Project 100,000" an experiment to train category IV men to accept useful positions in the services. The people who directed that effort can take considerable satisfaction in the accomplishment: many youths learned to read, to do relatively simple tasks, to find a new place in society. But clearly this was a sociological experiment to help young people make a new start, not to improve the capability of the armed forces. Few of the men thus trained ever undertook the complicated tasks of maintaining and operating sophisticated hardware; many proved untrainable, regardless of the generous hours devoted by the most skilled teachers in the services.

In 1977 the Army began giving skill qualification tests to determine how well its people could undertake their assignments. Senator Sam Nunn and Congressman Robin Beard, who gained information on test scores for 1977 and 1978, reported that for 370 occupational specialties, those tested had a failure rate of 40% or higher. These included key combat specialties. In the 1979 tests, failures were 86% for artillery crewmen, 89% for tracked-vehicle mechanics, 90% on nuclear weapons maintenance, 98% on tank turret and artillery repair, and 91% on aviation maintenance.[13]

Responding to criticism of test results, the Army replied that testing still is in the development stage and that scores cannot be considered valid. There may be merit in this position. But apparently Army leaders had sufficient confidence in the tests to use them for a large sample. Furthermore, even though the test results did not correlate perfectly with adequate job performance, it is difficult to imagine that there was no correlation whatsoever.

Former Secretary of the Army Clifford Alexander, testifying before the House Armed Services Committee in June of 1980, took an even more intransigent position on testing when he proclaimed that AFQT scores were "fundamentally irrelevant" and that he was "not sure that it (the test) measures anything." To emphasize the point, he ordered that the scores be removed from the personnel records of soldiers to prevent abuse.[14]

Even after admitting that tests contain biases and are sometimes slightly inaccurate, are they "fundamentally irrelevant?" Although a score is not a certain indication of a person's ability to perform a job well, it is a reliable predictor of persons who will succeed in training programs. One must ask bluntly if young personnel with these limited capabilities will be able to defend the nation with expensive hardware? Probably, many Americans would not welcome them as repairmen for their cars or dishwashers or telephones. Yet the armed forces are being asked somehow to prepare them for assignments that in an emergency would be more crucial than any of these.

FORCE COMPOSITION

Males constituted 86% of the new recruits for the Department of Defense through February, 1981; 83% of Army recruits were men.[15] The number of women in the armed services increased from 38,000 in 1968 to 150,000 in 1980, or from 1.6% to 8%. In 1985, the services plan for 254,000 women, or 13%, in the active force.[16] The women have had somewhat higher qualifications than the males: thus far in 1981, 90% of them had high school diplomas, compared to 74% of the men.[17] But they have not tested much higher than males: in 1980, 33% of the male recruits in the Department of Defense were category IVs, compared to 28% of the females; in the Army, 52% of the males and 51% of the females were category IVs.[18]

Women bring strengths to the armed forces, as well as problems. Until they are given combat assignments, an increase in their numbers reduces the possibility for rotation of male combat personnel to more desirable jobs, thus reducing the reenlistment of males. Pregnancy is a problem: it is estimated that 14% of the women in the Army during 1979 were pregnant.[19] Many military women are the single parents of children (men are as well), and they could be torn during mobilization between responsibility toward their units and toward their children. One study estimated that one woman in five, owing to pregnancy or parental responsibility, could not move with her unit in an emergency.[20] Moreover, women tend to leave the service sooner than men. The Army estimates that in FY 1982, female attrition will be 45.8%, compared to 30.6% for males.[21]

The racial composition of the All-Volunteer Force is changing as well. Blacks constituted 18% of the new recruits for the Department of Defense through February 1981, compared to 26% for the Army.[22] In 1979, blacks were 21% of the Department of Defense recruits, 32% for the Army. During the same year, 40% of the women entering the Army were black.[23] About one-eighth of the American population is black, and blacks constituted about the same share of our drafted forces.

The causes of this increase in black service people are several. For one, blacks test higher now than they did just after World War II, when more than half of them were in category V. Recently blacks have shown a dramatic increase in test results, not only moving from category V to category IV, but increasing in the top three categories as well. Blacks are also more likely to enlist than are whites, partly because the services have a reputation as a place where blacks can advance. Also blacks tend to remain in the service: in 1980, 57% of the black first term recruits reenlisted, compared with 35% of the others; among career people, blacks reenlisted at a rate of 80%, compared to 68% for others.[24] As a consequence of these factors, half of the soldiers in some Army and Marine combat battalions are black.

Despite improvements in test results, black recruits still fall largely into category IV. In the Department of Defense, 61% did so in 1980, 76% in the Army. This compares with 23% whites in the Department of Defense, and 40% in the Army. Only 3% of the Army black recruits in 1980 fell into categories I and II, compared to 20% for whites.[25]

A lively debate continues on whether the numbers of blacks in the services soon will discourage whites from joining, or in the event of war, if heavy black casualties would cause a national problem, or finally whether blacks might restrict the missions on which troops could be sent. This writer has no reservations on any of these three issues, but the qualifications of both blacks and whites who enlist into the services seem disturbing.

—Why do these problems exist?

Clearly the All-Volunteer Force of today is not the force envisioned by members of the Gates Commission. Recruits are not as qualified, they do not remain in the service as long, and the services are much more dependent upon blacks and women than the Commission predicted. What has gone wrong?

Apologists for the All-Volunteer Force argue that military pay scales have been too low to attract qualified people. It is true that military pay has not kept pace with that of civilians, as *Business Week* has noted: military pay was 89% of civilian pay in 1973, but only 82% in 1980.[26] Sadly, young men working at sea on aircraft carriers for one hundred hours a week, separated from loved ones for months, make less than a cashier at a fast-food restaurant working forty hours. Many families of enlisted men are forced to rely heavily on food stamps.[27]

But more than pay may be involved. In 1971 the writer went to Great Britain to talk with British defence officials about their program of volunteerism. Two points were strongly emphasized: First, while they found that higher pay did help to attract qualified people, they noted that the process of increasing pay in government is so slow that civilian organizations quickly equal and surpass what the armed forces are able to offer. The young people coming into the armed forces are such a large percentage of those entering the work force that military pay tends to set a minimum expectation rather than a competitive offering. Second, the British noted that in every population there are some men who will join military forces regardless of pay; these they termed the "French Foreign Legion" element. Some others can be induced by high pay to join. Finally there are those in the population, a large group, who will never join regardless of pay. The British believed then that they were attracting nearly all of the qualified people they could hope to recruit into their armed forces. An equivalent force for our population would number about 1.4 million, considerably smaller than our present force. The British might suggest that the United States has tried to maintain forces larger than volunteerism will support by sacrificing quality.

Others, including Senator Bill Armstrong of Colorado, argue that the armed forces lost their ability to attract qualified people when Congress terminated the GI Bill in 1976.[28] The GI Bill did attract many able young men to the services. But at about the same time Congress terminated the GI Bill, they increased programs of financial aid to young people attending colleges or universities; most of the states did the same. If these programs continue in some form, then the GI Bill at present would not be as attractive as once it was.

Recruiting a Reserve Force

Reserve forces constitute a vital part of our defense establishment. They supply one-half of the Army's combat strength and two-thirds of its support forces. Air National Guard and Reserve units are the world's fifth largest air force. Marine reserve forces make up one-fourth of the total Marine Corps.[29]

In 1980, reserve units recruited almost 222,000 young men and women, meeting their objectives for the year. All forces have reached desired strength levels except for the Army National Guard, which is at 86% strength, and the Army Reserve, only 80% of strength. Shortages in Army forces still are serious, because inevitably they exist among enlisted personnel in combat assignments that are unattractive to many young men. Among reserve recruits, 79% had completed high school, 8% were category IVs, 16% were blacks, and 11% were females.[30]

The Department of Defense continues to have serious shortages in the Individual Ready Reserve, people who have served with the armed forces who can be called up as combat loss replacements. (One who enlists has an obligation for six years, and thus one who serves on active duty for three years and is discharged is a member of the IRR for another three years.) The IRR should be large enough, under this planning, to provide replacements until a draft can be organized and people can be trained.

Too much confidence in the IRR as a source of troops in an emergency may be unwise. Rather than being called as a combat loss replacement, most members of the IRR would go into an organized reserve unit if they could find an opening. Others would be unable to serve, owing either to a physical or family problem. The Defense Department has never found a satisfactory way to maintain contact with these reservists. Finally, if the reservist is taken, there is the problem of assimilating him into a unit where he does not know his job, or is overrated for it, or must direct others doing something he does not understand. For these reasons, draftees must be called upon in a future emergency, from the outset, and thus the United States needs the machinery to insure their availability.

Retention

Through February 1981, the armed forces had retained 85,000 people, compared with 80,000 for the comparable period in 1980. Re-

Recruitment and Personnel Retention

enlistment rates improved for each of the services, both for first term and career personnel, reflecting the benefits of the 11.7% pay increase at the start of the year.[31]

But total numbers provide an incomplete measure, because it is in the critical specialties that retention counts most. History reveals that experience makes the commitment of forces practicable.

A close look at the Army shows that 263,000 senior noncommissioned officers are needed, but only 248,000 are serving. The Army has an imbalance in 37 out of 349 military occupation specialties resulting in shortages of about 30,000 people. As a consequence, 55% of those trained in these 37 specialties are assigned outside of the United States, compared with 43% of Army forces. This not only hurts retention but it exacerbates the problem of readiness in the units stationed in the United States.[32]

The Army remains in need of combat arms noncommissioned officers, although that condition improved during the last year. It also requires more junior officers, including about 3,700 captains and nearly 1,000 warrant officer aviators. The Army needs 5,273 physicians to maintain its health and hospital programs, but it had only 4,627 at the end of 1980.[33]

The other services have similar problems. The Air Force must keep 60% of its fighter pilots to remain combat-effective, but it is retaining only about 25%.[34] The Navy in 1979 retained about 31% of its pilots.[35] It costs more than $1 million to train a pilot to be effective in combat, and experience is a vital factor in gauging a pilot's effectiveness.

Critical to our defense is the Navy submarine force. It is short 10% of its officers and about the same amount in career enlisted submariners. In 1979 the Navy had 138 nuclear-qualified petty officers, with ten to thirteen years of experience, up for reenlistment. Only 36 decided to remain in the Navy.[36] The Navy lacks 20,000 key petty officers. Of these, 14,000 are required for the fleet at sea, making it impossible to operate our ships as they were designed to perform.[37] Thus some insight is gained into what General Meyer meant when he said that the Army had become a "hollow" force. The same might be said about our other forces as well.

The difficulty with retention is that problems cannot be cured by a pay increase alone. Pay must be improved to stop the hemorrhage, and this is imperative to save the volunteer force we always must rely upon in emergencies. But a pay increase will not make up for the losses already incurred. It will take years following corrective action before replacements are fully trained and ready to accept the responsibilities of those who have retired from the service. In this respect, the nation will pay for years because of the neglect of the past.

Many have argued that recruitment and retention are different problems. But they are linked in one significant way. When substantial rewards are offered to young people to attract them to the services, the relative economic position of the professional force is automatically lowered, and a large share of limited resources is allocated to the attraction of untrained people. Ultimately, this will reduce what is available for retaining the trained ones.

Another problem of retention is that the services cannot retain people better than those who originally come to them. Insofar as they have inadequate quality among recruits, military leaders can only select prudently from these. Some jobs can be done only by category I and II personnel. For instance, most of the positions in maintaining an Air Force F-15 wing require individuals of this caliber. All of the positions on a Navy Poseidon submarine must be filled by category I and II people. If these people are not attracted initially they cannot be developed through training.

Does the Nation Require a Draft?

Difficult as these times appear to be for recruitment of qualified people, the problem will become more demanding during the decade of the 1980s. In 1980, about 2.15 million young men became 18 years of age, the peak since World War II. By 1987 that number will decline to just over 1.8 million, and by 1993 it will fall below 1.7 million. The pool from which the services must draw will shrink dramatically.

What are the alternatives? There are several. More civilian personnel can be used for tasks that military people traditionally have performed, but when we do so, service life becomes less attractive because career people must perform a larger share of less desirable assignments. More women can be used, and each of the armed forces plans to do so.

One alternative, of course, is a return to selective service. As the former director of that effort, I am not particularly enthusiastic about doing so. We would have difficult and perhaps nearly insurmountable problems in making the system work. Few know how close we came to a complete collapse of the system during the last stages of the war in Southeast Asia. Many government records could not be used and thus we had no assurance that men had registered. About 10% of our youth had been classified as conscientious objectors. We had miserable success in enforcing the law. All of these difficulties would continue, and perhaps increase, in a future use of selective service. Nevertheless the draft may eventually be the nation's only prudent course of action.

When I asked former British Minister of Defence Denis Healey if Britain could fulfill its commitments with a volunteer force, he told me that I had confused the priorities: "First you must assemble the best force you can with volunteers," he said. "Then you tailor your commitments to those manpower realities. That is the only way defence can be handled in a democracy," he concluded.

I countered by saying that if we rely upon volunteers, then we place into the hands of our young people a veto on the formulation of our nation's strategic interests. "Exactly," he replied.

Should the United States do the same?

Although this seems to place a veto on the formulation of our nation's strategic policy in the hands of America's young people, we probably cannot avoid Mr. Healey's observation in the short run. For now, the Services must set prudent and firm standards both for entrance and retention, looking upon a compromise of these as a national disgrace. Reasonable pay scales should be established and maintained, and the military must work hard to attract the best force it can under these limitations. Such an armed force may not be as large as many Americans believe we require. But every unit in it must be the most effective unit possible, one that the American people can depend upon in an emergency.

Then, if the nation comes to a point where voluntary means will not provide the forces required, we must look again at conscription. My own guess is that the public will have come to that conclusion by 1985.

NOTES

1. Constance Holden, "Doubts Mounting About All-Volunteer Force," *Science*, 5 Sept. 1980, pp. 1095-1099.
2. Ralph Kinney Binnett, "Our Army Is Unprepared," *Reader's Digest*, March 1981, pp. 70-74; "A Sickly Volunteer Army Feels a Draft On Its Neck," *Business Week*, pp. 92N-92R; "Needed: Money, Ships, Pilots—and the Draft," *Time*, 23 Feb. 1981, p. 56; and Norman C. Miller, "Real Manpower Problems Pose Threat to Defense Consensus," *Wall Street Journal*, 21 May 1981, and "A National Service Debate," (editorial), *Wall Street Journal*, 29 May 1981.
3. "Divergent Views on Problems of the Volunteer Armed Forces," *National Review* V. 33, No. 4, (6 March 1981) p. 215.
4. William C. Westmoreland, "U.S. Readiness Requires a Draft," *Wall Street Journal*, 26 May 1981.
5. Office of the Assistant Secretary of Defense for Manpower, Reserve Affairs and Logistics, 25 March 1981. (Hereafter cited as OASD, MRA & L.)
6. OASD, MRA & L, 31 Oct. 1980.
7. U.S. Secretary of Defense, *Annual Report FY 1981*, 262-63.
8. OASD, MRA & L, 25 March 1981.
9. OASD, MRA & L, 31 Oct. 1980.
10. Congressional Record, 1 July 1980, S 9032; OASD, MRA & L, 25 March 1981.
11. OASD, MRA & L, 25 March 1981.
12. Congressional Record, 1 July 1980, S 9094.
13. Holden, Op. Cit.; *National Review*, Op. Cit.

14. Holden, Op. Cit., 1096.
15. OASD, MRA & L, 25 March 1981.
16. OASD, MRA & L, 31 Oct. 1980.
17. OASD, MRA & L, 25 March 1981.
18. OASD, MRA & L, 5 Jan. 1980.
19. Binnett, Op. Cit.
20. Ibid.
21. Department of the Army, *Program Objective Memorandum, FY 1982-86*.
22. OASD, MRA & L, 25 March 1981.
23. OASD, MRA & L, Oct. 1980.
24. OASD, MRA & L, Dec. 1980.
25. OASD, MRA & L, 5 Jan. 1980.
26. *Business Week*, Op. Cit.
27. *National Review*, Op. Cit., p. 216.
28. Ibid., p. 217.
29. Statement of Robert A. Stone, Acting Assistant Secretary of Defense for Manpower, Reserve Affairs and Logistics, before the Manpower and Personnel Subcommittee of the Senate Armed Services Committee, 10 March 1981.
30. Office of Assistant Secretary of Defense (Public Affairs), 30 Dec. 1980.
31. OASD, MRA & L, 25 March 1981.
32. Statement of LTG Robert G. Yerks, Deputy Chief of Staff for Personnel, U.S. Army, before the Subcommittee on Defense, Committee on Appropriations, U.S. Senate, 19 March 1981.
33. Ibid.
34. *National Review*, p. 216.
35. *Time*, Op. Cit.
36. *National Review*, p. 216.
37. Department of the Navy Statement on "Navy Sea Pay," (n.d.).

6

Surge Mobilization: Ground Forces

*Norman Friedman**

In 1981 the United States and the Soviet Union confront each other with very different stated surge mobilization policies and potentials. These policies are the consequence of differing national perceptions of the international environment, of differing political and economic systems, and of radically differing histories. Although there is a widespread perception that any future war will in no way resemble previous military experience, it appears that national perceptions of the content and value of mobilization resources are largely the consequence of the historical experience, with other factors tending to modify already existing tendencies.

Here, surge mobilization is defined as that effort available immediately upon the beginning of war, certainly within the first months. The widely noted difficulties the United States has in "surging" its military production relate to this period, during which existing production lines must be expanded. Numerous studies have shown that past U.S. prowess in industrial mobilization was most often a consequence, not of the use of existing facilities but rather of the conversion of parts of the large civilian economy to military ends. Such conversion is necessarily much slower than modification of existing production lines, where unutilized capacity exists in those lines. The burden of recent studies, then, is that the U.S. defense industry is running close to its current net capacity. That is why, for example, large increases in defense spending are often equated with considerable inflation in defense goods.

The Soviet Union is often credited with the maintenance, in peacetime, of "cold" production lines specifically intended for utilization in a crisis. However, the steadiness (in numbers, not cost) of Soviet production of many defense goods suggests strongly that short-term Soviet

---

* This chapter represents the views of its author. There has been only limited circulation of the chapter to the Hudson Institute staff and no formal review procedure. No opinions, statements of fact, or conclusions contained in this document can properly be attributed to the Institute, its staff, its members, or its contracting agencies.

industrial mobilization capacity is not large: the Soviet Union has a steady-state peacetime economy, and emergency shifts in that economy must take some time. If weapon complexity explains the sluggishness predicted for U.S. industrial mobilization, then the same factor must afflict the Soviet Union.

Surge mobilization takes on a new significance as the United States shifts towards a national strategy more aligned to a lengthy conventional war in Europe than towards quick escalation to a strategic nuclear exchange. That is, in order to keep its forces supplied during any lengthy ground war, the United States must either produce far greater quantities of materiel in peacetime (as reserves) or else must be willing very greatly to increase its production rate in wartime, or in the event of strategic warning. Materiel during any protracted war are likely to be very considerable, not merely in the theater but also enroute to it. Yet, current U.S. military procurement policy does not provide significant reserves of major elements of materiel, such as tanks and aircraft. Discussions of buildups of war reserve stocks tend to emphasize the increased production of ammunition and other expendables.

Experience in the October 1973 Middle East War suggests strongly that even in a purely conventional environment the rates of loss of equipment are likely to be very great. Moreover, in many cases crews will survive the loss of their tanks and aircraft, so that the supply of the latter may be a determinate of national military endurance. Of course, combat losses are hardly the only factor to be considered. For example, if the war lasts any length of time and if there are substantial stockpiles built up in the continental United States (CONUS), then the security of their transit across the Atlantic takes on a very great significance. Unfortunately, given previous U.S. attention to short-war scenarios, the United States has neglected important elements of port and transit security after the outbreak of war. For example, the U.S. antisubmarine warfare (ASW) strategy is a war of attrition against Soviet submarine forces, with only very limited forces assigned to the direct protection of merchant shipping (convoys). The Soviet naval mine warfare potential has gone largely uncountered. Depending upon the performance of the American industrial base during a surge, the security of prestockpiled equipment in Western Europe may be crucial to the survival of American army units in the theater.

Classical industrial mobilization has aroused relatively little interest in the United States since World War II, largely because nuclear weapons seem to negate the type of war to which American mobilization practices were most applicable. For example, if all wars are very short, and if nuclear weapons tend to dominate all others, then excessive attention paid to ground forces and to the production of their equipment is merely unrealistic: the equipment will arrive in the theater after the end of the

Ground Forces

war, because the lead time for its production will most likely exceed strategic warning and warfighting time. However, with the increasing perception of the Soviet threat and with increasing interest in crises short of war, mobilization is coming to be seen as an element of long-term escalation. Moreover, some prewar mobilization capacity may make it possible for the United States to redress the current extremely adverse balance of conventional forces in the theater.

Mobilization modifies any calculation of the relative military power of the United States, its allies, and the Soviet Union and its allies. In principle, the Atlantic Alliance, together with other countries of the West, retains immense long-term advantages in terms of productive capacity, net manpower, trained manpower, and technology. The Soviet Union benefits from a more docile population (in peacetime) and from a willingness, therefore, to devote a greater proportion of its productive base to peacetime military investment. Consequently, although it may well be that the U.S.S.R. has a far lower ultimate mobilization potential than does the West, it already possesses significantly larger stocks of equipment and ammunition—and trained manpower. It also has a far more systematic appreciation of the value of its form of mobilization than appears to obtain in the West.

That is, the Soviet military plans to mobilize by filling out existing cadre formation with reservists, pulling the reservists' equipment out of storage. The political system of the Soviet Union makes such a policy attractive, and indeed feasible. Except for West Germany, no Western nation has a large-scale reserve intended for quick mobilization, and no Western nation appears to maintain either large-scale materiel reserves or the ability very rapidly (within, for example, six months) to increase those reserves. In short, the United States has virtually no surge mobilization policy or current capability, the chief exception being an Army program for automated production of advanced ammunition.

The reasons for this disparity are rooted in a combination of historical factors and current political and economic realities. If this disparity is indeed a major danger to a United States embarked upon a new national strategy oriented towards protracted conventional conflict, then it is to those longstanding causes that attention should be directed.

Mobilization can be defined as a scheme for rapidly increasing military power; generally it can be subdivided into materiel and manpower categories. Materiel mobilization seeks to expand production of military equipment, including ammunition. Manpower mobilization is the call-up of (generally pretrained) reserves, the rapid increase in the sheer size of the armed forces. Most policies are mixtures of the two, but generally one or the other predominates. For example, the U.S. Korean War mobilization emphasized materiel production, and much of the manpower (for NATO, for example) was supplied by U.S. allies:

the United States functioned, as it had in World War II as the "Arsenal of Democracy." Indeed, in World War II there appears to have been a tacit American decision to direct manpower to military production rather than to the Armed Forces, as the United States contributed a smaller proportion in its adult male population to combat arms than did its allies and its enemies.

There must be some question as to whether modern forms of warfare any longer admit a clear distinction between manpower and materiel. As weapons become much more complex, war becomes less and less labor intensive, and the number of men required per unit military effect would seem to fall. If that perception is correct, then expansion of the power of the armed forces should involve a preponderance of materiel, taken either from stocks or from new production. Manpower should be a relatively minor element. To some extent, the American style of warfare so emphasizes this approach that American materiel mobilizations of the past may be less distinct from classical European manpower mobilizations than at first they appear. Even now, the maintenance of Air and Naval Reserve forces with their weapons and equipment forms a kind of manpower reserve against contingencies.

However, these air and naval forces are specialists; in some important cases, such as air transport and minesweeping, they represent an attempt to remove from the standing forces the military burden of a role which would be important only in an emergency. Ground reserve forces are a very different category. The ground forces in general tend to be less differentiated than are air and naval forces, and their effectiveness depends to a far greater degree on their total mass. That is, the Army profits little from the addition of a few specialists: it gains much more by a massive increase in size. It follows that a conscious national policy of ground forces manpower mobilization requires the formation of massive stocks of materiel with which to arm the expanded forces; or, at the least, it requires some means of very rapidly increasing the rate of production of existing weapons as the army is expanded. The Soviet leaders, in their manpower mobilization policy, appear to have chosen to maintain very large stocks of equipment against the need to fill out cadre formations in wartime.

However, a policy of maintaining large materiel reserves need not imply a manpower mobilization policy. Recent military experience, particularly in the Middle East, suggests that modern war materiel is expended extremely rapidly, even more rapidly than men. It follows that any modern war may soon exhaust stocks formerly considered sufficient for large manpower mobilizations. In NATO terms this problem is often expressed in terms of the requirement to prepare for a 30-, 60-, or 90-day war. However, experience in the 1973 war suggests that even the preparations now considered appropriate to relatively long wars may be grossly inadequate. For the United States, the great irony is that, having foregone most forms of materiel surge mobilization and all forms of manpower surge mobilization, it may well be that the policy of maintaining appropriate standing materiel stocks will also be inadequate.

It seems useful to return to classical concepts of mobilization in order to clarify terms and distinctions. Here "classical" means European, and one of the important issues is the extent to which the American experience has been so different from that of the Europeans that American mobilization concepts have not been adjusted to address the same problems that the Europeans have always faced. The classical European military problem was the nearby presence of enemy armies. Given any significant advantage, an enemy could generally overrun any European state very rapidly, simply because the distances are so short. The Soviet Union and its Czarist predecessor were far better situated than were other Continental states in this respect, but they shared a common strategic outlook.

Moreover, in an era of manpower-intensive military forces, advantage generally meant larger forces. However, there was a practical limit to the size of standing armies which could be maintained in peacetime. In labor intensive economies, the drain of too many men would in itself do sufficient economic damage to undermine the fiscal basis of the army itself. Thus, before 1914, for example, each European army was maintained in a balance between fiscal limits and the need to be able to repel or at least delay any assault by a more mobilized neighbor. In this situation, the extent to which mobilization reservists could function effectively in the frontline was extremely important: the "secret weapon" which the Germans deployed in 1914 was the combat use of reserve divisions.

This type of strategy leads to a distinction which remains useful: military forces can be divided between covering forces and mobilization forces. The covering force is the peacetime military, sufficient to handle contingencies up to some emergency limit, and also sufficient to stop or delay an attack long enough to permit mobilization to take effect. Just how large a covering force is required depends upon a combination of factors: the strength and needs of the national economy, the speed of mobilization, the level of contingencies which must be addressed without resort to mobilization.

In addition, a nation which follows a policy of manpower mobilization generally requires a standing reserve force of trained men. That, in turn, is generally achieved by rotating the male population through the armed forces, and by maintaining a list of reservists after separation. There were always tradeoffs involved. The larger the proportion of the army made up by short-service draftees, the lower the peacetime efficiency of the army; it becomes, in effect, a training organization. On the other hand, the faster men pass through the army, the larger is the trained or semitrained reserve available against major contingencies. To some extent, then, the choice of the character of the standing army depends upon perceptions as to the nature of the peacetime (i.e., nonmobilization) contingencies that an army must cover.

In a nuclear era, strategic forces may be considered the "cover" which permits industrial mobilization to proceed. For example, given the American style of war and the size of the Western industrial base, it might be argued that the Soviet leaders would find it difficult passively to accept a NATO-wide rearmament program. Moreover, inevitable industrial inertia would give them a long time during which to act—as long as they did not have to contend with the covering force.

At least since the late 1940s, the United States has followed a policy of very limited surge mobilization potential. There have been attempts to maintain the kind of industrial mobilization base which proved so valuable during and after World War II, but manpower reserves have generally been neglected. More and more the emphasis has been on the standing force, which is not considered a covering force. That is, the United States has not envisaged the transition from peace to war as a process of upgrading capability. Rather, it has been assumed that wars will have to be fought with men and with equipment already in place. Such a policy is consistent with experience suggesting that new equipment cannot be made available for over a year after the decision to obtain it.

The position of the draft in such a policy is one of short-term replacements for men, rather than one of upgrading the total force to some greatly increased size. That is, in a lengthy war such as Vietnam the draft was used to maintain the size of the standing army but there was no serious consideration of mobilization, i.e., of drafting men in large numbers for the duration. In a materiel (nonammunition) sense, the standing military force was almost static.

It should be noted here that American materiel mobilization policy in both World Wars was based largely on the size and capacity of an industrial base not normally devoted to military production. Given the long warning time assumed, it always seemed evident that that base could be turned to military production without extensive preparation beyond planning. The impact of nuclear weapons and thus of wars which could involve the United States very soon after their outbreak was to call such a policy into doubt. The apparent decline of American industrial capacity, particularly relative to that of other Western nations, has further reduced the credibility of an American policy based on massive increases in military production.

For the United States, the great historical factor in two World Wars was the long period available for mobilization, which in itself was a consequence of the protection afforded by two wide oceans. The oceans, in addition, greatly reduced the size of the covering force the United States needed to protect itself during mobilization, so that in peacetime the United States could make do with very limited military forces indeed. Although these factors have not been relevant since the late 1940s, American thinking continues to be influenced by them. That is, the American political system does not consider it natural to maintain very large military forces in peacetime, although it recognizes the need for such forces in the face of the Soviet military threat. Moreover, with the advent of nuclear weapons, the American response was that traditional forms of mobilization were less and less valuable: wars might come to the United States without the necessary warning period, and they would be over well before the American mobilization base could be activated. Here the role of history is evident in the American definition of adequate warning time (on the order of years) and the mobilization base (heavy industry, not manpower).

Manpower did not figure in American mobilization calculations because, on the scale of warning time assumed, very large armies could be raised essentially without much preparation. Thus, it was entirely acceptable to raise and train large ground forces in 1917 and in 1940, the standing Navy forming strategic cover, in 1940 the Army had essentially no combat capability because of its training role, and indeed it had little capability as late as 1942. This manpower element of American mobilization required far less preparation than did the massive increase in the production of ships, vehicles, and aircraft accomplished at the same time, for which planning had been proceeding for many years. The latter required industrial conversion on a large scale. Men were far more easily trained. Moreover, because of the character of the threat and of the mobilization, they could be retained "for the duration," so that the loss of capability due to large-scale training washed out over a few years, long before most of the troops entered combat.

The Soviet leadership (and, for that matter, many West Europeans) had a very different historical experience, typified by the events of 1914. Classical European mobilization planning envisaged relatively little warning, and that by a neighbor who might be able to project his land forces through the border quite soon after the outbreak of war. Mobilization had to provide a large enough land army to oppose the largest army that a potential enemy could field. In peacetime, there had to be large enough standing forces to cover the mobilization period. That is, there was always the fear than an enemy might be able to mobilize sufficiently (in secret) to overcome the covering force and win a war before the main force could be mobilized. In the world of 1914, there was no expectation that standing forces could win wars; it was necessary to mobilize a substantial fraction of the manpower of each country, at the cost of immense industrial disruption. Industrial mobilization as such was not a viable policy, since warning time would almost certainly be very short, on the order of weeks rather than years.

This concept is fundamentally geographical in its basis: the enemy is already at the border, and if he is sufficiently prepared he need give very little strategic warning. Geography remains vital after very considerable developments in military technology: in 1981 NATO remains concerned with the possibility of a surprise Soviet descent into Western Europe at the end of a large-scale military exercise. NATO concepts of strategic warning are not very different from those current in 1914, although the time scale of the war which would follow is considerably compressed.

For their part, the Soviet leaders profess themselves to be concerned with the threat of a NATO attack; they, too, appear to think in terms of relatively short warning. Moreover, they have often stated that modern war will consume far greater quantities of materiel and manpower than classical war, i.e., that it must be fought by forces far larger than those which can be maintained comfortably in peacetime. Evidences of such thinking include the maintenance of large numbers of under-strength (cadre) divisions, which are to be filled out in wartime, and also the Soviet willingness to produce weapons at rates far above those needed to fill training and equipment needs of their standing forces. The entire structure of the Soviet military, from the draft through the maintenance of standing reserves, testifies to a willingness to mobilize manpower at the outset of a crisis. Just how well the Soviet Union will be able to carry out its plans is of course open to question. The issue here is its policy and its rationale.

The Soviet surge mobilization concept is hardly unique to the Soviet Union; for example, West Germany relies heavily on a reserve structure in the event of war. However, it does satisfy some uniquely Soviet requirements, and it does correspond well to the Soviet military economy. That is, the Soviet Union has a planned, i.e., ideally a steady-state, economy. Radical changes (such as materiel mobilization) are to be avoided for a host of essentially political reasons. It follows that a prudent Soviet leadership must maintain a relatively high rate of military production, as rapid acceleration (even given some considerable strategic warning) is difficult at best. In effect, then, the rate of production has little relation to the level of standing forces. Political forces within the Soviet Union favor continued steady production rather than the redirection of effort from military objectives. Such production practices favor the maintenance of large reserve equipment stocks, and make manpower mobilization attractive.

By way of contrast, in the West in general, and particularly in the United States, overproduction of military equipment in peacetime carries great political costs. It is necessary to justify equipment purchases on the basis of the needs of the standing forces, as all such purchases divert funds and resources from other (often more powerful) pressure groups. In such circumstances the accumulation of reserve materiel stocks is often politically dangerous, as such stocks in themselves represent a reason to forego new production.

This is not a new problem. For example, one reason France produced relatively few new weapons (such as new tanks) during the 1930s was that she already had on hand a very large stock of serviceable weapons left over from the mobilization of World War I. The United States services, particularly the Air Force, took pains to destroy the large stocks of obsolescent aircraft left over from World War I so as to preclude Congress from avoiding new production. The British, with a much weaker economy, had no such luxury available to them, and indeed had to make do with World War II types through the early 1950s. It was the Navy's misfortune that it could not dispose of the very large (and largely obsolete) fleet left over from its wartime building program, even though much of that fleet was never recommissioned for postwar service. In this context the Army found that it could not obtain new tanks in any numbers until it had used up its (quite obsolescent) *Sherman* and *Pershing* tanks in the mid-1950s.

Given the reluctance of Western governments to finance very large programs of new weapons, and the need to maintain weapons production facilities, Western governments cannot help but arrange for long production runs at moderate levels, the total size of the buy determined by the size of the standing force. Economics, moreover, precludes the creation of large additional industrial capacity earmarked for mobilization. In consequence, peacetime production rates cannot approach those common in the Soviet Union. Unit costs are inevitably high, but any attempt to buy many units over a short period of time encounters the objection that any company agreeing to such a program is putting itself out of business. This problem of justifying production in peacetime is also closely related to the issue of excessive "goldplating": any contractor (or program manager) must justify new programs on the basis that they represent massive increases in performance. Merely keeping the industrial base alive is not an effective argument.

Until Vietnam, the draft represented a relatively low political cost in the United States, as indeed it still does in the Soviet Union. Both nations maintained large standing forces essentially on the basis of short-term draft enlistments. However, both nations saw their standing forces very differently. To the Soviets, the army was both a covering force and a means of training reservists who would, collectively, constitute a mobilization resource. Given this point of view, the cost of training establishments in a draftee army is quite acceptable.

Moreover, for the Soviet Union the draft is a means of assuring that a large fraction of an ethnically diverse population is put through a unifying experience. In this sense, the Soviet military fulfills a function similar to that of the military in an emerging nation: it helps to overcome the sense of regional nationalism. A serious reserve program keeps that sense of unity alive, and also maintains national awareness of the need for armed vigilance, itself an important unifying force. Reportedly, the Soviets used reservists in Czechoslovakia in 1968, in Afghanistan in 1979, and in Poland in 1980-81. In each case the mobilization policy allowed the Soviets to avoid regular-army personnel dislocations, at least at first.

To Americans, on the other hand, the standing army represents both strategic cover and, in many cases, the army which will be called upon to fight wars. Mobilization is so long term that the structure of the peacetime army is almost irrelevant to that of the war army, should the war be so large as to call for mobilization. On the other hand, the mobilization potential of the country is irrelevant in most wars, as in Vietnam. The effect of current perceptions is to change "most" to "all," as the time scale of mobilization currently exceeds even an optimistic estimate of strategic warning time. Even if it is accepted that mobilization is practicable in a grave crisis, the Army existing in peacetime must be able to prevail in a variety of limited-war situations which in a state like the Soviet Union would demand limited mobilization.

Given such a view of the role of the peacetime army, and so great a reluctance to mobilize reservists, the draftee Army is perceived as extremely inefficient. Even though it is not designed to maximize the size of the trained reserve, it must still devote a large proportion of its efforts to training—which is considered a gross inefficiency, soaking up a large fraction of the resources and energies of the long-term army. After all, if the reserve is considered relatively valueless, then the Army loses at least a year of training each time it releases a two-year draftee. It gains nothing. This reasoning was used to justify the "all-volunteer" army as a cost effective solution to the problem of U.S. national security requirements. In theory, there would be fewer men, but then again many fewer would be wasted in training, and the long-term enlistees would be more efficient than draftees.

Even now, with the all-volunteer force clearly a failure, the draft is justified in terms of the peacetime character of the Army. That is, it is now perceived that there are insufficient numbers of satisfactory volunteers and that the rate of reenlistment is far too low. Thus, the all-volunteer force suffers from the inefficiency of the draft but has not its benefit, the induction of sufficient high-quality troops. The problem is particularly acute, given the rising level of technology in the Army.

Thus resumption of the draft seems likely. However, such a step will not solve the U.S. surge mobilization problem. The only improvement—and it is a slight one—will be an enhanced ability to make up for combat losses and for the loss of manpower over time, and even then that will require considerable lead times for training.

British experience in World War I provides a sobering example. The prewar British Army had very little mobilization base, partly because, like the United States, Britain faced no enemy capable of instant descent across her borders. Her small standing Army was designed primarily for imperial policing, i.e., for small overseas wars. It appears that her military leaders were genuinely unaware of the consequences, in manpower terms, of their guarantee of ground forces to the French. Certainly, they had built up no mobilization structure: no stocks of materiel, of ammunition, of battle-worthy reservists. Nor was there provision for a draft. The very professional British Army of 1914 acquitted itself extremely well in the first battles of the war—which, however, destroyed men and equipment at an unprecedented rate. The size of the force which had then to be raised staggered most British planners. Indeed, the very speed with which the "Kitchener Army" of 1915-1916 was raised caused serious tactical problems. For example, it was considered so little trained that it could not be employed very effectively, and it is sometimes suggested that its lack of training led directly to the tactics which killed so large a fraction of it in battles like the Somme.

It is true that the United States has maintained organized reserves through much of its history; for example, State Militia formed a large part of the Union Army in the Civil War. However, these forces have never been very large nor have they, at least in this century, been particularly effective in wartime. In World War II, the Army found that it was faster to create new (draftee) divisions than to mobilize National Guard units, and often it broke up such reserve units rather than field them. The reserve function was somewhat better performed by specialist Navy and Air Force units, and indeed these units train and perform their military duties on a regular basis. It should be noted, too, that they can be considered part of the national strategic cover, and they fulfill essential duties at a relatively low cost in manpower. Army reserves are a very different issue, as they do not make an important difference unless they are available in great numbers.

To the Soviets, manpower mobilization policies make it possible for the Soviet Union to react rapidly (albeit on a short-term basis) to emergencies. For example, the Soviets mobilized some reservists to expand their forces around the Polish border during the recent crisis in Poland. They were thus spared the need, again in the short term, to draw down forces in other sensitive areas, such as the German border and the Far East. Again, the standing force is primarily a combination of cover and a training organization. The reserves are used for unexpected contingencies, contingencies against which the standing forces may not suffice.

Such a policy carries considerable costs. For example, twice each year the Soviet Army must adjust to a massive influx of new trainees while men who have served their full terms are released. The training-camp aspect of the Army is emphasized, and combat is difficult unless the planned transfers of personnel are voided by decree. Such a step carries with it considerable economic and social costs, and will not be accepted casually.

However, to a militarized state such as the Soviet Union even relatively minor contingencies carry the need for large forces beyond those required in a peacetime which the leadership considers fraught with danger. Ready reserves and large stockpiles represent the minimum margin of safety. Soviet ideology predicts that war is entirely possible, though deterrence may also prevent it. Survival in war is the first function of the State, and justifies the social costs of heavy peacetime production, and of the continual replacement of obsolescent equipment. It is a useful coincidence that the same policy is attractive to the military-industrial complex which dominates the Soviet state. Even so, a Soviet state mindful of its geography and of the feelings of its neighbors probably could not but maintain approximately the mobilization base and practice which the Soviets currently operate.

The American problem is that just this Soviet policy represents a considerable advantage to the Soviet Union. The United States can make the decision that war is probable within X years and can mobilize its industrial base to match that schedule. It was done in the period immediately after 1950, and it can probably be done again, quite possibly more effectively than the Soviet Union can countermobilize. However, any such policy carries extremely high costs. The highest is the cost in the event the war occurs—but not until a few years later than expected. History is replete with examples of major rearmament programs which fell afoul because of rapidly evolving military technology. The Soviet program of the 1930s (which produced the largest air and tank forces in the world) is a prime example. Given Western politics and economics, any massive buildup carries with it a disinclination to scrap or replace the large force build up. This problem of course extends well beyond ground forces.

Several courses are open to us. One is to return to a draft, but to take ready reserves far more seriously than we have in the past. We can, for example, retain men in the Army for a slightly shorter period, but train them for (say) four weeks a year for four years after they leave the service. We can expand our standing force materiel reserve by providing modern equipment for the expanded reserves, and we can assure interest in the reserves by giving them more important wartime missions—as the Navy and the Air Force already do. It may even be possible to reduce somewhat the size of the standing Army while increasing the size and the service commitment of the reserves. The key to such an arrangement is the draft, as only the draft can produce the flow of trained men into the reserves in the first place.

We can also seek to expand our production base. One measure is simply to increase our own budget figures, our own estimates of the forces and equipment needed to fight a modern war. That kind of self-discipline seems difficult to impose, however, particularly if it is combined with greater increases in the manpower costs of standing and reserve forces. The other possibility is greatly to relax our constraints on foreign military sales, to consider FMS a means of maintaining rates of production we consider valuable. Only FMS can provide a reserve of equipment awaiting shipment, equipment which can be sequestered in an emergency. FMS (to Great Britain) was an extremely valuable contribution to American industrial mobilization in World War II.

Unless we take some such steps, it will be impossible for the United States to make up for the losses its ground forces can be expected to sustain early in a European war. Nor will it be possible for the United States to make effective use of the strategic warning which still seems likely. NATO planners constantly write about up to two weeks of warning. That will suffice to move some American troops into position to break their prepositioned unit equipment (POMCUS) out of storage dumps, and to move their dependents home. However, there will be precious few troops remaining in the pipeline once those units have flown to Europe, and the United States will have little ability to fight elsewhere in the world with its ground troops. Nor will there be much materiel available to replace that lost in the first few days—or, for that matter, in the sabotage of the POMCUS dumps.

Nor is it necessary to envisage a protracted conventional European war to see the need for an American reserve system for ground forces. For example, the Rapid Deployment Force represents a very significant fraction of American ground forces, particularly when its logistical support is taken into account. Should it become engaged in the Persian Gulf, and should further large forces be required, there would not be sufficient ground forces remaining to accomplish the usual roles of the standing army: for example, the force in Europe would probably have to be drastically drawn down.

An ability to accelerate the production of advanced artillery shells will not solve that type of problem.

7

Civil Reserve Air Fleet

Ralph P. Novak

The Civil Reserve Air Fleet (CRAF) is an element in the logistics systems the United States depends on to transport forces and materiel in a variety of contingencies. Since its inception in the early 1950s, the CRAF has been like the understudy in a play, always ready to perform, but never called upon for one reason or another. Over the years CRAF has become used to its role and its inactivity. As a consequence, CRAF and the force it supports have grown complacent about its potential and its problems.

The organization and planning that have built CRAF reveal that a lot of hard work and thought went into developing its current capabilities. Unfortunately, the fact that CRAF does not take advantage of the full potential of America's airlines and the problem of competing requirements for the aircrews counted on to man CRAF pose serious questions for mobilization planning. This chapter will consider these issues and offer recommendations for improving the capability of CRAF.

One of the most serious problems facing American military planners today is transportation: how can enough men and materiel be moved quickly enough to a trouble spot to control a crisis or successfully fight a war? This chapter looks at that problem in the context of a Soviet attack against NATO—a contingency which would require a rapid and massive response by the United States. In an attack against NATO, it seems reasonable to assume that immediate reinforcement and resupply efforts would be made and that the Military Airlift Command (MAC) would be totally occupied transporting preplanned loads of combat troops and equipment, and support elements for tactical aviation units. Further, CRAF planning must also consider the possibility that the Reserve and National Guard forces of the United States have been totally mobilized.

In order to determine if CRAF has the capability to handle its role it is necessary to understand its history, organization and equipment.

CRAF is a voluntary program with the participating airlines signing contracts with the Air Force to provide aircraft and crews in times of emergency.[1] In order to give the system some flexibility and some leverage in getting airlines to cooperate, CRAF is broken down into three stages. Stage one provides enough capacity to take care of most of the Military Airlift Command's (MAC) routine "channel" or route traffic and can be activated by the Commander-in-Chief (Cinc) of MAC. Stage two provides about a 140% increase in the number of aircraft in the system over Stage one and it must be activated by the Secretary of Defense. Airlines participating in either of these first two stages are given priority in obtaining military airlift contracts.

Stage three of CRAF is activated by the Secretary of Defense only after the President or Congress has declared a state of emergency or general war. When this happens, the current total of approximately 430 aircraft in CRAF will be pressed into service on one of four route segments: long-range international, short-range international, Alaskan or domestic, depending on aircraft type, range and load carrying capabilities. For planning purposes, MAC schedules the CRAF aircraft and their crews at the same flying hour rates used by the airlines in normal civil operations.

The strength of CRAF, as currently organized, is that the number and types of available aircraft are known to the Air Force. In addition, the internal configuration of each aircraft is known and, therefore, initial loads of cargo and/or troops can be planned for it. Further, plans have been made for the utilization of civil airfields by CRAF, thus spreading the logistical load out among as many airfields in both the mainland United States and Europe.[2] As a part of the plan to use civilian fields, participating airlines with the greatest capability at a given field have been designated as Senior Lodger, giving them the responsibility for all CRAF operations at the field.[3]

In sum, CRAF appears to be a well-planned effort to insure that the nation has the airlift capability to respond to any emergency. However, a number of serious deficiencies exist in CRAF as presently constituted.

The first question to ask is, "Is CRAF large enough and composed of the right type of equipment to perform the tasks required of it in the strategies being considered today?" A complete analysis of the logistical effort required to prosecute successfully a conventional war in Europe is beyond the scope of this chapter. However, it is worth noting that the Air Force is seriously concerned about the shortfall of cargo aircraft within its own fleet and is pressing hard for an aircraft that not only could transport large sized military equipment, but could transport this equipment to forward bases, thus freeing tactical, or theater, airlift for short-range requirements that now go unmet.[4]

The next major problem that confronts CRAF is the imprecise information the Air National Guard, Air Reserve and the Airlines have about the competing commitments their crews may have in a general mobilization. The depth of the problem can best be illustrated by the following facts: neither the National Guard or Reserve forces keep central records on the civilian occupations of members.[5] Individual units do, but only so members can be contracted during working hours. The commercial airlines, including the ones involved in CRAF, do not know which of their pilots belong to the reserve components. The office in the Department of Defense (DOD) charged with determining if there is any conflict between critical civilian industries and reserve participation, in its 1980 annual report to Congress, stated that "according to airline industry publications, only 7% of civilian pilots and flight engineers have Guard or Reserve affiliation." To back up an earlier claim that recall of all Reserve flyers would not have a seriously disruptive impact on the airline industry, the report goes on to state that "with specific reference to recall of Air Reserve pilots in the 100,000 package (selected Reserve call-up as permitted by the War Powers Act), the impact would be negligible as only about 1,300 are included."[6] However, the report fails to take into consideration the effect that such a call-up would have if the airlines themselves found their CRAF committed aircraft and crews suddenly called upon at the same time the reserve components were totally (not partially, as in the DOD report) mobilized. The problem grows in magnitude when it is understood that a large portion of the Military Airlift Command's C-5 and C-141 day-to-day crew force comes from what are known as reserve associate units.[7] Also, during the past four years the Strategic Air Command has turned over 128 KC-135 airborne tanker aircraft (approximately 20% of the total of this type of aircraft)[8] to the reserve forces. The KC-10, a derivative of the McDonnell-Douglas DC-10 commercial aircraft, and U.S.A.F.'s new tanker will be crewed primarily by reserve component crews.[9] Above that, some 30% of the Air Force's tactical fighter force is composed of reserve units.[10] Clearly, the reserve components play a critical and growing role in the Air Force's capacity to defend the United States and its allies. The people who man these units will be essential to their unit's ability to carry out their assigned missions. And yet, they may be just as important in their civilian occupations as air crew members in the country's commercial aviation industry.

The role this civilian industry can play in fighting a war is realized in the United States by the mere existence of CRAF. The European allies in NATO nations also understand this need and have started work on forming a 1,000 aircraft CRAF of their own.[11] If one needs to be convinced of the military utility of efficiently utilizing civil aviation during a military emergency, one only has to look at Aeroflot, the Soviet national airline. It is headed by a Soviet Air Force general officer and it regularly exercises with Soviet forces during major war games.[12]

The 1980 Department of Defense report to Congress on reserve manning concluded that the 7% figure of civilian pilots and flight engineers who were members of the reserve components was considered to pose no problem to the airline industry if they were recalled to active duty. The report's preceding paragraph notes that 800 of some 27,400 Federal Aviation Administration (FAA) air traffic controllers were members of the ready reserve. The FAA categorically declared them as key employees and had them processed out of the ready reserves.[13] Losing this 2.9% of its work force in time of a national crisis was considered serious enough by the FAA to force it to take a step that would undoubtedly prove unpopular with the affected employees and inhibit some highly trained individuals leaving the service from coming to work for them.

Yet, when it comes to aircrews, at least as important to air transportation as controllers, there is no concern over the losing of twice as high a percentage (7%) of the available manpower. The problem becomes serious because aircrews are not interchangeable among aircraft without retraining, a luxury a major conflict will not allow. A Boeing 747 crew cannot fly a DC-10 or L-1011. All three types of aircraft are important to CRAF, but if reserve commitments cause manning problems, CRAF could be required to choose between manning aircraft with untrained crews and denying key personnel to reserve units.

The size of CRAF is constrained by what the Air Force can get out of the airlines, rather than the airlines' capacity to support an all-out effort. Two possible explanations can be offered. The first is that CRAF was formed in the days when a major conventional conflict between the United States and the Soviet Union was not thought possible. It was, in fact, formed out of U.S. experience in the Korean conflict and was designed to give forces in some foreign battle area the logistical support required while not disrupting the civilian economy. The second explanation is that the Air Force has aimed at having CRAF consist of aircraft that can be quickly configured to haul cargo. This fits the apparent pattern of having CRAF support a military action not involving direct confrontation with the Soviet Union and thus not requiring instant, massive reinforcement. Just as importantly, it limits the number of aircraft that can be brought into the CRAF system since most commercial aircraft are not built to be converted from a passenger to cargo carrying configurations.

Today, CRAF has its required strength of approximately 430 aircraft and it will be increased in size over the next few years by adding more wide body, high capacity aircraft. It also has the manpower, based on gross numbers, to man it effectively throughout the range of its requirements.

What can be done or should be done to correct the problems of CRAF? First, all commercial airline aircraft of a certain size (DC-9/Boeing 737 and larger) should automatically be included in CRAF. Industry figures show that there were over 2,100 aircraft of the required size in service with the U.S. airlines at the end of 1979.[14] The current three stages of CRAF should remain intact with a fourth one added to take in the additional aircraft. Flexibility should be built into the stages by assigning each stage three categories of aircraft. These would be all cargo, all passenger, and cargo-passenger convertible. By selecting a stage and a category MAC could tailor a CRAF fleet that would meet the needs of a particular crisis while maintaining a reserve of the proper type of aircraft at home in case of a larger or more urgent crisis in some other part of the world.

In any case, the most important accomplishment of an expansion of CRAF is that plans for the use of the United States' full aviation capacity could be drawn up and be ready for use. It would also allow military planners to insure that an additional airlift force would be in place, at known locations, within hours of notification. Instead, they are now limited to using current CRAF and then having to fit, willy-nilly, the rest of the civil fleet into a system ill-prepared to take them and their militarily limited capabilities, should the President take control of the airlines.

Expanding CRAF, in itself a mostly bureaucratic action, would also serve as an indication of our will to both ally and adversary alike. In the case of a major conflict in Europe both sides recognize the importance of the United States and its manufacturing capacity in determining the outcome. Both sides also recognize that even with a large capability to produce, the United States' effect on a war in Europe would amount to little if transportation of large quantities of men and materiel to the war zone became bottlenecked. In any long war surface shipping will make the major contribution to the hauling of supplies, but air transport alone will be able to react to emergency situations and take advantage quickly of any enemy weakness. The United States must have the plans to use civil aviation—all of it—before any conflict starts.

Perhaps the larger problem concerning the use of the civil aviation industry in a major military emergency is manpower. Regardless of whether CRAF is expanded or remains in its present form, the aircraft are identifiable and available. This is not the case with the aircrews who are supposed to fly them. Any plan to expand CRAF or to solve its current problems cannot succeed if it does not take into account the effect any solution may have on participation in the reserve components by commercial airline pilots.

There is probably no occupation more uniquely suited to reserve participation than airline pilots. Most airline pilots flying today got their flight training and first few years of operational flying as members of the U.S. military. Some, when they left active military service, were required to join a reserve unit in order to complete their service obligation under the selective service system.

Certain types of reserve units and programs seem almost designed to take advantage of the free time airline pilots are able to garner. The MAC associate unit program, for instance, teams reserve crews with active duty C-5 or C-141 units. The active units "own" the aircraft and schedule all missions, assigning crew members according to their availability. This gives MAC the crew force it needs efficiently to use its aircraft and it provides the reserve crew member the scheduling flexibility he needs in order to fit his reserve responsibilities in with his civilian occupation.

The same applies to the reserve crew member who belongs to a unit flying the KC-135 aircraft for the Strategic Air Command. Organized differently than the MAC reserve associate units, the reserve KC-135 squadrons control their own aircraft and are responsible for their entire operation. However, since they are required to keep one aircraft on alert at all times as part of SAC's quick response force, these units offer a convenient opportunity for someone with the time, such as an airline pilot, to serve in the reserves.[15]

In other words, flying for the airlines and belonging to a reserve unit could be called a natural fit in peacetime. A large number of airline pilots have previous Air Force experience and some affinity toward the service. The reserves recognize that a large portion of the pilot resources they can recruit work for the airlines and therefore design their operations to take advantage of that resource.

That is the crux of the problem. In order to man the reserve units the Air Force must recruit from the airlines which, in turn, make suspect the airline capability to man CRAF fully. Unless the airlines and the Air Force planners responsible for CRAF know who is going to be available for what role during a general mobilization, confusion will result. Even in today's CRAF the airlines need to know if there are any serious manning shortfalls in any particular aircraft or area when their crew members who are reservists are not available. If CRAF is expanded, as it should be, to take instant advantage of the entire air transportation industry, this problem will only worsen.

On the other hand, the air reserves could not exist without the participation of airline pilots. Nor should the airline pilots who want, or need, to participate in reserve programs be penalized by having to give up their reserve affiliation or possibly be denied promotion to a better aircraft within the airline due to their reserve status.

The Air Force needs to know if there is any major conflict between individual reserve commitments and airline commitments to CRAF. If there is a problem, or even a suspected problem, further steps should be taken to assess the extent of the problem and to correct it.

The Air Force reserve programs have been leaders in coming up with innovative programs such as the reserve associate units and the SAC tanker units in response to unique manning or duty problems. Insuring adequate air crews to fulfill all the requirements of a major crisis or conflict can be solved if the scope of the problem is known and if a fresh approach to it is taken.

In conclusion, CRAF plays a vital role in our ability to respond to contingencies around the world. However, in attempting to play its part, CRAF does not now use the greater share of commercial airliners in service in this country. In addition, the manpower base behind the system is suspect for a variety of reasons. The problems and shortfalls of CRAF can be addressed and solved by relatively simple and direct fixes. Expand CRAF to its full potential in equipment and then insure that it is backed by sufficient numbers of trained crews.

NOTES

1. *United States Air Force Fact Sheet* number 80-29, prepared by the Secretary of the Air Force, Office of Public Affairs, Washington, D.C. 20330.
2. Ibid.
3. Ibid.
4. General Robert E. Huyser, Commander-in-Chief, Military Airlift Command, in a speech reprinted in the *Supplement to the Air Force Policy Letters for Commanders, March 1981*, page 17.
5. This information was provided during interviews with several individuals from the Office, Deputy Assistant Secretary of Defense (Reserve Affairs) and the Reserve Affairs Office Headquarters, Tactical Air Command.
6. *1980 Report to the House Appropriations Committee: Screening Ready Reservists Employed by the Federal Government*, prepared by the Office, Deputy Assistant Secretary of Defense (Reserve Affairs) para. c of the Air National Guard Study section.
7. Compiled from the Forces section of the 1981 U.S.A.F. Summary prepared by the Directorate of Cost and Management Analysis, Comptroller of the Air Force.
8. Ibid.
9. *United States Air Force Fact Sheet 80-81*, Secretary of the Air Force, Office of Public Affairs, Washington, D.C. 20330.
10. U.S.A.F. Summary, Forces section, page 5, Op. Cit.

11. Information obtained during discussions at DOD and FEMA in February, 1981.

12. C. Kenneth Allard, "A Clear and Present Danger: Soviet Airborne Forces in the 1980s," page 13. From a paper presented at the Ninth Annual Conference of the International Security Studies Program, The Fletcher School of Law and Diplomacy, Tufts University, April 23-25, 1980, published in *Projection of Power: Perspectives, Perceptions and Problems* (Hamden, Conn.: Archon Books, 1982).

13. *1980 Report to the House Appropriations Committee*, Air National Guard Study section, para. b, Op. Cit.

14. Information obtained from the Air Transport Association shows that there were over 2,300 Boeing 707, 720, 727, 737, and 747, McDonnell-Douglas OC-8, DC-9 and DC-10, Lockheed L-1011 and Air Bus Industries A-300 aircraft in service with U.S. airlines at the end of 1979.

15. Knowledge of reserve forces' operations and organization comes from the author's own experience as a staff member of Headquarters, Tactical Air Command, working with Air National Guard and Air Reserve units.

8

RX: The Industrial Preparedness Planning Program—Bad Medicine or Poorly Administered?

*John C. McLaurin**

For good reason, there has been growing concern among national policy and opinion makers about the United States defense posture. Some of this concern has focused on a key element—the condition of the industrial base. Groups such as the Defense Science Board, the General Accounting Office (GAO), the American Defense Preparedness Association, and the House Armed Services Committee have addressed the industrial base and its ability to respond to defense needs during national emergencies. In the course of these discussions one hears few good things about the Industrial Preparedness Planning (IPP) Program.

As its name implies, the IPP Program was designed to ensure that the defense industry was prepared for national emergencies. But it has failed to reach that goal: The current U.S. industrial base is not able to respond adequately to defense mobilization requirements. This chapter discusses the condition of the industrial base and how it relates to defense concerns. This condition will illustrate the need for a governmental program designed to cure some of its ills. The chapter then examines the IPP Program and how it has been executed. Finally, it explores reasons for the program being executed as described. This discussion should enable the reader to determine whether industry's lack of preparedness results from a poor policy or poor implementation of that policy.

The Condition of the Patient

When the stockpile of war reserve materiel falls short of predicted requirements, the logical way to decrease risk to a warfighting strategy is to ensure an industrial base capable of adding to the stockpile at an accelerated pace sufficient to meet the strategy. This step does not suggest that we stop peacetime production. Instead, this approach advocates

* The opinions, conclusions, and recommendations expressed or implied in this chapter are solely those of the author, and do not necessarily represent the views of the National Defense University, the Department of Defense, or any other U.S. government agency.

producing as many weapons as defense budget priorities will allow. If upon approaching the budget ceiling the level of production is still below that needed, then we should go one step further and invest in the strengthening of the capability of the industrial base to produce the needed quantities in reasonable time once the "go" signal is given.

This implies that when the "go" signal is given, conditions will be such that funding will be made available for production at maximum capacity. This accelerated production pace will call for such added expenses as multiple work shifts, overtime, expedited transportation, continuous vice batch processing, and opening up new lines. But in an emergency, efficiency is not the key factor. The emphasis shifts from cost to time. The key is to put ourselves in a position to take maximum advantage of increased funds without sacrificing peacetime production, to make wartime industrial capability and peacetime production enhance each other. For example, a manufacturer can accelerate his output much faster from a base where some production is in progress (warm base) than from a base where production has stopped (cold base). For air-to-air missiles, for example, this means a loss in time between six and twelve months if production must be initiated without benefit of a warm mobilization base.

In the absence of the proper amount of preparation the industrial base will not respond to our needs. At the outset of the Korean War, production was accelerated but, because the industrial base had been inactive, not much of the materiel made it to the battlefield. "None of the thousands of tanks which were produced by Ford, General Motors, and Chrysler, the planned producers, for example, was deployed."[1]

One might point to the accomplishments of United States industry in World War II and assert with pride, "They said it couldn't be done then, but we did it." He should recall, however, that the United States had two years' head start through Britain's arms purchases, lend-lease, and "anticipatory measures by the Roosevelt Administration."[2] The United States may not have two years' warning next time, and certainly should not depend on it.

Today's industrial base indicates that we have not paid sufficient attention to accelerated production needs. Consider the aircraft and missile producers' capabilities in Figures 1 and 2. During an emergency it would take nearly five years for the production of the A-7 to increase to its maximum rate of 33 aircraft per month. It would take nearly two years for the production of the SPARROW missile to reach its maximum rate.

One reason for this lack of responsiveness is that today's weapons systems are far more complex and lead times continue to grow. Weapons system technology has increased faster than the associated manufacturing technology. Dr. Hans Mark, former Secretary of the Air Force, compared World War II's P-38 with today's equivalent, the F-15, "...time to create the F-15 was a decade whereas the P-38 was ready to fly less than two years after the first contract was signed..."[3] From 1978 to 1980, the lead time for titanium forgings increased by 255%, aluminum forgings by 153%, integrated circuits by 115%. These factors have contributed to the situation in which in 1981 it takes fifteen months to produce a SPARROW missile, in contrast to nine months in 1961.

Another reason can be attributed to producers being (understandably) more concerned with return on investment than mobilization. Looking for ways to increase the number of SPARROW missiles that can be produced over a given period, one finds Raytheon's Bristol Plant operating its radome assembly schedule at three shifts a day, eight hours a shift, six days a week. Obviously, there is no room for expansion without building additional facilities. Corning Glass Works, another contractor for the radome, politely declined to support the activities of the Industrial Preparedness Planning Program. How much pressure could be exerted by the Department of Defense when all of Corning's defense business amounts to less than 0.5% of its sales?[4]

Moreover, concerned observers agree that there is a trend away from defense business, especially at the subcontractor level.[5] Contractors cite the following as detractors for defense business: high risks and low profit margins, changing and unclear Department of Defense requirements, cumbersome and expensive regulations and paperwork, and small orders. One contractor pointed out that in 1979 more money was made on television computer games than on electronic warfare equipment.

Yet another reason for inadequate industrial ability to respond to accelerated production needs is the way the government usually does business, i.e., annual contracts. The budget must be approved, the contract let, and the prime contractors in turn negotiate with their subcontractors. The second step along, government-to-prime contractor, averages three months. Meanwhile, production decisions wait. Understandably, some companies do not commit funds to protect lead times by prestocking until they have a contract. Moreover, in 1979 at least one state discouraged prestocking by taxing inventories.[6]

As a result of physical plant capabilities, competition for nondefense items, and governmental policies and procedures, many factors operate to reduce the responsiveness of the industrial base to defense needs and the trends are adverse. But the potential for improvement exists. The costs involved are those of peacetime costs, since defense procurement must compete with other priorities. Today's capability is worrisome. Even though one can safely assume that money will be available during an emergency, such funds will not produce early results with our existing industrial base. Lead times have lengthened over the years. Industry is leaning away from defense business and either not able or not willing to invest in greater productivity. Government policies and actions are partly to blame.

Preparedness Planning Program

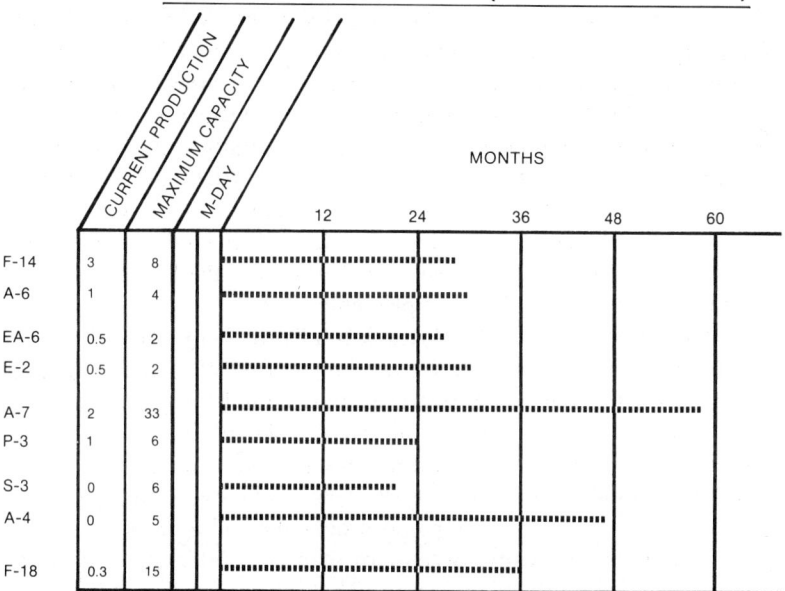

Figure 1

Source: Naval Air Systems Command

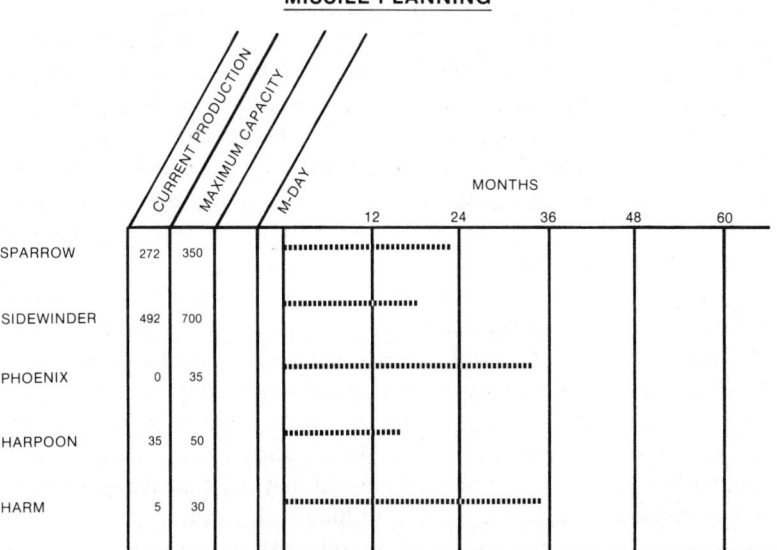

Figure 2

Source: Naval Air Systems Command

The Prescription

Stemming from Executive Order 11490 dated 28 October 1969, the Industrial Preparedness Planning Program was designed to cure the ills of the U.S. industrial base. But the patient still shows symptoms of lethargy. In 1977, the Government Accounting Office observed, "The present Department of Defense mobilization planning with private industry does little to strengthen United States industrial capacity to meet emergency requirements...GAO recommends that the program be restructured."[7] To try to determine why the medicine did not work, this section takes a macroscopic view (see Figure 3) of the IPP process and examines the way it has been implemented.

The first step in the IPP process is to identify items for which surge and mobilization are desired. We need to set priorities among the tens of thousands of defense items to prevent overloading the system. In Fiscal Year 1980, the Department of the Navy included 1,813 items on its planning list. This does not mean that the Navy alone planned to acquire all of these items. Many were items sought by another service or agency. A tow truck, for example, is procured by all four services but is planned only by the Army. Because of their size and complexity, ships are not included on the planning list. The current practice of including complete aircraft is questionable. The planning for such a large system requires a great deal of effort and the actual production extends over a long period. It may be better to spend that time planning for spare parts and ammunition for existing aircraft.

The second step is to calculate surge and mobilization requirements. We need to provide industry with a production schedule that will meet defense needs. In some cases, however, defense planners have not calculated requirements. Instead they have planned the end items according to the producers' current capabilities. In other cases, they have expressed requirements as a total number of units to be produced as rapidly as possible. Such maneuvers are confusing and unrealistic to the producers who must plan on meeting the requirements. They may satisfy the immediate task as viewed by the operations planner, but do not enhance industrial preparedness.

An example is drawn from Fiscal Year 1981 mobilization planning data. It involves the pacing item for an air-to-air missile. The Department of Defense passed to a manufacturer for this component a requirement for 3,240 units. The manufacturer planned to produce this item over a period of thirty-six months. Moreover, he was under the impression that once those units were delivered, the production line would go cold, while the planners actually had anticipated that some postsurge or postwar production would be needed. Fulfilling such requirements in thirty-six months would pose an unacceptable risk to United States' air superiority in most scenarios, but this was where the process ended. The manufacturer was not asked to improve his plan.

Since the requirements for the other components of the missile were expressed the same way, and their producers' capabilities varied, their delivery schedules were different. Had such a plan been executed, components would have arrived at the assembly center at scattered times and ultimate completion of the order would have been later than desired. In sum, it is not enough just to state requirements as total numbers or capabilities. We also need to prepare to build the missiles by specifying a desired production rate.

The third step in the IPP process is to select contractors to be "planned producers." A "planned producer" is an industrial firm which has indicated a willingness to produce the specific military item under IPP procedures.[8] This important step should be understood and appreciated by all who are involved in weapons procurement. The producer's qualifications should be examined carefully, including those of his subcontractors and vendors. No materiel or components should come from non-U.S. manufacturers (with the exception of Canada) for mobilization planning. His subcontractors should be able to accelerate production at least as well as the prime producer. He does not necessarily have to be currently producing the item to be a planned producer, but it certainly would be an advantage. He should have proven his capabilities where possible.

A planned producer who takes the job seriously can be of great assistance in developing a responsible industrial base. Not only can he provide to the Department of Defense data on which to make informed decisions, but can take measures on his own to improve his productivity and capacity. This will only happen if he has confidence in the system and his role in it, and if he is given clear, realistic requirements.

Not all manufacturers are willing to participate. Time and effort are required to do the job properly. Unfortunately, the government has not always been helpful. In Fiscal Years 1980 and 1981 the government did finance some indepth studies of planned producer capabilities. However, nearsighted decisions like granting production contracts to manufacturers other than planned producers negate any incentive they might have had and undermine the entire program. Prior to the Vietnam War, the Department of Defense had identified certain corporations as "planned producers"—those firms which indicated a willingness to produce items during a national emergency. When the war came, the government contracts in many cases went to low bidders who were not planned producers, thus wasting any investment a firm might have made as a result of agreeing to be a part of the preparedness program. As recently as Fiscal Year 1980, the government did the same thing for a component of the SIDEWINDER missile. This is not to assert capriciousness on the part of government decision-makers. There were likely good reasons for the decisions. However, it is not clear that the consequences of these decisions were fully appreciated. Industrial base capabilities should have been given a greater weight in production decisions.

The fourth step is for government and the planned producers to agree on surge and/or mobilization production schedules. One might visualize the task for threat-oriented weapons to be shown in Figure 4. We need to draw a line from the "stockpile" point at Mobilization Day (M-day) to a point somewhere on the requirements line. The factors bearing on the choice of the end point are wartime risks and peacetime costs. The further to the right the point is, the higher the risks; the more to the left, the higher the costs.

Developing a schedule is voluntary on the part of a producer unless a contract specifically calls for it. The Naval Air Systems Command is experiencing about a 25% return rate on its requests for planning. Prime contractors do not wish to expend the time and effort to plan with their subcontractors. As a result, in most cases we do not have the data on which to make sound industrial base investment decisions.

Figure 3

IPP Process

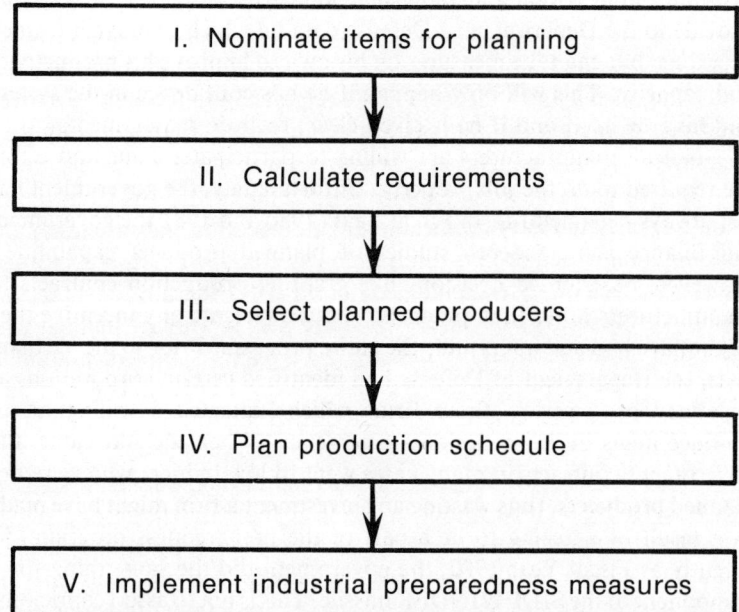

Figure 4

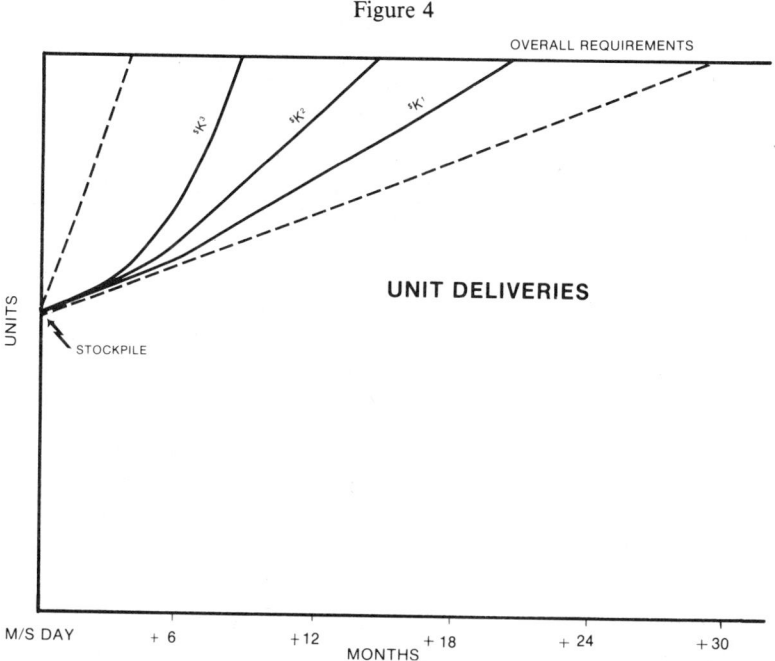

The final step is to finance improvements in the planned producers' capabilities to meet the accelerated production schedules agreed upon as a result of step IV. These improvements are called "industrial preparedness measures" (IPMs). Some producers have been very conscientious and have provided cost estimates for prestocking long lead time materiel and components and for special test equipment and tooling. Moreover, they have estimated the improved capabilities that will result from these measures.

But the government has not invested in the IPMs. The mobilization planners solicit industry for meaningful mobilization and surge data, but lack the clout to acquire the funds to finance the IPMs. Moreover, there is a general lack of understanding about the IPP Program and its accomplishments. It seems that the only military people who are familiar with the Program are either those directly involved in its implementation or students at the Industrial College of the Armed Forces. This can only lead to less than full support (especially when support = program $) for the Program.

The same discontinuity can be observed throughout all the steps of the process. No one person or group is at fault. In the second step—calculating requirements—each of the participants (operations planner, program manager, mobilization planner, and industrialist) was carrying out his part of the task as he saw it. The key to defining fully our problem, then, may be the way each player saw his respective role.

The Diagnosis

It will be useful to examine why the IPP program has been carried out in this manner. The overriding reason could be termed the "stockpile syndrome"—the belief that anything done to improve the industrial base will detract from the stockpile of war reserve items. There is not enough data to support this conclusion, especially in light of the very real possibility that increased productivity resulting from capital investment and revised contracting procedures may in fact improve the stockpile posture. Nevertheless, it is a prevailing attitude that must be addressed.

This attitude is sharpened by the fact that the current United States stockpile of armaments falls far short of requirements. The Chief of Naval Materiel testified:

> ...we are below inventory objectives in all categories of our war reserve materiel, and I submit that when you are below these objectives, there is little incentive to do industrial preparedness planning, which is the planning that is necessary to take place after those war reserves have been used.[9]

Among the victims of the stockpile syndrome are those who subscribe to a "first things first" philosophy; i.e., produce the items needed for the first few weeks of a war and then worry about having an industrial base that can deliver additional items. While acknowledging the prospect of a long war, they argue that it makes little sense to worry about the capability to deliver items seventeen months after the war begins when one lacks the items needed for the first six months. In constrained peacetime budgets, however, this approach has become a "first things *only*" philosophy. In fact, the United States does not have even the "first things" in the storage bins.

A second group clings to the likelihood that the next war will be a short one preceded by little warning. It is argued that the specter of escalating to nuclear warfare will furnish irresistible pressure to reach an early resolution of the conflict. The 1973 Arab-Israeli war is an example of what this group anticipates. The advocates of the short-war scenario disavow the utility of industrial preparedness. This line of reasoning is critiqued by Dr. Fred Iklé who, at the time of this writing, is Under Secretary of Defense for Policy:

> One is reminded of a bridge builder whose bridge fails to span the river. When asked whether he does not need additional timbers to complete the job, he answers that none are needed since he is planning for a "short bridge."[10]

Again, in reality, there are not enough weapons to fight even a short war. If one were to agree either that we should plan on a short warning followed by a short war or that we should do first things first, one should also agree that it would not be prudent to put all of our efforts into one scenario. In these scenarios there is a substantial risk of being wrong about the length of the war or about what and how much will be needed. Richard Danzig, former Principal Deputy Assistant Secretary of Defense (Manpower, Reserve Affairs, and Logistics), relates this philosophy to the man who buys life insurance because he believes that death is the worst thing that could happen to his family. The man would be foolish if that were all he bought, if every time someone approached him with a fire insurance policy, he said, "Oh no, I only invest in the worst case. What I'm going to do is buy myself a million dollars of life insurance and if I've got any extra money, I'm going to buy some more life insurance, but I'll never invest a penny in fire insurance."[11]

At a minimum, we would want to be very careful not to reduce our industrial capability through concern for the near term. An example of reducing capability involves a recent contract for a key component of an air-to-air missile that was allowed to expire. Two producers had been operating in parallel but one picked up the entire contract; i.e., he became the sole source for that component. The government saved $1.7 million. But, in effect what it did was trade the capability to produce 350 missiles a month for the price of 16.5 missiles. Moreover, sabotage or a union strike against the remaining plant could result in no missiles being produced for at least eight months until an alternate source began delivering. The marginal return on an investment of $1.7 million in this case is clearly greater for dual rather than single source.

The stockpile syndrome is especially apparent at the final step in the IPP process—financing the industrial preparedness measures. But it affects decisions throughout all the steps. When the participant feels that his primary allegiance is toward improving the stockpile this feeling tempers his support for IPP and obstructs his view of the Program as a whole.

This difficulty in seeing the whole introduces a second reason for executing the Program as reported above—organizational pressures. Referring again to the example of determining requirements, we find that the operations planner states his requirement and then turns his back on the problem and waits for the stockpile to grow. The mobilization planner determines what can be accomplished by industry—which usually is not enough. Meanwhile, the program manager is trying to track down shipping containers for the next lot coming off the production line.

Mobilizers and operators seem to move in separate circles even though both groups are centered on the same goal: a strong defense. Current military organization seems to institutionalize this concentricity. The military tends to assign mobilization matters to logisticians and allows operators to ignore the mobilization problem. This separation may also have been influenced by the decision during the Vietnam War to have both guns and butter. It may have given the impression that the United States could fight a war without mobilizing. That is a type of confidence that the United States does not deserve. Developing the means to counter the Soviet Union is a much more formidable problem, and mobilization and/or surge represents an indispensable ingredient in an effective defense capability.

Another example involves planned producers. They should receive preferential treatment for government contracts. Whether for new United States production (including surge and/or mobilization), or foreign military sales programs, the contracts for items on the IPP list should go to firms who have planned with the government and agreed to accelerate production during a crisis. They should at least be given the opportunity to bid. Such action would ensure a warm base, lend credibility to the IPP Program, and provide incentive for participation in the Program.

Unfortunately, with the 1950s came the label "military-industrial complex" followed by safeguards against conflicts of interest. This philosophy has contributed to decreased cooperation between individuals in government and industry, with effects detrimental to our defense production capability. There can be a better appreciation of each other's concerns, capabilities, and interests without sacrificing the ideals of fair competition and free enterprise. Put another way, there can be competition at fair prices without discouraging industry's capital investment. Actions like combining surge and peacetime production contracts, removing bureaucratic obstacles, providing incentives for capital investment, and prestocking, represent ways of dealing with industrial defense needs. They do not compromise ideals and do not necessarily cost more money. It can be argued that in the long run, as a result of improved efficiencies and competition, the country will come out ahead financially while accruing greater industrial preparedness.

A final reason for the way we executed IPP is that there is a lack of incentive for industry or Defense planners to apply themselves to the Program. If money is not being spent on industrial preparedness measures, industry is understandably reluctant to expend dollars and manhours in developing them. Subcontractors and vendors often lack critical path networks and expertise in forecasting capabilities and markets. They are especially sensitive to releasing proprietary information to prime contractors. A disincentive for industry is that government purchases may fluctuate radically. For example, the 1981-1985 planned production of F-16 aircraft dropped from 180 to 120 per year. There is a high risk of a producer losing any capital investment in increased capability.

On the Defense side, no one official is held responsible for the condition of the industrial base associated with a weapons system. In 1977 and 1981, the GAO criticized the IPP Program. In 1976 and 1980 the Defense Science Board did the same. The second reports by both bodies pointed out that little had been accomplished since the first report. Their suggestions and criticisms are not reaching the working level for there is no one charged with the preparedness of the industrial base except the Secretary of Defense, and he is faced with a large number of critically important issues and choices.

Conclusions

Problems of the Industrial Preparedness Planning Program stem more from poor execution than from poor policy. To be sure, there have been accomplishments. For example, there is detailed planning for surge and mobilization. Choke points for selected planned items have been identified. Some indepth surge studies, specifying the capabilities for contractors in selected systems, have been conducted. The Program itself is a logical one. It makes sense first to decide what we want, then who should do it, how it should be done, and then to close the gap between goals and capabilities.

Although there are some weak spots in the *planning* part of the Program, it seems that the largest shortcoming lies in the *preparedness* area. The present United States industrial base is not able adequately to respond to surge and mobilization requirements. Lead times are long and manufacturers are not able to shorten them during a national emergency. For example, multiple-shift production during peacetime leaves little room for expansion. Moreover, small subcontractors find nondefense business more attractive, thus reducing the sources for critical material and components.

Our execution of the IPP Program, from a systemic viewpoint, has diminished the Program's credibility, which has further precipitated a lowered priority for scarce resources. Mobilization and surge requirements have been confusing and unrealistic in the contractors' eyes. Awarding contracts to other than planned producers, even for the best of near-term reasons, has not endeared businessmen to the Program. Failing to finance industrial preparedness measures has been the most significant indicator of the degree of government nonsupport for its own IPP Program.

The most pervasive reason for the way the Program has been executed is the stockpile syndrome. Government and industry need to understand that U.S. national security interests can best be served by investment in both the stockpile and the industrial base. Other reasons for the way we executed the Program can be attributed to organizational pressures and a lack of incentives to support IPP.

The Government Accounting Office recommended that the Program be restructured. However, we should be cautious about building a new one. Our government has demonstrated time and again a greater proclivity for policy formulation than for policy execution.[12] Recognizing the reasons for the unsuccessful execution of the Industrial Preparedness Planning Program and taking the necessary corrective measures, will accomplish far more than building another structure. IPP is not bad medicine; it has been administered poorly.

NOTES

1. Henry A. Miley, Jr., "Future Industrial Mobilization," *National Defense*, v. 63, (July-August 1978), p. 55.
2. Fred Charles Ikle, "Preparing for Industrial Mobilization: The First Step Toward Full Strength," *National Security in the 1980s: From Weakness to Strength*, edited by W. Scott Thompson, et al. (San Francisco, Ca.: Institute for Contemporary Studies, 1980), p. 61.
3. Hans M. Mark, "Productivity, Technology, and the Illusion of the Free Lunch," *Defense 80*, August 1980, p. 8.
4. Lt. Col. Howard E. Bethel, U.S.A.F., et al, "Industrial Preparedness Planning—An Evaluation and Proposal" (Final Report of Defense Management Issue Analysis No. 11—Vertical Slice Real-Time Planning to the Industrial College of the Armed Forces, 11 June 1979), p. G-24.
5. See American Defense Preparedness Association, *Proceedings of the Defense Readiness and Requirements Symposium, Andrews Air Force Base, 24-25 September 1980* (Arlington, Va.: American Defense Preparedness Association, 1980).
6. Bethel, Op. Cit., p. G-28.
7. U.S. Comptroller General, *Report to the Congress, Restructuring Needed of Department of Defense Program for Planning with Private Industry for Mobilization Production Requirements*, Report No. PSAD -77-108 (Washington, D.C.: General Accounting Office, 1977), title page.
8. U.S. Department of Defense, *Industrial Preparedness Planning Manual, DOD 4005.3-M* (Washington, D.C.: U.S. Government Printing Office, July 1972), p. viii.
9. Admiral A.J. Whittle, U.S.N., Chief of Naval Materiel, as quoted in U.S., Congress, House, Committee on Armed Services, *Capability of U.S. Defense Industrial Base, Hearings before the Committee on Armed Services and the Panel on Defense Industrial Base*, 96th Cong., 2nd sess., 1980, p. 678.
10. Iklé, Op. Cit., p. 63.
11. Richard Danzig, as quoted in American Defense Preparedness Association, *Proceedings of the Defense Readiness and Requirements Symposium, Andrews Air Force Base, 24-25 September 1980* (Arlington, Va.: American Defense Preparedness Association, 1980), pp. 30-44.
12. Jacques S. Gansler, *The Defense Industry* (Cambridge, Ma.: MIT Press, 1980) p. 279.

Section III

The Lead-Time Required
for Upgrading the Mobilization Base

Obsolescence, Declining Productivity, and the American Defense Mobilization Infrastructure

Leon S. Reed

Introduction

Industrial mobilization capability and the degree of obsolescence and declining productivity of the defense industrial base are closely related. If we were to project *current* capabilities into an environment of rapidly increasing demand for defense products, it would be likely to mean mobilization of an increasingly inefficient and unproductive defense industrial base. Inattention to the fact that mobilization may be necessary—that preparedness for war is the ultimate purpose of defense production programs—may account, at least in part, for this declining productivity and capability. Although many other factors contribute to defense mobilization capability—in a positive or negative fashion—the levels and relevance of investment in new processes and technology may be the most important single determinant of industrial readiness. An obsolete and unproductive industrial base cannot mobilize, or even meet, near-term demands effectively.

What follows is an assessment of the current status of defense industrial responsiveness, some of the factors which account for the present situation, and some alternative programs and reforms which could improve the current situation. Although many other factors are vital for mobilization capability—such as military manpower, maintenance and repair depots and operations, and transportation facilities—this chapter will consider only industrial production capability.

Efforts to understand mobilization capability must begin with an analysis of industry's ability to meet present-day defense requirements, because it is this capability which provides the baseline for expansion of production. If the defense industry cannot meet near-term needs, its prospects for meeting vastly increased mobilization requirements cannot be considered promising. Many reforms which could improve mobilization capability would also, if implemented today, improve the ability of defense industry to meet near-term, continuing needs; conversely, failure to address these problems in the near term would likely result in continued deterioration of defense capability and of mobilization potential.

It is useful at the outset to establish distinctions between two terms: surge and mobilization. Aside from stipulating that surge falls somewhere short of mobilization (in terms of increased rate of production and stress on society), there is little agreement on the distinction between the two terms. When does surge stop and mobilization begin, or, for that matter, when does everyday defense contracting let off and "surging" begin?

However, two useful distinctions can be made. First, while everyday production and surge would be carried on, for the most part by existing contractors, full mobilization would undoubtedly involve massive conversion of commercial producers. Second, while situations short of mobilization would be carried out under existing legal authorities and constraints (at least given current planning), mobilization would undoubtedly involve wholesale suspensions of present legal requirements and augmentation of existing Presidential authority to control production and stabilize the economy. These two characteristics have a significant effect in determining the adequacy of industrial response under these two scenarios.

Many factors influence the ability of industry to mobilize or to meet increased demand for defense materiel. Some of the most important factors are:
— the raw materials stream, including mining and processing;
— the adequacy and productivity of contractors; and subcontractors' industrial facilities, including especially the ability of the machine tool industry to meet increased demand;
— the availability of skilled labor in adequate quantities and with sufficient skills to operate the available machines;
— the adequacy of the government-industry planning system;
— the legal structure underlying the system, both in terms of the authority it grants the government to conduct mobilization planning and in terms of any special obstacles which these requirements impose on near-term procurement and/or surge/mobilization planning and requirements satisfaction.

Serious deficiencies have been identified in all of the previously described areas. Many of these problems are closely related. For instance, raw materials supply problems can result in limiting the capacity of processing and refining industries. Efforts to increase stockpile holdings of some critically short materials (e.g., titanium sponge) could further strain existing supplies and have a serious impact on defense production programs. Similarly, shortages of skilled labor can affect the willingness of industry to expand capacity by installing new equipment.

Moreover, it is not clear that attempted solutions to any single problem can be accomplished without implications for other problems. For instance, investment incentives could have a variety of impacts on defense industry. In terms of manpower, some types of investment could greatly increase demand for machinists, computer programmers, engineers, and other skills which are presently experiencing shortages. Other types of investment, in robots or computer-aided machinery, for instance, could moderate the demand for some labor skills, such as machinists, while increasing the need for other skills. Efforts to encourage industry to invest in new machinery could also strain the capacity of the machine tool and similar industries, which because of severely limited capacity and expansion capability, have long been a critical bottleneck to defense expansion efforts. Thus, efforts to improve mobilization potential must attack the problem on a broad front. Uncoordinated efforts could solve one problem at the expense of others.

Legal and Administrative System for Preparedness and Mobilization

Any effort to understand defense production and mobilization capabilities must consider the system of laws which establishes emergency preparedness planning and guides the defense production and mobilization system. Two acts of Congress, both more than thirty years old, establish the basic structure for industrial preparedness and mobilization planning. These are:
— the National Security Act of 1947 (50 U.S.C. 401 et. seq.);
— the Defense Production Act of 1950 (50 U.S.C. App. 2061 et seq.)

Both Acts reflect the style of their times. They are very flexible, provide only general policy guidance, and grant authority in a relatively unconstrained fashion.

The National Security Act of 1947 directs the National Security Resources Board (now, as a result of many executive branch reorganizations, the Federal Emergency Management Agency (FEMA)) to undertake, and to advise the President on, mobilization planning. Specifically, FEMA is directed to develop plans for:
— industrial and civilian mobilization to make the maximum use of the nation's manpower in time of war;
— the stabilization and conversion to a wartime footing of the civilian economy;
— unifying the activities of federal departments and agencies engaged in activities important to the war effort or mobilization;
— rationalizing potential supplies of and requirements for man-

power, resources and productive facilities;
— establishing adequate reserves of strategic and critical materials (i.e., the National Defense Stockpile); and
— the strategic relocation of industries, services, government and other essential economic activities.

The National Security Act is potentially very powerful legislation. Only two weaknesses have been identified, both of which could probably be corrected by administrative action. First, the Act defines and contemplates a relatively small coordinating entity within the Executive Office of the President (EOP). This function has been reorganized on numerous occasions, but it was not until the 1974 creation of the Office of Preparedness, within the General Services Administration, that the function left the EOP. It is possible that the lack of harmony between FEMA's legislative charter and its current organizational status accounts for some (though by no means all) of the confusion about FEMA's proper role in emergency planning.

Second, while the Act provides a relatively complete definition of the types of actions that should be planned for, these authorities are all oriented toward mobilization. No official basis exists to plan for mobilization-type activities in situations short of mobilization, though the nonmobilization "surge," with greatly increased defense demand but without wholesale conversion of the economy, may be both more likely to occur and more stressful to defense industry. The failure to provide in the law for planning for this situation represents a major void in U.S. preparedness efforts.

By contrast, the Defense Production Act of 1950 contains both general authority for industrial preparedness and mobilization planning and specific authority for priority contract performance, allocation of materials, control of hoarding, financial support to assist defense contractors or to increase supplies of critical materiels, and consultation with industry on industrial preparedness programs. The scope of the authorities contained in the DPA was perhaps best described by Paul Kreuger, Assistant Associate Director of FEMA for Resource Preparedness, who stated:

> The easiest way to say what we can do and can't do under the DPA is that the entire synfuels program could have been funded, could have been authorized, using the existing authorities in Title III of the DPA. There was no necessity really for all of that legislation... We can make direct government loans. We can make loan guarantees. We can guarantee certain levels of production. We can guarantee prices. We can fund research and development. All of this is in the area of materials. If you look in the back of the Act, the materials are defined in a very

broad sense, to not only include what we think of as common materials, but also processes, ideas, concepts, so that the authorities are quite sweeping, quite broad.[1]

These authorities are available every day, and are not keyed to a state of war or declaration of national emergency.

Individual provisions in the DPA either affect or could affect nearly every one of the problems mentioned earlier. Because of the importance of the DPA, and because its provisions do provide a useful structure for discussion of these problems, the next sections of this chapter will discuss specific problems in the context of relevant provisions of the DPA which represent either problems or potential solutions to the problems.

Lead Times

Unlike the problems mentioned elsewhere, increasing lead times should be regarded as a *symptom*, rather than a cause, of ailments in the defense industrial base. Between 1977 and 1980, according to the Defense Science Board, lead times for many weapons systems, components, and subsystems increased rapidly. For example, in 1976, the lead time for aluminum forgings was 20 weeks; by 1980, this had increased to 120 weeks. The 1976 lead time for traveling wave tubes (35 weeks) had more than doubled to 95 weeks by 1980. Titanium lead times increased steadily, from 40 weeks in 1976 to 46 weeks in 1977, 60 weeks in 1978, 70 weeks in 1979, and 104 weeks in 1980. Aircraft landing gear lead times were 52 weeks in 1977, but had increased to 120 weeks in 1980.[2]

Even a "DX" priority rating, supposedly a recognition of utmost urgency and highest national priority, did not guarantee timely delivery or protect against growing lead times. DX-rated aluminum small forgings experienced lead time increases from 55 weeks in 1978 to 125 weeks in 1980. Similarly, lead times for DX-rated titanium large forgings increased from 65 weeks in 1978 to 108 weeks in 1980. Electronic parts showed similar lead time growth: DX-rated microcircuits increased from 25 weeks (1978) to 51 weeks (1980), while DX-rated integrated circuits rose from 25 weeks to 62 weeks (1980).[3]

There were many causes for increased lead times, including: insufficient capacity, or imbalanced capacity, at subcontractors and vendors; competition from commercial orders, especially in the then-booming commercial aircraft industry; labor problems at some key subcontractors and vendors; and failure to apply or enforce defense priorities.

Title I of the DPA provides authority to the President to "require that performance under contracts or orders (other than contracts of employment) which he deems necessary or appropriate to the national defense shall take priority over performance under any other contract or order." (50 U.S.C. App. 2071 (a)). Priority ratings of "DO" or "DX" are applied to virtually all defense weapons systems procurements, and regulations of the Office of Industrial Mobilization (Department of Commerce) stipulate that priority ratings attached to prime contracts must flow down through all subcontractors, vendors and suppliers. However, there is general agreement that the DPS has been used ineffectively.[4]

The parallel Defense Materials System (DMS), concerned with allocation of critical materials, appears to function effectively, but its utility is limited by the fact that its coverage represents, in essence, 1950s materials utilization patterns, and fails to consider changes in supply and utilization patterns since that time. Presently, the DMS establishes stockpiling guidelines for the following materials: steel, aluminum, copper and nickel alloy.[5] The former administrator of DPS/DMS testified: "The DMS is an outgrowth of experience that was gained during the Second World War and during the Korean conflict when it was found that through control of these particular commodities, we could basically control U.S. industrial production."[6]

The limited coverage of the DMS, not applying to such vital defense materials as titanium, cobalt, and other critical materials which are in short supply and/or suffer from processing industry capacity limitations, undoubtedly contributes to long lead times and higher program costs. Given the changes in usage and patterns and supply sufficiency since the 1950s, it is not necessarily true that control of the four named materials still permits *basic* control of production. Even if this were true, such a macroeconomic approach ignores the potential for materials allocation to mitigate *specific* supply shortfalls for materials such as titanium. Although no legislative permission would be needed to designate new materials, this has proved difficult. A recent effort to establish stocks of titanium was cancelled after the proposal was published in the Federal Register, principally due to titanium producer opposition to the proposed government control.

Priorities and allocations are important for other reasons than their potential for controlling lead time growth. In wartime, these systems would assume much greater importance. Bernard Baruch, head of the World War I mobilization effort, referred to priorities as the "synchronizing force" for war production efforts.[7] A critical shortcoming of industrial preparedness planning appears to be that the current DPS/DMS are uniquely ill-suited to wartime needs, when any or all of the following would be required:
— prioritization between different defense projects, based on relative urgency *and* on the degree to which the program could be completed in a timely fashion;
— broad allocation of many materials;

— priorities and allocations for industrial and essential civilian production; and,
— renewed enforcement efforts, to deal with a potentially higher degree of violations.

Although DPS/DMS has a potentially important role to play in reducing lead times, it is not a panacea. There is no substitute for capacity. Other industrial improvement and planning measures will be necessary to bring lead times under control. Lead times may be the most accurate gauge of the responsiveness of defense industry, and have a direct impact on defense readiness. Increased lead times have a direct impact on near-term readiness, by delaying delivery of programmed systems. Reducing lead times would mean automatic improvements in near-term readiness, due to the shortened delivery periods.

Lead times also affect surge and mobilization capabilities, but the relationship is not as direct. Although reduced lead times are a necessary precursor to improving mobilization capabilities, such reductions will not necessarily improve these capabilities. Instead, project-by-project analysis would be needed to determine the impact of reduced lead times in one area on other potential bottlenecks in an environment of increasing production rates.

Expansion of Productive Capacity and Supply for Strategic and Critical Materials

The United States is dangerously dependent on foreign suppliers for many strategic and critical materials, including some of the most important for defense programs. Shortages of critical materials can affect industrial responsiveness no fewer than five ways: (1) by increasing lead times, if materials are unavailable or in short supply; (2) by limiting domestic processing capacity; (3) by adding to costs, if suppliers increase prices; (4) by forcing use of substitutes; and (5) by making it impossible to meet existing or expanded program needs due to supply interruptions.

Stockpiling of critical raw and processed materials has been the traditional way of protecting against materials vulnerability. However, for many reasons, the present U.S. stockpile is seriously out of balance. Of 61 individual materials and family groups in the stockpile, shortfalls exist for 37. In the case of 23, stockpile holdings equal half or less of approved goals.[8] While serious questions exist about the realism of the present goals, and although many of the deficits are for relatively low-priority items, greater attention could probably be given to the potential for increasing imports "on warning." It is, nonetheless, clear that it will take a very expensive and long-term effort to bring the stockpile up to adequate levels.

It is possible, however, that stockpiling should be regarded only as a last resort. Actual purchase of a material can be quite expensive and can place an unacceptable strain on already limited supplies (e.g., titanium sponge). Furthermore, stockpile purchases alone cannot reduce foreign dependence, solve raw materials supply problems in times short of national emergency, or, perhaps most important, correct processing or industrial production capacity shortages. Indeed, it may be impossible to buy some of the most critically needed materials, precisely because the short-supply situation which creates the need for stockpiling prevents any action which would tighten supplies further.

An alternative exists in the form of Title III of the DPA, which authorizes virtually unlimited financial assistance for projects to expand domestic capacity and supply of critical materials, including energy resources. However, despite the potential for use of these authorities, no new awards of financial assistance have been made since 1967. FEMA has proposed four Title III projects—for titanium processing, cobalt, guayule rubber cultivation and refractory bauxite. All four of these projects are significant because they could increase domestic capacity for materials for which substantial stockpile shortfalls presently exist. At relatively small cost, these programs could reduce stockpile goals, thus freeing limited acquisition funds for other purchases.

Title III can also be used more broadly to grant loans or loan guarantees to government contractors for virtually any project which would promote improved defense production efforts. This authority, like the authority for critical materials, has remained unused for nearly fifteen years.

Contractor Investment

While lead times may be the most basic indicator of industrial responsiveness, investment in new processes and technologies may be the most important determinant of this responsiveness. A great deal of attention has recently been focused on the problem American industry is facing in forming capital for plant modernization. It should come as no surprise to find that defense contractors suffer from these problems which affect American industry generally.

However, defense industry also suffers unique investment disincentives which grow out of Department of Defense depreciation and cost reimbursement policies. Interest has traditionally been an unallowable expense on defense contracts. Depreciation of equipment has traditionally been allowed only at a very slow rate. However, while government cost-reimbursement policies have tended to ignore investment costs, labor has always been recognized as a legitimate, allowable input. In addition, cost projections have been based on historic (allowable) costs, and target profit rates have been based on these cost projections. Thus, as the Defense Department's Profit '76 Task Force acknowledged, contractors have had little incentive to reduce costs, especially if cost-reduction measures would involve reductions in allowable costs (labor), increases in unallowable costs (investment), and overall reductions in incurred costs (and thus profits). The Profit '76 Task Force reached very broad conclusions about the contribution of new investments to productivity and the negative impact of Defense's cost and profit policies on contractor investment and productivity. However, the reform initiated as a result of this study effort was comparatively modest, and, according to the General Accounting Office, was unlikely to provide a significant incentive for new investments.[9]

A second investment disincentive, the inability to allow interest, was partially corrected in 1976 with the issuance of Cost Accounting Standard (CAS) 414, which allowed the imputed rate of interest for facilities capital as a contract charge. Working capital is not covered by CAS 414, however, and the reimbursement rate for facilities capital is limited to the Treasury borrowing rate, which is presently below the rates that most contractors must pay for facilities capital.

Perhaps the most significant investment disincentive is posed by the Department of Defense's depreciation policy, mandated by CAS 409, which was issued by the Cost Accounting Standards Board in 1975 under the authority of Section 719 of the Defense Production Act. Because the cash flows resulting from any expenditure are vitally important, the rate at which a new investment can be depreciated plays an important role in determining a contractor's willingness to make new investments. CAS 409 requires that depreciation for contract costing be based on the historical useful life or the estimated economic useful life of the given piece of equipment, which is perhaps the slowest depreciation rate prescribed by any governmental body in the world. While this procedure undoubtedly minimizes short-term government expenditures, by limiting the rate at which contractors will be reimbursed for new investments, it can pose a substantial disincentive for contractors to make new investments. General acceleration of tax depreciation policies to spur corporate investment will have little impact on the defense industry unless CAS 409 is also modified. Due to an unique situation which has existed since September 30, 1980, CAS 409 and other cost accounting standards may be the only government regulations which can, at present, be modified only by Act of Congress.[10]

Government-Owned Machinery

Inadequate as industrial investment has been, it is probably in better shape than the government-owned tool base. Congress has given the government contradictory directions regarding government-owned tools. While the Defense Industrial Reserve Act specifies that the government should retain an "essential nucleus" of government-owned tools to meet current and emergency needs, it also directs the government to make the maximum use of privately owned industrial facilities. Short-term budget reductions have led to a sentiment to "do it next year," resulting in a rapidly aging machine tool base. While industry has relied heavily on government-owned tools, the government has failed to modernize its own machinery. According to the Defense Science Board, more than 20,000 of 26,000 government-owned metal cutting and metal forming tools in contractor plants (including government-owned, contractor-operated plants) are in excess of twenty years old. Little is being done to modernize this base.

Machine Tool Industry Capacity

Efforts to promote increased industry investment in new machinery are likely to be constrained by the limited capacity and responsiveness of the machine tool industry. In past mobilization efforts, this industry has constituted a critical bottleneck. One of the classic studies in the field concluded that "this component of production, relatively small in dollar value, was the main bottleneck of industrial mobilization in World War II and after the outbreak of war in Korea."[11]

The machine tool industry suffers from a variety of problems which all serve to limit its capacity and responsiveness. These include: decentralized structure; limited investment capital; fluctuations in demand; and skilled manpower shortages. For all these reasons, the machine tool industry has traditionally been unable, or unwilling, to expand its capacity to meet increased demand. To cope with this problem, the Machine Tool Trigger Order Program (or M-day Tool Program) existed until 1969, under the authority of the Defense Production Act, for the purpose of minimizing machine tool bottlenecks during emergencies. Under this program, standby contracts were signed with various machine tool producers, requiring them, in time of emergency or upon order, immediately to begin producing designated types and quantities of machine tools. In 1971, the Department of Defense requested that the Tool Program be reactivated, and in 1974, an interagency committee made the same recommendation. However, little has happened since that recommendation was made. Several years ago, standard contracts were developed and offered to machine tool producers, but these contracts were refused, reportedly because of the machine tool producers' reluctance to accept government requirements and contractual restraints at a time when a machine tool "seller's market" existed. It is ironic that the conditions which create the greatest need for such a program may also maximize the resistance of machine tool manufacturers to get involved in such a program.

Other Productivity Problems

Lack of investment, while important, is not the sole cause of unsatisfactory productivity in defense industry. Inefficient labor utilization practices also play no small role. For example, in the general turmoil surrounding release four years ago of the "DOD/OMB Aircraft Capacity Study," one conclusion which was generally overlooked was that most of the extra costs represented *people, not machinery*. For instance, the senior DOD procurement official, testifying about this report, stated:

> For the most part, this cost consists of indirect labor, i.e., engineering, marketing and administrative personnel, retained in anticipation of and to enhance obtaining additional government business. Twenty-five percent or less of the extra capacity costs is associated with under-utilized plant and equipment.[12]

Another study, by the Air Force Systems Command, found similar inefficient direct labor utilization:

> Manufacturing costs are about 42 percent of direct costs on a typical production contract. About 50 percent of this cost represents nonproductive labor caused by inefficiencies of one kind or another. If it were possible to achieve only a 20 percent improvement in labor productivity, approximately one billion dollars could be saved on contracts at 11 of the major Air Force contractors.[13]

Many factors may account for poor labor productivity. The DOD/OMB study recommended absolute limits on contractor indirect labor charges. Hand-in-hand with enforcement, however, should be increased stability in procurement and increased investment incentives, to achieve improvements in labor utilization. In addition, the impact of legal and administrative compliance and reporting requirements on contractor productivity should be considered.

Other Legal Requirements

Many other laws, most of which appear to have little bearing on defense contracting or mobilization, can also have a serious negative impact on industrial responsiveness, productivity, and mobilization capability. These are the numerous procurement and "socioeconomic" laws, many of which have been approved by Congress within the past fifteen years, and most of which have never been reviewed by the committees most concerned with defense production.

It is not unprecedented for the United States to apply socioeconomic policies to defense contracting efforts in time of war. In 1953 alone, the Office of Defense Mobilization issued several manpower policies dealing with some of the same subjects as present-day "affirmative action" policies. These included: (1) Defense Manpower Policy No. 7 (DMP-7), providing for more effective utilization of older workers in the defense program; (2) DMP-9, calling for emphasis on increasing opportunities for handicapped workers and more effective use of such workers in the mobilization program; and (3) DMP-11, providing for special assistance to returning Korean veterans in obtaining suitable training or employment.[14]

What is new is the breadth of coverage of present-day requirements, the detailed compliance requirements, and the punitive enforcement provisions. Socioeconomic legislation in the fields of environmental protection, employment practices, and subcontractor/prime contractor preference, as well as general procurement law, has become so detailed that the industrial response in World War II and in the Korean War should probably be considered irrelevant to the environment of the 1980s.

These new requirements can have any of the following negative impacts on defense procurement and on mobilization capabilities: diversion of effort, in order to comply with detailed reporting and review requirements; delay in approval of reports or in initiation of contracting efforts; and additional expense, due either to the delays or to additional compliance efforts. Reporting requirements under defense contracts can have a negative impact on contractor productivity, because the work necessary to comply with the requirements would be considered to be indirect, nonproductive labor.

Perhaps most serious in their effect on mobilization potential, however, are those requirements which act as barriers to entry for new firms or prevent initiation of production under new government contracts. These requirements include: preparation of Cost Accounting Standards disclosure statements, which must be approved before a new contractor or subcontractor can initiate production; a former CASB senior staff member estimated that preparation and approval of a disclosure statement for a new contractor or subcontractor could take as long as six months. They also make necessary the preparation and approval (and litigation, if necessary) of environmental impact statements, needed for any major federal actions significantly affecting the environment (including new plant construction, Title III projects, and weapons projects such as the MX); preparation and approval of an affirmative action employment plan; and preparation, approval, *and negotiation into the contract* of a detailed small and disadvantaged business subcontractor utilization plan. This requirement is especially burdensome, and must be developed anew *for each contract.*

None of these requirements was present, in anything like their present form, even during the Vietnam conflict. Significantly, none was written or considered by the Armed Services Committees, normally considered to be the committees in the Senate and House of Representatives, respectively, most concerned with defense matters. In most cases, enforcement authority, as well as waiver authority, lies with agencies other than the Department of Defense, and provisions for suspending the requirements during emergencies are not specified. It is important to remember that *bureaucratic bottlenecks can delay mobilization efforts just as much as production-capacity bottlenecks.* Defense procurement procedures, only some of which were mandated by Congress, such as qualified bidder's lists, first-article approval requirements, pre-award surveys, and complex specifications and quality control procedures, can also delay and add to the costs of defense programs.

In all likelihood, these requirements will not be repealed. They probably should not be repealed, even in wartime. The United States has always placed a high priority on protecting its values, and this may be even more important in wartime than in peacetime. As stated earlier, policies such as those under discussion were applied, to some extent, during World War II and the Korean War. Indeed, some socioeconomic policies—such as the requirement for contracting in labor surplus areas—may become *more important* in wartime, because of the impact of localized labor shortages and surpluses.

Instead, what is needed is a reassessment of the miscellaneous socioeconomic requirements and procurement procedures which can inhibit industry's ability to respond to near-term or mobilization requirements. The probable effect of these requirements on defense production was generally not considered at the time these requirements were enacted, and should be now. In some cases, such a review might disclose methods of avoiding impairment of defense production while still ensuring satisfaction of the original purpose of these requirements.

Conclusion

Preparation for industrial mobilization has been considered irrelevant for many years, because it has been assumed that future conventional wars will occur with little warning and will be very short. Clearly, the ability of industry to increase production significantly, or to mobilize, over the short term is so questionable (especially with existing legal constraints) that mobilization planning, at least on a broad scale, should be considered irrelevant under such a scenario. The increasing complexity of modern weapons systems, lengthening lead times, and the declining number and capacity of subcontractors contribute to this problem.

However, there is an element of self-fulfilling prophecy in these assumptions. If the United States assumes that it will not begin to mobilize industry "on warning," and if the United States continues to assume that industrial preparedness is irrelevant, then it probably will be. If the United States refuses to take advantage of "warning," and if it continues to allow mobilization capabilities to deteriorate, then mobilization plans will be lacking, mobilization capability will not be provided, and future conventional wars, in all probability, will be "short," due to the inability of U.S. industry to sustain its forces.

Since the Korean War, industrial preparedness planning has frequently been forced to take the "back seat"—first to the doctrine of massive retaliation, then to Vietnam War consumption requirements, and then to the requirements for force structure modernization. Declining defense budgets and the Department of Defense's self-imposed imperative to perpetuate the major aircraft manufacturers also contributed to the low priority for IPP.[15]

However, this does not need to be the case. Defense production capacity is not foreordained, nor is it static. This capability can improve or deteriorate. If legislative packages were introduced and approved to provide necessary legal authorities and reform burdensome requirements, if proper investment incentives were furnished, if government and industry initiated effective industrial preparedness planning to include both broad industrial improvements and planning for wartime expedient measures, if the Department of Defense initiated programs to correct deficiencies in the lower tiers and to attack known and prospective bottlenecks, and if effective programs were initiated, under the stockpiling program and the Defense Production Act, to correct raw materials and materials processing shortages, the result could be a robust defense industrial base which could support more realistic and useful military planning.

These improvements in defense industrial capability should be of concern to everyone, regardless of ideological perspective. Conservatives should favor programs to improve defense industrial capabilities, because their efforts over the near term to expand defense capabilities are likely to be frustrated if inadequacies in the defense industrial base are not corrected. Liberals and arms control advocates, likewise, should favor these initiatives, because they will ensure that defense dollars are not spent profligately and because a sound, economic and expandable defense industry, capable of responding to increasing needs, provides the assurance necessary to back up arms control agreements.

Efforts to improve industrial mobilization capabilities should begin with the strengthening of the ability of the industrial base to meet near-term defense needs. Failure to address these problems in the near-term will result in the continued erosion of defense capabilities and a continued decline in mobilization capabilities.

NOTES

1. Statement in *Capability of the U.S. Defense Industrial Base*, Hearings before the Panel on Defense Industrial Base, Committee on Armed Services, U.S. House of Representatives, 1980, pp. 1367-68.

2. *Report of the Defense Science Board Summer Study Panel on Industrial Responsiveness*, Office of the Undersecretary of Defense for Research and Engineering, January 1981, pp. 30-31.

3. Ibid., p. 31.

4. Defense Science Board, Op. Cit., pp. xvii and 63-64; also, testimony before House Armed Services Committee, Op. Cit., by the Honorable Dale Church (pp. 131, 135), Jerry R. Junkins (pp. 304-8, 318-21), General Alton Slay (pp. 475-77, 661-62), General John R. Guthrie (p. 743) and Wallace Brown (pp. 1010-52).

5. DMS regulations require that producers of these "controlled materials" "set aside" designated quantities and types of production each month for allocation to defense projects.

6. Testimony of Wallace Brown before House Armed Services Committee, Op. Cit., p. 1015; see also testimony of General Alton Slay, p. 509.

7. Bernard M. Baruch, "Priorities: The Synchronizing Force," *Harvard Business Review*, Spring 1941, pp. 261-70. For discussions of the application of priorities immediately before and during World War II, see John M. Martin, "Present Status of Priorities," in the same issue, pp. 271-85 and Donald M. Nelson, *Arsenal of Democracy, The Story of American War Production* (Harcourt, Brace and Co., 1946), pp. 90, 110-11, 119, and 349-90; and R. Elberton Smith, *The U.S. Army in World War II—The Army and Economic Mobilization* (Office of the Chief of Military History, 1958), pp. 507-49. Application of priorities in the Korean conflict is discussed in *Progress Report No. 10*, Joint Committee on Defense Production (JCDP), U.S. Congress, November 26-27, 1951, and in *Annual Reports* of the JCDP, 1951, and subsequent years. More recent status of the DPS/DMS was discussed in *Defense Priorities System*, Hearings before the Joint Committee on Defense Production, U.S. Congress, May 22 and 23, 1975, and in the *Annual Report* of the JCDP for 1975.

8. Federal Emergency Management Agency, *Stockpile Report to the Congress*, January 1981, p. 3.

9. General Accounting Office, *Recent Changes in the Defense Department's Profit Policy—Intended Results Not Achieved*, (PSAD-79-38), March 8, 1979. See also *Defense Industrial Base, Part II: Department of Defense Profit '76 Study*, Hearings before the Joint Committee on Defense Production, U.S. Congress, November 18, 1976; and *Department of Defense Contract Profit Policy*, Hearings before the Committee on Banking, Housing and Urban Affairs, U.S. Senate, March 21, 1979.

10. The Cost Accounting Standards Board was denied an appropriation for FY 81, and ceased to exist on September 30, 1980. Although the CAS remained in effect, no authority, other than Act of Congress, presently exists to modify, amend, repeal, or grant waivers from CAS requirements. An effort to transfer CASB authorities to the Office of Federal Procurement Policy, supported by OMB and the GAO, failed in the 96th Congress due to major

contractor opposition to elements of the proposed legislation.

11. George A. Lincoln, *The Economics of National Security*, (Englewood Cliffs, N.J.: Prentice-Hall, 1954), p. 209. See also Nelson, Op. Cit., pp. 127-28, 140, 152.

12. Testimony of the Honorable Dale Church, Deputy Director for Acquisition of the Directorate of Defense Research and Engineering at *Defense Industrial Base, Part IV: DOD Procurement Practices*, Hearings before the Joint Committee on Defense Production, September 30, 1977, p. 34.

13. Cited by Senator William Proxmire in *Federal Acquisition Act*, Hearings before the Committee on Armed Services, U.S. Senate, October 5, 1978, p. 44.

14. ODM submission to *Third Annual Report*, Joint Committee on Defense Production, U.S. Congress, 1954, p. 71.

15. For discussions of mid-1970s industrial base planning, see: *Defense Industrial Base, Part IV: DOD Procurement Practices*, Hearings before the Joint Committee on Defense Production, U.S. Congress, September 29 and 30, 1977; *Civil Preparedness Review, Part 1: Emergency Preparedness and Industrial Mobilization*, Report of the Joint Committee on Defense Production, February 1977, pp. 55-96; Colonel Harry E. Ennis, *Peacetime Industrial Preparedness for Wartime Ammunition Production* (Washington, D.C.: National Defense University, 1980); and Jacques S. Gansler, *The Defense Industry* (Cambridge, Ma.: MIT Press, 1980).

10

The Mobilization Aspect of the Soviet Economy as a Factor in Preparedness for War

Michael Checinski

According to the Soviet Military Encyclopedia, the term "mobilization" refers to a complex of activities designed to convert the armed forces and the national economy into a military state.[1]

> The mobilization of the economy involves the conversion of all sectors of the economy and their respective enterprises from a peace-time to a war-time state; to arrange the deployment of a mass-production of military goods, including military uniforms, armaments, technology and ammunition, so as to ensure all needs of the military and civilian population during times of war....

This entry does not touch upon the specific aspects of Soviet mobilization activity which exist as a result of the modern age of war, i.e., the development of nuclear weapons and missiles. This omission is not surprising given the extreme secrecy with which everything relating to military activity is treated in the Soviet Union. This applies in particular to all matters connected with mobilization activity.

In this same definition we read that planned mobilization activity must be performed within the shortest possible time span, as well as in a highly secretive manner, so as to enable this activity to be responsive to changes in the military-political situation. Based on the above, we must therefore acknowledge that a thorough analysis of Soviet mobilization policy is crucial to estimating correctly that country's preparedness for war. This chapter can only suggest the direction and framework for such an analysis. It is also crucial to evaluating the balance of military power between the Warsaw Pact and NATO countries, as well as estimating the military-political intentions of the U.S.S.R. However, a comparison of Soviet and Western mobilization activities is no simple undertaking.

An analysis of the economic mobilization of the U.S.S.R. must take into account that this activity occurs in a country with very specific economic, social and geopolitical features. No other system or country in the West has a comparable set of features. Thus, to discuss mobilization activity within the Soviet economy, the following specific conditions must be kept in mind:

1) the existence of a fully centralized, state-controlled economy which is developed according to a strict plan;
2) the fact that the U.S.S.R. is one of the largest countries in the world, almost self-sufficient in its raw material needs;
3) a totalitarian system in which all matters relating to military-economic activity are kept completely secret; and,
4) the potential to justify the building of a large military power by using communist propaganda to mask the imperialistic policy of the U.S.S.R.

In addition, other specific national characteristics are important. These include a historically rooted bureaucratic militaristic tradition and a deeply ingrained fear of the rest of the world. This paranoia is, in part, a result of the outside intervention during the Revolution, further intensified by the Nazi aggression in World War II. These factors, however, create after decades "a bureaucratic-industrial system that finds it very difficult to change a course once set."[2] Last but not least is the rich experience afforded by World War II in evacuating large masses of the population and rebuilding new places of living and production within a relatively short period of time.

All of these factors combined give the U.S.S.R. a number of distinct advantages in preparing and executing the mobilization of the economy for war. Writing in the mid-1920s about the preparation of the national economy for war, Mikhail Frunze stated:[3]

> The preparation of the country for future war is facilitated by the nature of the principal elements of our state economy. It would be a terrible crime if, having these distinct possibilities, we are not able to build up the defense of the U.S.S.R. on the highest level.

The problem, of course, lay in determining when and to what degree to use these mobilization potentials of the Soviet economy. The unfortunate experiences gained in World War I and the Civil War were used to justify and formulate the policy; almost all high-ranking Soviet strategists and military economists recommended that as soon as order was restored after the Civil War, heavy emphasis should be placed on preparing the economy for future war.[4] (This advice was ratified by all subsequent Party Congresses.) Because the U.S.S.R. at this time felt in danger of attack by its neighbors, it began economic preparation for war even before the adoption of the first Five-Year Plan in 1928-29. During the 1920s, when the country had still not recovered from the destruction caused by the Civil War, the Soviet Union began simultaneously to build up its military reserves, to develop the transportation systems needed by the military, and to build armament factories. Also at this time, a special department headed by S.I. Ventsov (replaced in 1925 by N.A. Efimov) was created as part of the staff of the Red Army. The name of this department and its successors has never been made known. This department was assigned the following tasks:[5]

1) to control all sectors of the economy, with special emphasis on industry, with the overall objective of preparing the country for war;
2) to monitor and check that the mobilization plans for the economy were being properly executed;
3) to prepare the necessary documents which would serve the government as a basis for decision-making in this area;
4) to coordinate the activities of the most important departments of the Red Army Staff in assessing their respective needs for armaments and equipment (plan *zakaz*) to be presented to Gosplan;
5) to work in cooperation with other departments of the Red Army to prepare the transport system for wartime needs; and
6) to prepare the deployment of medical and other related services to the military during time of war.

This department cooperated with the civilian administration of the economy in fulfilling the tasks described above, and collaborated very closely with Gosplan in drawing up the first One-Year and Five-Year Plans. The materiel needs of the army were incorporated into the Plans in such a way that it was very difficult to distinguish purely military needs from those of the civilian sector. This intertwining of military and civilian needs persist to the present day in Soviet economic planning. A recently published Soviet source describing the role of this department noted:

> The multifaceted work of this department, which embraces almost all of the defense functions of the state administration, results from the character of its organizational and employment structure. This includes the adoption of strict principles for selecting the most appropriate individuals for this work (of this department)....[6]

Just as it does today, this department included in its ranks military men with very different specialties and fields of expertise.⁷ In time, the mobilization activities of this department embraced the Party apparatus and the Gosplans of the various Soviet Republics as well as the planning authorities of the Obkoms and Raikoms. In this way, a military economic mobilization system, totally integrated into the civilian administrations of the country at all levels, was created and developed. This system, with a few modifications, is still in operation today. On the initiative of M. Frunze, a Department of Military-Industry was organized in the Military Academy to ensure a ready supply of experts to run this system.⁸ Graduates from the Military Academy in 1926–27 were sent to various civilian ministries with the purpose of more closely uniting the civilian and military sectors. In 1931, a Military-Economic faculty was organized in the Frunze Military Academy. The graduates of a two-year program were sent to head military departments organized in all civilian ministries and in the Gosplans of all Soviet Republics. This time marked, therefore, the beginning of the permanent institutional and functional ties which join the civilian and military economic administrations in the U.S.S.R. Also at this time, a classified quarterly journal was established by the General Staff of the Red Army, specifically to examine these military-economic problems. The publication of this journal was interrupted by Stalin in the 1930s, but was resumed again—probably by the end of the 1950s.⁹ It is interesting to note that almost all of these problems have significance today both from a theoretical and pragmatic point of view.

Although there were an extensive number of issues debated at that time, this analysis concentrates on the questions which dealt with the mobilization of the economy. That debate revealed an interesting phenomenon. Whereas all participants in the polemic agreed in principle upon what was to be done, they disagreed on when and how to accomplish this end. The various solutions offered depended largely on which military-economic strategy they believed in. Almost always the concept of economic mobilization was understood in a different way.¹⁰ Some theoreticians believed that the purpose of economic mobilization was only to accumulate reserves of materials needed for war. Others understood economic mobilization to mean a total conversion of the national economy to wartime needs, reserves representing only a small part of this program. The latter group prevailed. Then the most controversial issue centered around deciding when the exact moment was for beginning the mobilization and conversion of the economy. Some felt that mobilization should simply be a permanent state of affairs in the economic policy of the state; they promulgated a theoretical program for a long-term, step-by-step conversion of the whole economy to the needs of war. This involved adapting existing means of production so that they would be capable of producing goods of a military nature as well as regular, civilian products. This theory introduced a brand new set of problems.

It was commonly believed that accumulating strategic reserves was the first stage of military-economic mobilization. The second stage was seen as increasing production of the specialized military-industrial factories. The third stage involved the conversion of civilian factories so that they could produce military goods. This concept, that economic mobilization should be effected in three stages, was abandoned in the 1930s. Instead, the idea of a kind of permanent state of mobilization was accepted, whereby all newly built factories and enterprises were designed so that they could immediately begin mass-production of military goods should the need arise. The obvious advantage of this concept was that it greatly accelerated the process of economic mobilization, neglecting as a matter of principle the price which would have to be paid for this to occur.

Discounting the cost of mobilization in favor of speeding up the process has been an integral part of Soviet economic policy. It is important to note that this lack of concern with the issue of cost became official doctrine in the 1930s—it was forbidden to discuss publicly the cost of economic mobilization—and is in force up to the present day.[11] Thus, the whole question of how much the country would have to pay for mobilization ceased to be an issue of public debate at that time. The factors involved in this mobilization policy were kept so deeply secret that even the government could not truly estimate the costs—there was no basis for calculation. To enforce this policy, all theoreticians who had formerly debated the issue were either killed or removed from positions of influence.[12] The military academies were purged and new personnel instated, the most important among them being Elizaveta Khmelnitskaya.[13] To justify Stalin's policy she argued in her lectures that the issue of cost in economic mobilization was not crucial because profits and capitalist enterprises do not exist in the U.S.S.R. For this reason, she believed the U.S.S.R. could gear the entire economy toward military expenditures without concern. Any price would be paid for the sake of defense and for the purpose of fulfilling the extensive military production mobilization program. A special plan for adapting civilian industries for military needs was put into practice. The mobilization aspects of the economy, affecting industry in particular, were treated as integral parts of the whole economic planning process. A special military department of Gosplan collaborated with the military departments of the various ministries in drawing up the following components of the mobilization plan prior to World War II:[14]

1) to stockpile large reserves of strategic raw materials and semimanufactured goods;

2) to create and develop new, large industrial centers in the Kuznetz-Ural Basin;

3) to prepare conditions for a massive evacuation of the population and industry if a war should turn unfavorable for the U.S.S.R.

The events following the outbreak of World War II fully justified all the above-described mobilization activities prepared by the U.S.S.R. Still, there are many who think that even what they did then was not enough. As emphasized above, the experience of World War II is of crucial importance in understanding the current mobilization philosophy of the U.S.S.R.[15]

Beginning with the first Five-Year Plan, the civilian sectors of the economy were designed largely to function as a support system for the military sector. Hence the enormous price paid by the population in order to fulfill the military-industrial mobilization plans. But despite such a concentration of resources and manpower on military needs, there still remained a number of unanswered problems. These involved the coordination and solution of two conflicting concepts in the development of armament and strategic tasks. The first concept stressed a very rapid technological modernization of the armament and military industries; the second concept emphasized the issue of supplying mass armies with the already existing models of armaments. One problem was deciding which kinds and models of weapons could be produced on a massive scale without being outmoded by the time war started, bearing in mind that the army had to fight against an enemy equipped with the most sophisticated and modern weapons.

This dilemma still exists today, and it is important to note how Soviet experts have resolved the question. The problem was that not only could the mass-produced weaponry become outmoded by the time of the next conflict, but also the industries themselves which produced the weapons. The logistics system, the training of the military, and various other aspects of the military's readiness to wage war, was also in danger of being outmoded. The problem of supplying the military with the most modern weapons and equipment on a mass scale was not made easier by the fact that the Soviet Union at this time had a limited industrial potential, incapable of producing new models of armaments every few years. Another problem confronting Soviet military experts was when to begin supplying the military with the most modern weapons if the time of the next war could not be predicted. This question would be much easier if a country were planning an aggressive war. But for a country in a defensive position, as the Soviet Union was at that time vis-a-vis the Third Reich, the problem is much more complicated. In this context, one ought to consider the opinion of Vishnev, a respected expert in the 1930s:[16]

The newest models of weaponry, even those of the highest quality, cannot have the desired effect if they are used for the first time in a war on a small scale. Furthermore, the use of these new weapons may be counterproductive. Once you have revealed your hand to your enemy before the appropriate time, you risk undermining the morale of your own army....

Vishnev's solution to this contradiction in armament policy was to continue the massive production of military equipment while simultaneously improving and modernizing armaments, which were to be designed in such a way that their models could be continually improved upon. This reduced the possibility of supplying already outmoded equipment to the military.

This policy, it is interesting to note, is still carried out today under Soviet armament and mobilization planning. To some degree we can find this practice in the recent development of tanks, airplanes, warships, artillery, and various other military equipment. The highest level Soviet military commanders still heartily support this process of modernization. Marshal A.A. Grechko, while discussing the problem of mobilization and modernization, stated:[17]

> Another important feature of modern scientific-technological progress is that it is manifested not only in the creation of qualitatively new military technology, *but also in improvements in combat performance characteristics of existing items.* Therefore, a very current trend in scientific-technological progress in military affairs has been *the modernization of combat equipment which has been in an army's inventory for a long while. Figuratively speaking, this gives it a second life if there is purpose in this both from a military and from an economic point of view.* (emphasis added)

From the point of view of mobilization readiness, the policy of improving existing items of Soviet military equipment, combined with the creation of new models and types of armaments, is extremely important. This differs in some respects from the policy of modernization exercised in the West, which is based largely on creating totally new (or almost new) models of weaponry. The Soviet approach makes it easier to continue the mass production of armaments and military equipment, as well as aiding in the accumulation of large reserves of military materials. It is also more convenient from the point of view of training, logistics, stockpiling, and many other areas of the mobilization policy.

However, this policy of rearmament has its drawbacks, and the large number of military-political consequences are worth noting. The Western concept of military production differs from that of the U.S.S.R. insofar as it prefers major changes in newly produced models and equipment. This makes possible the potential for a situation in which a large proportion of Soviet armaments and equipment could be outmoded within a very short time. The example of the neutron bomb can be used to illustrate this point. From the economic and strategic point of view, the use of neutron bombs would represent a true catastrophe for the Soviet Union. Theoretically, these bombs could, very quickly, destroy the entire superiority the Soviets presently have in Europe in terms of being able to supply their armies with large numbers of tanks and military vehicles. Therefore, billions of rubles would be wasted. This strategic and economic blow to Soviet military preparedness for war in Europe contains political and military consequences worth mentioning.

The U.S.S.R. could try to use the temporary superiority of its large reserves of tanks and armored vehicles to procure military and political advantages in areas of the world where direct confrontation with NATO is not expected, i.e., Afghanistan, the Persian Gulf region, Africa, etc. However, other possibilities cannot be excluded. It is entirely possible that the Soviet Union could press for a direct confrontation with NATO before neutron bombs are supplied on an operational scale. In this way they could wage a war using the above-described, conventional means of military superiority.

Soviet leaders and military theoreticians both acknowledge that their mobilization and armament policy is risky from an economic and military point of view. However, they firmly believe that in an age of nuclear weapons and missiles the only rational course is to be prepared to wage and win a war at any given moment. Soviet leaders, having analyzed the failures of the first stage of war with Germany (WW II), believe that the very fact that the Germans initiated the war explains why the Red Army was not fully prepared to defend the country. Stalin concurred with this position in a speech delivered in 1944, asserting that the aggressor is always in a better position at the outset of a war, and the defending countries are never adequately prepared. In other words, the problems of coordinating mobilization plans with rearming the army are intertwined with calculating the exact moment of the next war.[18]

It would be an oversimplification to discuss all of Soviet mobilization policy solely within the framework of these problems. Modern Soviet military doctrine, including mobilization doctrine and policy, is influenced by a number of factors involving a complexity of military, economic, political, and social developments. In order to understand this doctrine, a more detailed analysis of these factors is necessary. In this context, however, we will restrict ourselves to the most important element of this topic.

The changes in Soviet economic mobilization policy over the past two decades (1960-80) were influenced primarily by the advent of nuclear weapons and ICBM systems which "brought about changes in the methods of waging war."[19] However, the economic mobilization policy is not only a military, but also a political-economic matter. We should consider in this context the polemic concerning the definition of military strategy, discussed in the Foreword to the second edition of Marshal Sokolovskiy's classic, *Soviet Military Strategy*:

> The authors did not find it possible to agree with the recommendation of some reviewers (of the first edition) to exclude from the scope of the military the investigation of the problems of directing the preparation of the country for war....[20]

This point is strongly underlined in the 1979 edition of the Soviet Military Encyclopedia, where we read that military strategy "...embraces the theory and practice *of preparing the country* and the military forces for war, and the planning and conducting of war...."[21] A close reading of the quoted entry left no doubt that the mobilization of the economy is considered part of the military strategy of the U.S.S.R. Of course this is a practice rooted in all of Soviet history, as we noted above. However, it was only in the 1960s that the influence of the military strategy on the development of the mobilization activity of the whole country took on such a broad and general character. At this time the whole pattern of Soviet economic development established in the past twenty years changed dramatically. Supporting this thesis requires an explanation of the changes in the concept of economic mobilization in an era of missiles and nuclear weapons.

The present Soviet mobilization program is not, as in the past, limited merely to directing the civilian sector of industry for military tasks and enlarging military and state reserves; rather, it embraces a wide range of activities. Today the program of preparing the military and the economy for war includes new elements; in addition, several other important activities performed in the past for this task have been considerably altered. Thus, until the 1950s, the location policy of industry was heavily influenced by military programs which demanded that concentrated industrial centers be built deep within the interior of the country (e.g., the Ural-Kuznetz Basin). Beginning in the early 1960s, however, a time when the U.S.S.R. was just beginning to work out a new strategy and military doctrine for the possibility of nuclear war, the former concept regarding the location of industry was changed totally. In this new era of nuclear weapons, it was most advantageous, from the military's point of view, to disperse industrial centers as much as possible in small units throughout the country. It was also recommended that part of the new factories be built underground. This program, although extremely costly, brings a strong influence to bear on all of Soviet economic planning. Some recently prepared studies and information from the U.S.S.R.

support this statement.²² From these we can deduce that policies in the areas of civil defense and military mobilization of the economy are intertwined. Soviet measures to protect the economy are based on two kinds of solutions:

1) to build part of new and important plants deep underground; and,
2) to prepare specific facilities about 35-50 km from the cities that would enable an immediate evacuation to these places of a number of important factories and to continue production immediately.

The factories that are built underground have to keep about 25% to 50% of their production capacity in such a way that it will enable them to continue their work even in time of an atomic war, provided, of course, that these factories are not located in the center of a nuclear blast. Such underground departments were also added in old, but important factories, which are expected to be targets of an American atomic exchange. Specific information is known about the following plants:

1) In Liubertsy, 50-60 km from Moscow, on the road to Riazan, is located one of the biggest optical and special glass factories in the U.S.S.R. that has worked only for the Ministry of Defense (Liuberetsky Opticheskii Zavod). This factory is built mostly inside small mountains, about 50-60 meters high, or underground.
2) Along the same railroad line to Riazan, in a small town 10 km from Kratovo, is located one of the biggest Soviet construction plants of military planes, one of the "hearts" and "brains" of the R & D institutes and construction factories of the famous constructor Tupolev. With about 10,000 engineers and technicians, these facilities are located mostly underground.
3) Near Volgograd, but on the other side of the Volga, a new city, Volzskyi, has been built together with a totally new chemical factory employing about 20,000 workers. A large part of this factory is built underground.
4) In a small town, Novay, in the Uzbek Republic, between Samarkand and Bukhara, a new chemical factory was built only fifteen years ago, which employs about 10,000 workers, half of the town's population. Three floors of this factory are above ground, but *six floors* are built underground. A second chemical factory is also built in the same way (i.e., underground) in this town. These factories were built by criminal prisoners with life sentences. Three big prison camps in this town also serve as a reservoir of workers in these factories.
5) In a forest, about 35 km from Riga (Latvia), accessible only by a secret road which is closely guarded, is a reserve, wartime

place for the biggest metal factory in Riga, which would have to be evacuated in time of crisis. Buildings have been prepared, water and energy supply facilities, the most important machines and raw materials, etc. Special exercises with a selected group of the factory's managers and workers are provided from time to time about how to carry out the evacuation and to start production in this new location.

Of course, the above mentioned activities would not be sufficient to protect all of industry or the population from the consequences of a nuclear attack, but the Soviet leaders are confident that they will be able to protect a substantial proportion of their population and production capacity. Under the camouflage of civil defense and military training, a great effort is made to keep the mobilization plans completely secret. We must underline here the principal differences in the function of civil defense in the U.S.S.R. and in the West. The primary goal of Soviet civil defense is not the saving of as many human lives as possible per se, but rather protecting its means of production, particularly military production crucial to winning the war. Human life is valued first of all from the standpoint of manpower, a necessary component of production. This attitude is widely acknowledged in currently published Soviet literature.[23] The Central Intelligence Agency paper published in 1978, *Soviet Civil Defense*, confirmed that a number of its activities are a real military factor, and "the Soviets certainly believe their present civil defenses would improve their ability to conduct military operations and could enhance the U.S.S.R.'s chances for survival following a nuclear exchange...."[24]

The preparation of industry for war is, therefore, combined with civil defense activity and with a large number of organizational and administrative changes. The administrative system is constructed so that each microregion can be governed, if necessary, independently from the Central Administration, but this would occur only in a situation where communications had completely broken down. The strategy of developing microregions is important in understanding the present policy of strategic reserves allocation. The reserves necessary for survival, however, are not evenly dispersed throughout the microregions, but are allocated heavily in favor of military needs. Since Soviet military experts predict that a maximum of two-thirds of the population will survive a nuclear attack, they base their calculations of reserves for civilians on this reduced figure. Most important, in their view, is the necessity for keeping these reserves secure—preferably underground.

Providing reserves for the military sector is a more complicated issue. The supplies must be sufficient to wage and win the war. The following regulations for military reserves were put forth by the Polish military at the end of the 1960s by the demand of the Warsaw Pact Treaty Organization Command: the regiments or divisions were provided with a seven-day fighting capacity (especially armaments and ammunition); the armies were allocated sufficient reserves for two to three weeks of active fighting. In addition, large state reserves (probably enough for six months of fighting) are available for use by the Defense Council. These allocations were calculated sufficient to push the NATO units out of Europe in three to four weeks, and to attain such an advantage that surviving industries would then be able to produce new supplies of military equipment.

The structure and size of military reserves, as well as their location, are calculated to wage all three possible kinds of war: 1) limited local wars, 2) conventional war with NATO, and 3) a total nuclear war. The logistic systems of the Soviet and Warsaw Pact armies are integrated with the infrastructure of the civil defense systems of all of Eastern Europe. This affects the transportation system, especially junctions and bridges, medical facilities and sanitary investments, the water supply system, including a program for preparing a network of artesian water sources. Public schools and theaters are prepared to accommodate the evacuated population, providing all services necessary for survival (showers, baths, and sanitation arrangements, kitchens, medical and sanitary facilities, etc.).

Of course, all the above listed investments and mobilization activities are possible because "tyranny is always better organized than freedom."[25] If this is correct, we cannot neglect all these preparations of the economy for future war in the balance of power between NATO and Warsaw Pact forces. Mobilization readiness is primarily a military-economic factor, which has tremendous importance if we calculate the "reciprocal measures for arms stabilization" between NATO and the Warsaw Pact, and the possibility of an unexpected surprise Soviet nuclear attack. Is the unthinkable thinkable?

In the quoted collection of Marshal Sokolovskiy, we read that "the most important task is the destruction of the military-economic potential of the enemy", while "the economy of the socialist countries is in a more favorable position."[26] Fred M. Kaplan argues that "there is no sign that any measures have actually been implemented to protect the Soviet industry... to survive a nuclear blast and most of the rest to be regenerated within a short time." He is also sure that "the United States would have at least three days' warning time for an evacuation—more than enough time to retarget ICBM's."[27] Kaplan's approach ignores the obvious indications of industrial preparedness presented earlier. The economic mobilization readiness of the United States is beyond the scope of this chapter; some sources view this link in the chain of the American defense system as quite weak.[28] However, even if the civil defense of the

United States were to be improved, it would be difficult in a democratic society to take the hard decision to prepare a preventive attack if, for example, the U.S.S.R. were to start mass scale civil defense exercises; i.e., evacuating a large part of its population from the cities, and even announcing this through the mass media. A high-ranking officer in the Polish Civil Defense system suggested to the author in an interview that such a scenario of starting a war with NATO was included in the Warsaw Pact countries' military planning in the 1960s.

Robert Kennedy, writing about the consequences of the Yom Kippur War, noted:

> In an age of sophisticated electronics and expanded intelligence capabilities, warning time was found to be not simply a function of the amount of relevant information gathered, but also of the perceptions of that information as clouded by events and filtered through human imperfections. *So the surprise scenario is one with which Western planners must contend*, not just because it is one of many options which might be selected by the Soviet Union, but because it is a tactic which promises to have the effect of significantly offsetting the Western technological lead in precision-guided weaponry. . . . (emphasis added)[29]

And most observers would agree that the Soviet Union is much more sophisticated and devious in preparing surprises than is Egypt. To understand the balance of power between NATO and the Warsaw Pact, the mobilization policy of the U.S.S.R., particularly as it affects industry, must receive serious and extensive study.

NOTES

1. Sovietskaia Voennaia Entsiklopediia (hereafter quoted as SVE), Moscow 1978, Vol. 5, pp. 342-343.

2. Colin S. Gray, "Strategic Stability Reconsidered" in *Rethinking U.S. Security Policy for the 1980s*, Proceedings of the Seventh Annual National Security Affairs Conference, 21-23 July 1980. (Washington, D.C.: National Defense University Press, 1980), p. 170

3. M.V. Frunze, *Izbrannye Proizvedenia*. Voenizdat. Moscow 1977, p. 169.

4. Compare the writings of:
M.V. Frunze, M.N. Tukhachevskii, P.M. Zaionchkovsky, J. Vacetis, P.P. Lebedev, A. Svechin, P. Karatygin, B. Saposhnikov, S. Pugachev, Yu. Sviatlovskyi, P. Sharov, and in the thirties: L. Amiragov, M.I. Savitskyi, S.M. Vishnev, G.J. Shigalin, and E. Khmelnitskaia.

5. P. Kalinovskii, "Iz istorii voenno-ekonomicheskoi raboty shtaba RKKA" (From the History of the Military-Economic Activity of the Staff of

the Red Army), *Voenno-Istoricheskii Zhurnal*, 1972, No. 5, pp. 66-67.
  6. Ibid., p. 67.
  7. Michael Checinski, *A Comparison of the Polish and Soviet Armaments Decision-making Systems*. Rand Report R-2662-AF, (Santa Monica, Ca.: Rand Corporation, 1981).
  8. Frunze, Op. Cit., p. 214; *50 let voennoi akademii im. M.V. Frunze* (50 Years of the Frunze Military Academy), (Moscow, 1968), p. 114; I.A. Korotkov, *Istoria Sovetskoi voennoi mysli*, (Moscow, 1980), p. 187.
  9. Kalinovskii, Op. Cit., p. 68; It is interesting to note that the Editing Board of this Journal includes officials (most probably from the Military Departments) of Gosplan, various ministries and the staff of the Red Army. The Secretary of the Editorial Board was A.L. Karpushin, an expert from the staff of the Red Army.
  10. The discussion about the economic mobilization is one of the most interesting and important issues in the development of the Soviet war-economic doctrine. In this context it is necessary to underline the differences between the *concept* and the *doctrine* of economic mobilization. According to a Soviet expert, "...Military doctrine includes the most essential, stable, and relatively long-term military concepts. *'Military Policy' is a concept* that is both more sweeping and more dynamic. *In addition to the doctrinal provisions*, it encompasses a broad range of both future and current problems..." Colonel B. Kanevsky, "Military Policy of the CPSU; Content and Main Directions", *Voennaya Mysl* 1973, No. 9, p. 3. (Emph. added.) From the large number of articles in which the problem of economic mobilization was discussed in the 1930s in the U.S.S.R., we will mention some of them: A. Volpe, *Sovremennaia voina i rol' ekonomicheskoi podgotovki*, (Moscow, 1926); S. Ventsov, *Narodnoe khoziastvo i oborona SSSR.*, (Moscow-Leningrad, 1928); P. Karatygin, *Obschye osnovy mobilizatsii promyslennosti dlia nuzhd voiny*, (Moscow, 1925); G. Shygalin, *Podgotovka promyshlennosti k voine*, (Moscow, 1928); S. Pugachev, *Osnovy podgotovki strany k oboronie*, (Moscow, 1926); S.M. Vishnev, "Problemy perevooruzhenia innostrannykh armii," *Voina i revolutsia*, 1932, Vol. 4, pp. 68-78.
  11. E.L. Khmelnitskaia, "SSSR v borbie za ekonomicheskuiu niezavisimost", *Bolshevik*, 1932, No. 13, pp. 34-37. It is worthwhile to note that only in the last fifteen years (1965-1980), were published in the U.S.S.R. some articles in which the importance of a more careful cost-accounting and cost analysis of the armament production was emphasized. In preparing the methods for such an analysis, the famous book of Ch. Hitch and R. McKean, (*The Economics of Defense in the Nuclear Age*) was translated into Russian, *Voennaia ekonomika v yadernyi vek*, Moskow 1962; and SVE, Vol. 7, Moscow 1979, pp. 635-636.
  12. Waclaw Stankiewicz, *Socialistyczna mysl wojenno-ekonnomiczna* (The Socialist Military-Economic Thought) (Warsaw: Ministry of Defense Publishing House, 1972) p. 221.
  13. Stankiewicz, Op. Cit., pp. 228-231.
  14. Kalinovskii, Op. Cit., G.S. Kravchenko, *Ekonomika SSSR v gody Velikoi Otechestvennoi Voiny* (The Economy of the U.S.S.R. in WW II) (Moscow 1970), pp. 66-67. Of course, the highest level decision-making body was at this time (until 1937) the Council of Labor and Defense (Sovet Truda i Oborony).
  15. Marshal A.A. Grechko, *The Armed Forces of the Soviet State*, (Moscow 1975) (translated and published under the auspices of the U.S. Air

Force, Washington, D.C.: U.S. Government Printing House, 1975), pp. 62-74; V.D. Sokolovskiy, *Soviet Military Strategy*, edited with an analysis and commentary by Harriet Fast Scott. (New York: Crane Russak, 1975), pp. 136-166.

16. Korotkov, Op. Cit., p. 191.
17. Grechko, Op. Cit., p. 148.
18. Korotkov, Op. Cit., pp. 190-194; Marshal Sokolovskiy argued that, "...the development of the Armed Forces in peacetime is planned for certain periods related to the overall plans of the national economy, new scientific achievements in the field of weaponry and combat equipment, and the nature of the international situation..." Op. Cit., p. 313.
19. Sokolovskiy, Op. Cit., p. 274.
20. Sokolovskiy, Op. Cit., p. XIII.
21. SVE, 1979, V. VII, pp. 555-556.
22. Boris Rumer, *The Dynamics of the Capital Coefficient of U.S.S.R. Industrial Output. Investment Process in Soviet Industry*. Russian Research Center, Harvard University, Cambridge, Ma., December 1980. (mimeograph); Information collected from a number of Soviet immigrants. Almost 20 years ago the former Chief of the Soviet Rear Services argued: "the (Warsaw Pact) countries have large territories, on which are located hundreds of thousands of various economic objects, of which the most important are defended with air defense installations *including those hidden underground*..." (Emph. added) A.N. Lagovskii, *Rol' ekonomicheskogo faktora v voine*, (The Role of the Economic Factor in War), Znanie, Moscow 1959, p. 18.
23. "...The principal tasks of civil defense are to ensure the required conditions for normal activity of all governmental control agencies during the course of the war and the effective functioning of the national economy..." Sokolovskiy, Op. Cit., p. 332; See also General Major A.S. Milovidov and Colonel V.G. Kozlov (edit.) *Problems of Contemporary War*, Moscow, 1972. Translated and published under the auspices of the U.S. Air Force, (Washington, D.C.: U.S. Government Printing Office, *1974*), pp. 240-244.
24. *Soviet Civil Defense*, Director of Central Intelligence, Washington, D.C., July 1978, N. 178-10003.
25. Charles Pierre Peguy, quoted by John L. Morrison, *The Weapons Procurement System of the Soviet Union*, National Defense College, Latimer, May 1978, p. 1.
26. Sokolovskiy, Op. Cit., p. 290.
27. Fred M. Kaplan, "Soviet Civil Defense: Some Myths in the Western Debate", *Survival*, (May/June 1978), pp. 113-120.
28. Lieutenant Colonel Edward G. Rapp, *Construction Support For Mobilization: A National Emergency Planning Issue*. National Security Affairs Monograph Series (Washington, D.C.: National Defense University Research Directorate, 1980), pp. 80-89.
29. Robert Kennedy, "Precision ATGMs and NATO Defense", *Orbis*, V. 22, No. 4, (1979), p. 913.

11

Construction Support for Mobilization: A Pacing Issue

Edward G. Rapp

The First Step

"Construction is not only the biggest single part of defense, it is also the first step in defense."

Sidney Hillman
Truman Committee Hearings, 1941

When mobilization is mentioned today, debate and analysis center usually on the preeminent problems of manpower. Production expansion generally is the second most important issue. Construction, if thought of at all, is well down the list of priorities. Yet in each war in this century the nation's ability to marshal quickly and to focus its construction capabilities was the controlling factor in expanding both manpower and production capabilities. The United States has grossly underestimated facility requirements and costs for construction in previous wars and consistently undervalued the response capability of the construction industry in mobilization planning.[1] Certainly a positive attitude has a lot to do with success in earlier conflicts. But the technology explosion that has occurred since World War II makes reliance on the past a shaky proposition. America can no longer count on a three-year warning or a protected industrial base. Technology changes place great stress on both organization and doctrine for the construction support of mobilization.

There is evidence that construction will be a problem in any future mobilization. NIFTY NUGGET, a mobilization exercise conducted in 1978, uncovered shortages in troop housing and outloading facilities.[2] A recent U.S. Army study indicates a mobilization troop housing shortfall on the order of a quarter of a million spaces to support even a NATO short war scenario.[3] In spite of history and recent evidence that a problem exists, it would appear that planning for the next mobilization construction surge has undergone considerable decline. The problem may be an unwillingness to think through the issues, or an overreliance on strategic forces to deter war. More likely the problem is an inability to visualize requirements beyond a hypothetical M-day. This lack of awareness of a mobilization construction requirement is reminiscent of the period preceding both world wars where planners did not visualize the magnitude of the discontinuity imposed by war preparations.

A mobilization day is a significant discontinuity in the processes of the nation. It is a legal declaration by the President that national defense and survival, beyond quality of life, are the dominant national goals. On that day emergency provisions of law begin to be implemented and position responsibility and authority, particularly in the Department of Defense, increase greatly. Peacetime management systems and tools have a problem dealing with such a discontinuity. Even the Five Year Defense Plan (FYDP) presupposes peacetime continuity; as a result, preparations for war in the programming and budgeting world take the form of a continuum, as if an actual M-day might not occur during this program and budget horizon. What the Department of Defense would do if M-day were tomorrow is different from what is contained in the current budget which assumes war can come—sometime. Congress, with its responsibility to raise an army, needs to know what must be done if M-day were tomorrow. Neither the current budget nor the budget proposal before Congress contain answers to that question. Understanding steps beyond an M-day discontinuity is essential if Congress is to assess the readiness posture of the nation. Since construction is a prerequisite for manpower and production expansion, a deeper understanding of this issue provides valuable insights into the total posture of the nation for mobilization as well.

The central question is: What is the minimum upgrading required now to support requirements in future mobilizations? Most of what anyone needs to know about mobilization is contained in America's history. This chapter attempts to synthesize that history and relate it to contemporary conditions. The purpose is to present issues and recommendations for resolution so that construction will be reduced as a pacing factor in defense emergency should one occur during the late twentieth century.

Mobilization construction support for mobilization does not just happen. The U.S. Contract Construction Industry must be directed into action. Historically the source of direction, technical expertise, and engineering management in a national emergency has been Army engineers. Before developing the issues it is necessary to portray some basic facts about the size and character of the U.S. Contract Construction Industry and the U.S. Army Corps of Engineers.

The Industry

The U.S. Contract Construction Industry is the nation's largest category of industrial employers.[4] Even though the industry has generated a consistent 9% to 12% of the gross national product since 1950, it is made up of thousands of independent contractors. As a result, the industry exhibits great flexibility with regard to demand. During non-mobilization periods defense uses less than 1% of the industry's capacity. Yet in World War I this utilization jumped to 30%, in World War II to 60%, and for Korea to 10%.[5] Such a shift does not occur without major efforts both by industry and government to resolve labor, materials, real estate, funding, and contracting problems. The plans and mechanisms to obtain this shift of effort constitute the focus of this chapter.

Corps of Engineers

Decentralization and size are the key features of the Corps' civil works structure. The civil functions are performed by 37 district offices and 12 division offices located throughout the continental United States, Alaska, and Hawaii. Within this structure are 800 officers and 48,000 civilian employees controlling and operating a $3 billion annual program of water resource management and flood control.[6] Incidentally, this was the approximate size of the structure prior to World War II.

The Corps of Engineers Civil Works program is the nation's strategic reserve for mobilizing defense construction.[7] Although to some this may appear as a paradox, the linkage of civil works to mobilization is traceable both in intent and Act of Congress from the early inception of the Corps.[8] The earliest missions given to the Corps were for surveys of public routes and properties. In preparation for the War of 1812, districts were formed under the director of engineer officers to mobilize civilian labor forces for construction of coastal defenses. These districts were expanded after the war to serve in a nation building capacity. Work was primarily centered on improving harbors for commercial shipping. In 1824 Congress institutionalized and codified the use of Army engineers for nation building when it passed into law the forerunner of the Rivers and Harbors Act.[9] The Corps of Engineers Civil Works districts continue to serve the nation in a dual capacity—"nation building" during periods of peace and defense construction in times of conflict.[10]

The Corps of Engineers is responsible under law for actions in a broad spectrum of emergency conditions that range from natural disaster to nuclear holocaust. Fundamental authority and responsibilities are contained in the Title 10 (Armed Forces). Responsibilities for water resources protection and disaster relief are found in Title 16 (Conservation), Title 33 (Navigation and Navigable Waters), Title 42 (Public Health and Welfare), and Title 43 (Public Lands). Civil defense responsibilities are contained in Title 10. All these missions have one thing in common. The Corps is directed to mitigate loss of life and property in national disasters whether the source of events is natural or manmade. The spectrum of emergency scenarios for which the Corps must be prepared is graphically depicted in Figure 1, which reveals that the tasks performed under all scenarios are essentially the same. Many of the tasks performed in the cleanup following a hurricane are similar to the tasks to be performed following a nuclear attack; the variation lies in the scale of the workload and long term effects. The peace side of this emergency response matrix is exercised almost continuously by natural disasters and occasionally by large industrial accidents. The country averages about thirty disasters a year of a size requiring the Corps of Engineers to make a contribution. The Corps is proud of its results and is good at mitigating losses under these conditions.[11] But these events do not compare in magnitude to those experienced and postulated in preparation for, conduct of, and recovery from war. This generates a series of questions about what has to be done, what rules have to be changed, and what organizational shifts are needed as the nation shifts toward the war side of the matrix.

Figure 1

EMERGENCY RESPONSE SPECTRUM

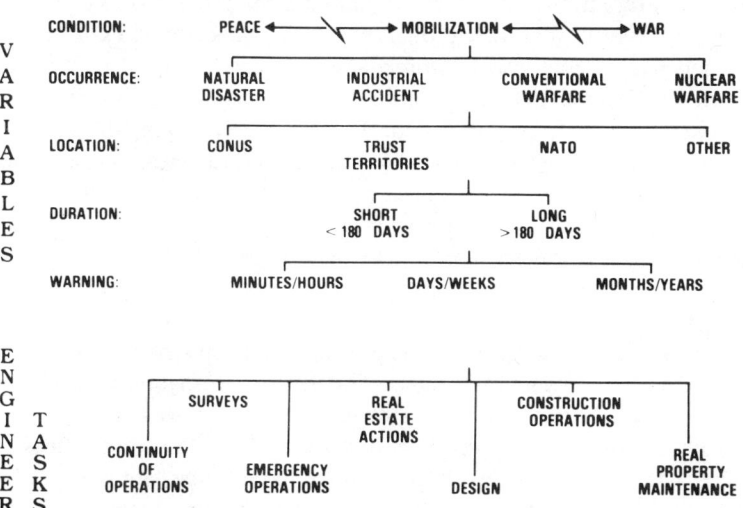

The Issues—Lessons Forgotten

It is dangerous to assume that all the lessons of past mobilizations are now incorporated into existing war plans, policies, and procedures. The issues presented here are not necessarily new; most represent an updated version of a lesson learned in previous mobilizations. The challenge will be to avoid repeating the bitter experiences of the past.

ISSUE: THE SHORT WAR SYNDROME

Some theorists argue that the next war, large or small, will be short. Limited war for limited objectives fought on the boundaries of superpower interests supposedly will be short, intense affairs characterized by rapid deployment and lethal fires. We are told war for total objectives will be fought with nuclear weapons and will terminate rapidly when exchange ratios clearly favor one adversary or the other. In either case there will not be time for creation of additional forces or production base expansion. Thus, the concept of total mobilization in the manner of past world wars is passé. These theorists hypothesize that there might not even be time for full mobilization of the reserve components, and that to minimize risk the United States should concentrate all resources on forward deployment and a short war strategy. But what if the short war theory is wrong? General E.C. Meyer, the Army Chief of Staff, says, "One who plans a short war is apt to get a short losing war."[12]

All "next wars" are short wars. History is replete with optimistic predictions about "the duration." The truth of the matter is that the current infatuation with short war planning defies the lessons of history. Prior to World War II the buzz word equivalent to the current day "rapid deployment" was "immediate readiness." Mobilization plans called for immediately ready units to begin deploying five days after M-day.[13] As the preparations for World War II began, the ramifications of this optimistic concept became abundantly clear. America was mobilizing a million men without a declared war and with no place to put them, no space to train them, and no production base to support them. Congress was incensed at the lack of prior planning.

In the spring of 1941 each House of Congress began to investigate allegations of undue delay, cost overruns, and malfeasance in the Army's mobilization activities. Land acquisition and construction programs were the initial targets for inquiry. The Senate investigation was chaired by Harry S. Truman and the House investigation was chaired by R. Ewing Thomason. The hearings and reports of these committees are filled with stinging lessons about what ought not to be forgotten in planning for mobilization. This gist of the Senate findings is summarized in this Truman rebuke: "Plans for mobilization of a million men contem-

Construction Support 163

plate a place to put them and a place to train them. Evidently you did not have it,"[14] The Thomason investigation laid the blame for inadequate mobilization plans as follows: "It is obvious that Congress must share with the Army any censure for failing to foresee a situation that seems so clear today."[15]

It was clear that there had been no investment in planning for mobilization construction. In addition no mobilization plans were made for circumstances where forward bases were unavailable or where early deployments were not desirable. Both investigations cite this lack of visualization and plans as the root cause for the problems then being experienced. Truman, in an attempt to fix blame on an individual, bore in on this failure and called before his committee both active and retired generals for questioning. In reading the testimony one can visualize the same questions being asked and the same answers reluctantly being given in today's environment.

Question: What plan did you have to take care of them?
Answer: We were going to put them in tents.
Question: And where?
Answer: I don't know...
Question: Did you have any detailed layouts for those— (camps)—?
Answer: No.
Question: Did you have any plans for utilities for them?
Answer: No, no.[16]

All of the thought and planning had been geared to immediate readiness of existing forces using existing facilities and peacetime resource levels. But in 1942 6% of the Gross National Product was generated by more than 1 million defense contract construction workers.[17] The construction surge of World War II converted a $200 million per year Corps of Engineers' waterway and flood control construction program into a military construction surge that emplaced $18.2 billion worth of cantonments, airfields and defense plants.[18] The value of this construction would be more than $100 billion in FY 1981 dollars.

World War II was not an isolated incident. Figure 2 shows the relationships of construction in the United States to total defense outlays and to Gross National Product (GNP) from 1915 to present. Defense construction reflects the military construction by the Army Corps of Engineers and the Navy Civil Engineer Corps. Both the Army and the Navy serve as construction agents for the Air Force. Civil works construction is that work performed for the civil sector by the Corps of Engineers and is convertible to military construction to support defense construction surges. The surges of defense construction necessary to support mobilization are readily apparent. Notice in a defense emergency that the Corps' nation-building resources and efforts were converted to military construction to support mobilization. Notice also that the shapes of the mobilization surges are strikingly similar. Even the size of the surges in World War I and World War II is the same relative to GNP for those periods. Both experiences were *total* mobilizations—the reserve components together with individual replacements were called, and additional forces were created.

The character of the Korean War hump is also the same, although the relative magnitude was less. The Korean conflict constituted full, not total, mobilization, in that only existing units of the reserve components and individual replacements were called. The period of a relatively high level of defense construction following Korea shows the magnitude of effort required to emplace strategic nuclear missile bases. Vietnam does not appear significant on this plot because the nation did not mobilize. Almost no reserves were called and base construction was implemented outside the continental United States.

Figure 2 reveals the surges of emergency construction needed to fight the major wars of this century. Some important lessons can be drawn from this historical plot.

— Mobilization is a discontinuity. World War I and World War II indicate that a construction surge on the order of 50 times prewar levels can be expected in a total mobilization. Korea provides an experience base for full mobilization of reserve components short of total war.

— Construction is a pacing issue. It should be noted that the construction peaks precede the Total Defense Outlay (production) peaks. This is graphic evidence of the pacing nature of construction in a national defense emergency.

— Construction surges were huge enterprises. In World War I and World War II construction outlays exceeded prior year defense outlays.

— None of the past global conflicts were short wars; in fact, none were predictable as to size, scope, or duration.

The bottom line is that short war thinking defies our history and denies that perspective for the future.

ISSUE: AFFORDABILITY

The Truman committee hearings raise an important question: How did competent officers, whose experience base included mobilization and camp construction in World War I, produce such ill-conceived and inadequate planning? According to the testimony, the General Staff evidently assumed that the nation could never again "afford" the great cantonments built for World War I. They had witnessed the investigations of malfeasance and profiteering following World War I and had become so used to doing without during the 1930s that their requests were limited

Figure 2

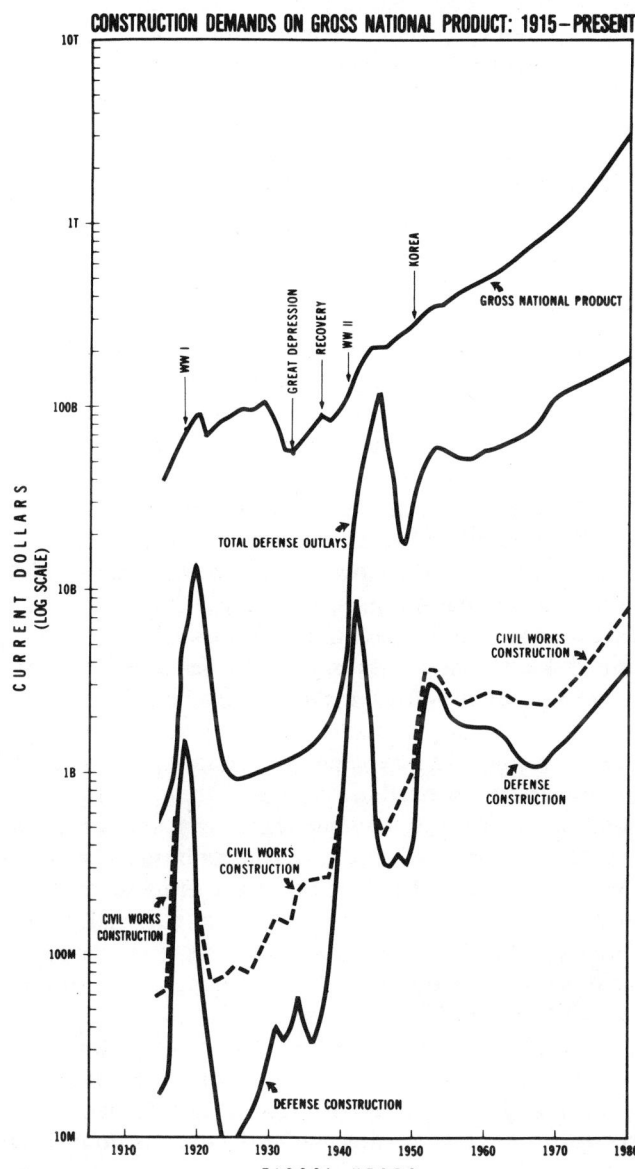

Sources: 1. Newspaper Enterprise Assoc., Inc.,
            The World Almanac and Book of Facts 1979.
         2. Dept. of Commerce, Bureau of the Census,
            Statistical Abstract of the United States: 1978.
         3. *Historical Statistics of the United States—Colonial Times to 1970.*

to what they thought they could obtain from a Congress concerned primarily with social and economic problems. Truman questioned why the Army had not asked for planning money when it was obvious that one dollar in planning would have saved at least seven dollars in haste and waste then being experienced. The Under Secretary of War, the Honorable Robert P. Patterson, testified: "If any officer a couple of years ago had said, 'I want $15,000,000 to lay out possible camps,' I submit that they would have made short shrift of him. Why, they would have said that it was fanciful. They would have wanted that officer looked into as to his ability and capacity."[19] All of the thought and planning was geared to "immediate readiness" of existing forces using existing facilities and peacetime resources levels.

This is not 1938 but the United States is suffering from a similar malady. The current planning view is constrained by considerations of what can be afforded in peacetime. Plans have not been made to employ efficiently and effectively all the resources of the nation if war were suddenly imminent. There are no comprehensive M-day construction and support programs to lay before Congress. There are no comprehensive project listings and real estate acquisition plans and few cantonment schematics. All that exists now is a short war mobilization concept that visualizes double bunks, tents, and rented motel space until the troops deploy to overseas or until the crisis passes.[20]

Who is at fault? The system is at fault, including the continuum management tools currently used. In the crunch of peacetime zero basing and affordability, spending money to draw up plans for camps that may never be used, to design and build production facilities that may never be needed has been considered fanciful even for the limited requirements of full mobilization. The system places these items in priority after the backlog of maintenance and repair, traditionally the lowest priority construction item funded. Further, no one asks to see mobilization plans. No one, as in Truman's days in Congress, has said, "*Show me* the layouts and plans for housing the force, *show me* the real estate requirements and acquisition plans for the training areas." No one has asked what we must build if we activate the full force.

Figure 3 shows what ought to be contained in a mobilization construction program. It is relatively easy to define the customers and determine in general what needs to be done. But the "how much" column is not defined for any of the probable mobilization conditions. Based on the current level of the economy and historical precedent, full mobilization construction requirements could cost on the order of $10 billion to $30 billion. A total mobilization construction program would cost $100 billion to $150 billion.[21] Where are the plans for that? The Department of Defense has not defined the requirements.

Currently the resources for emergency preparedness fall into that unwashed category of overhead. In the press of day-to-day activities, planning for general emergencies is slighted. Resources for emergency preparedness planning, including mobilization, should be identified as a separate line item in both military and civil works appropriations. Given that one dollar in prior planning would have saved seven dollars in haste and waste, investment in detailed mobilization construction plans is not fanciful. That is not only a high cost-benefit ratio, it is a requirement for a viable national strategy.

Figure 3

Full Mobilization Workload—A Framework

Who	What	How Much
Peacetime Customers	Program Reorientation	
	Terminate Nonessential Contracts	Unknown
FORSCOM	Troop/Installation Support	
TRADOC	Construct Troop Facilities	250,000 Men*
DARCOM	Expand Utilities	58,000 Men*
Air Force	Expand Training Areas	Unknown
	Enhance Nonindustrial Facilities	Unknown
	Expand Covered Storage	Unknown
DARCOM	Production Base Support	
Air Force	Accelerate Maintenance	Unknown
	Expand Facilities	Unknown
	Rehabilitate Rail Spurs	Unknown
MTMC	Transportation Support	
NAVY	Dredge	Unknown
	Expand Port Facilities	Unknown
	Expand Choke Points	Unknown
Health Services COMD	Facilities Support	Unknown
Communications COMD	Facilities Support	Unknown
Others	Other Support	
	(Nuclear Preparations)	
	Acquire/Develop Real Estate	Unknown
	Manage Construction	Unknown

*Army data only, currently under revision

ISSUE: EMERGENCY POWERS

Significant lessons pertinent to mobilization are embodied by law, but these lessons are seldom appreciated until a crisis occurs. For instance, in the Civil War, Congress recognized that it could not adequately visualize needs and appropriate funds to meet the fluid conditions of mobile warfare. The result was the Feed and Forage Act of 1861,[22] which permits the Secretary of a military department to expend funds for the immediate needs of the Service without an appropriation from Congress. The lesson is that the public goals and expectations change with the degree of emergency. Whereas law in peacetime attempts to promote social reform, strengthen the free enterprise system, and appeal to perceptions of fair play, the law in war provides certain emergency capabilities to protect the national interests.

It would be inaccurate to say that all of the emergency provisions must be employed or that all provisions needed are already contained in law. Since the last major mobilization, significant new bodies of social, environmental, and safety law have come into being and few of these laws were written with war in mind. Figure 4 contains a listing of those provisions of law which have an impact on mobilization construction. The point here is that significant provisions in law reflect the value systems of this nation at war. Prudent use of these provisions, not necessarily new law, is required on M-day.

The authority to exercise emergency powers in law is not automatic. The President must specify in his declaration of a national emergency or in subsequent Executive orders "those provisions of law under which he, or other officers will act."[23] It is through these means that the President can control the transition to emergency powers. A surprise attack may dictate a Presidential declaration specifically imposing all or nearly all emergency provisions contained in the U.S. Code. For other scenarios the President may selectively choose emergency powers appropriate in that particular time frame. Historically the United States has done neither; instead, the nation has tended to slide in and out of states of emergency amid confusion and with no clear indication as to the specific emergency powers governing in any time frame. Standby Executive orders specifying those provisions listed in Figure 4 need to be drafted prior to M-day. Procedures for use of these provisions must be described in regulations and other implementing instructions prior to M-day.

The executive branch must be prepared to decentralize contracting authority, in particular by expanding dollar thresholds. Early in World War II it became necessary to decentralize authority in order to handle the magnitude of contract work. Authorities were expanded by a factor of ten or more in most areas where dollar-thresholds were imposed. For instance, division engineers were given authority to negotiate contracts up to $5 million and district engineers had a ceiling set at $3 million.[24] At present the ceiling for minor construction that can be accomplished without specific authorization by Congress is $500,000. This limitation is only one example of thresholds that ought to be expanded on M-day. The increased contracting workload must be handled by decentralizing

Figure 4

Emergency Powers Summary (U.S. Code)

Title Number	Section	Summary
5	3326	Permits the appointment of retired members of the Armed Forces to positions in the Department of Defense (DOD) when a state of national emergency exists.
5	7902 and implementing Federal regulations	Permits waivers of national safety standards and procedures.
10	2231, 2233	The Secretary of Defense (SECDEF) is authorized to acquire and expand facilities necessary for use of reserve components in time of war or national emergency.
10	2304	Permits contracts for supplies and services to be negotiated without advertising if determined to be necessary in the public interest "during a national emergency declared by Congress or the President."
10	2663, 2664	The Secretary of a military department may "in time of war or when war is imminent," take and use property, including property for lumber production, immediately upon filing of petition for condemnation.
10	4501, 4502 9501, 9502i	"In time of war or when war is imminent" the President may order necessary products to be manufactured at private plants or take over such plants upon refusal to comply with such orders; and maintain lists of plants capable of war production.
10	4742, 9742	Relates to Presidential control of transportation systems "in time of war."

Figure 4 (Concluded)

Title Number	Section	Summary
10	4776, 9776	If in "an emergency" the President considers it urgent, a temporary air base, fort, or fortifications may be built on private land if the owner consents in writing.
10	4780	Relates to acquisition of buildings in the District of Columbia in time of war or when war is imminent.
10	9773	Relates to the acquisition and construction of air bases and depots during national emergencies.
15	2621	Provides waiver procedures of pollution abatement requirements for toxic substances.
16	470	Provides relief from the Endangered Species Act.
33	1323	Provides waiver procedures of water pollution standard for Federal facilities.
41	11	Permits the Armed Services to purchase clothing, subsistence, forage, fuel, quarters, transportation, medical and hospital supplies, which, however, shall not exceed the necessities of the current year, without an appropriation from Congress.
42	300J-6(b), 4903 7412, 7418, 7606	Provides exemptions to water, air, and noise pollution abatement provisions.
42	6961	Provides exemptions to solid waste disposal standards.
50	1431	Relates to authorization to enter into defense contracts or into amendments or modifications of defense contracts without regard to certain other provisions of law.
50	1211, 1213, 1216	Relates to renegotiation of contracts.
50	2291-2295	Relates to authorities in a Civil Defense emergency.

selection and award. It is necessary to establish policy controls and broadly expanded levels of authority now so that mobilization planning can proceed using M-day rules, not peacetime rules.

Contracting procedures to be used in mobilization must be laid down in advance. In each previous mobilization experience, the use of "cost plus a fixed fee" (CPFF) contracts has been a hotly debated issue.[25] In 1917 and again in 1940, the initial pulse of mobilization construction was accomplished by CPFF contracts. The widespread use of this type of contract is controversial and trouble-prone because it cuts short competitive bidding and contains no incentive to increase productivity or to reduce cost. The utility of the procedure is that it allows construction to begin before plans and specifications are finalized and it provides guarantees to the contractor that he will not be broken by rapidly rising and unpredictable labor and material costs. The decision to use CPFF under certain conditions where rapid construction is essential should be made in peacetime to ensure a clear course during mobilization.

Even with prescribed contracting procedures, there are problems that must be resolved at the civil-military interface. CPFF is a negotiated contract wherein issues of policy, contractor selection, negotiation, execution, and review surface. In each instance of its use it has been necessary to establish civilian advisory boards in order to settle industry and government differences.[26] These boards should be set up in peacetime on a standby basis to be used during the emergency period. Such advisory boards can provide valuable information not only on contracting and war profits but also on labor relations, wages, overtime policies, materials, equipment rentals, and public relations.

Since World War II and Korea, significant bodies of law have come into being, particularly in the areas of socio-economic reform, environmental protection, and safety. Although certain emergency relief procedures are contained in these bodies of law, they have not been tested. It would be natural for agencies newly created for peacetime protection of our society to attempt to perpetuate rules and regulations in wartime. The Federal Emergency Management Agency (FEMA) was formed to adjudicate emergency procedures between departments and agencies of the federal bureaucracy.[27] Procedures and letters of understanding need to be established prior to the emergency so that mobilization planning can be accomplished within this framework. The Corps of Engineers should take the lead in initiating this interchange for construction. This is essential so that both district engineers and contractors can approach mobilization planning with mobilization, not peacetime, rules.

ISSUE: CRISIS REALLOCATION OF CONSTRUCTION RESOURCES

When national priorities become dominated by defense and national survival issues, mechanisms for reallocating resources are needed. On

M-day the budget and the Five Year Defense Plan are overcome by events. What is the process that replaces these peacetime procedures? At the start of the World War II mobilization period there was no overt action to stop work on nonessential programs already authorized and funded in order to conserve and reallocate resources. Peacetime construction merely wound down as projects were completed.[28] In the future this process may not be satisfactory where time and other resource constraints make it imperative to turn off construction in those sectors not essential to defense. For instance, there should be a mechanism to stop work on certain Corps of Engineers water projects to generate resources for cantonments and production facilities. Similarly it may be desirable to stop investing in inner city housing and block improvement projects to increase housing capacities in outlying host areas. There are numerous nation-building and quality of life construction projects that could be delayed or cancelled to allow greater efforts in support of the emergency.

There is a precedent for project review and stop work orders for nonessential construction in the records of the Facility Review Committee of the War Production Board (WPB) during 1942 and 1943. This board was able to stop projects amounting to $1.3 billion from government programs including much of the civil works construction of the Corps of Engineers. In addition, the deterrent value of these review procedures caused a significant reduction in nonemergency related proposals.[29] Unfortunately these mechanisms did not come into being until 1942, well into the war. The Facility Review Committee was composed of members of the WPB, Army, Navy, and the Maritime Commission. A similar organization in today's environment would involve membership from FEMA, Army, Navy, and the Maritime Commission. The challenge is to establish the organization, the authority, the criteria for review and the procedures now, prior to M-day.

From the perspective of contractors who must disengage peacetime work and reengage in the mobilization effort, it is vital to know who is in charge. The lesson is that responsibilities, organizations and procedures must be established before a crisis begins, and the organization must be kept simple and constant.

ISSUE: CONGRESSIONAL OVERSIGHT

In World War I formal investigation of emergency construction began with the 1918 inquiry by the Senate into war expenditures. This occurred nine months after the war had begun.[30] In World War II formal inquiry began in 1941 with investigations conducted within both House and Senate.[31] Within a year and a half after mobilization had begun, but still six months prior to the outbreak of war, effective oversight of emergency construction was established. This oversight was

Construction Support 173

maintained throughout the war and well into the recovery period. The failing in these previous experiences was that no oversight was given during the mobilization planning phase.

Congress is responsible under the Constitution to raise and support armies and to provide for organizing, arming, and disciplining the militia. Oversight of mobilization construction planning would appear to be a necessary requirement in fulfilling these constitutional responsibilities. Currently it does not appear that Congress is concerned with mobilization beyond the manpower issues. History clearly shows that construction is a national policy issue. As Thomason stated in 1941, "Congress must share in any censure."

If one waits until after the fact, there can only be censure and recommendations for future generations. One reason that no effective Congressional oversight exists may be the fact that at least three committees are involved. Civil Works are within the purview of the Public Works Committees; military construction is within the purview of the Armed Services Committees; and the health of the contract construction industry is within the purview of Small Business and Commerce Committees.

Congressional inquiry before the fact is necessary to prevent history from repeating itself. Construction need not be a pacing issue of significant magnitude. Requiring that viable mobilization construction plans be laid out for public inspection can only add to the defense potential of the nation, thereby enhancing the deterrent value of the Total Force Policy. Without having a detailed M-day construction program to support mobilization plans, the strategies of forward basing, ready reserves, and rapid deployment are in serious question no matter what scenario is hypothesized.

Posturing for the Future

Despite the numerous improvements needed, there are many strengths associated with the nation's emergency preparedness in the area of construction support. Many of the lessons of the past are incorporated in institutions and national processes. There exists on the positive side of the nation's construction capabilities ledger:
— a strong and responsive contract construction industry,
— a large decentralized Army civil works program throughout the country,
— a continuing history of effective response in preparing for and mitigating damage in natural disasters, and
— a healthy civil-military synergism between industry and the Corps of Engineers in large civil works enterprises.

But on the other side of the ledger there exists considerable deterioration through shortcomings:
— to plan construction requirements for M-day and beyond and to pro-

vide resources for detailed planning, design, and dormant contracting (DOD),
— to provide resources for the planning and design requirement (DOD, OMB, Congress),
— to plan the prudent use of emergency powers (DOD),
— to develop procedures for rapid reallocation and refocus of national construction resources during mobilization (DOD and FEMA), and
— to maintain effective oversight of mobilization preparedness (Congress).

Correcting these shortcomings would materially improve the posture of the Corps of Engineers to support the nation in a national defense emergency.

Recommendations for Action

In view of evident weaknesses in planning for mobilization, the following directions are recommended to lessen the impact of construction on any future mobilization and to take advantage of the fundamental strength of the U.S. contract construction industry.

For Congress:
— establish oversight of national emergency preparedness with particular emphasis on mobilization; and,
— authorize and appropriate funds to design a M-day to M + 180 Construction Program.

For the Federal Emergency Management Agency:
— require all agencies with national emergency preparedness responsibilities to review emergency provisions in law and establish procedures for rapid implementation in times of emergency;
— examine the reliefs contained in the new bodies of law, particularly environmental, safety, and social law, for applicability to the full spectrum of national emergency conditions and create legislative proposals where reliefs are inadequate for the emergency conditions hypothesized;
— include mobilization within the spectrum of national emergency conditions, while insuring that other agencies with a role in defense mobilization integrate their plans into DOD mobilization plans; and,
— cause national emergency preparedness resources to be programmed as separate line items within each agency's program and budget so that the total resources for emergency preparation and execution are visible for management.

For the Department of Defense:
— cause the services to develop a detailed M-day to M + 180–day construction support plan for full mobilization rapid deployment, with the development of detailed plans for the historical contingency

of delayed deployment;
— cause the Services to define construction requirements for total mobilization and develop concepts and plans for meeting the requirements;
— review historical precedent and procedures for implementing emergency provisions contained in the U.S. Code and provide guidance for planning the use of these provisions;
— establish criteria and policies for the use of Cost Plus Fixed Fee construction contracts and publish guidance; and,
— allocate resources for negotiating dormant contracts for certain critical mobilization construction projects.

For the Secretary of the Army:
— make the Assistant Secretary of the Army (CW) the executive agent for integrating civil works construction assets into DOD construction plans beyond M-day.

For the Assistant Secretary of the Army (CW):
— cause national emergency preparedness planning for civil works, including planning for mobilization construction using civil works resources, to be presented to Congress as a single line item rather than as the "overhead" part of all civil works projects; and,
— take action to bring the construction industry into mobilization planning by establishing advisory boards utilizing distinguished membership of the Society of American Military Engineers and other professional engineer societies.

Among all the disasters that befall man, war must surely be the worst. It would appear that war is the one disaster whose occurrence humans could avoid. The United States can design and build great breastworks to protect its heartland from the devastating thirty-year flood and provide earthquake protection in the tallest buildings. These precautions work—not perfectly—but loss of life and property can be substantially reduced. In almost all cases, the benefits returned far exceed the costs.

The lessons of history demonstrate that a prudent national posture would allow for a mobilization requiring construction on the order of 5% of current GNP. Construction is not only a mobilization pacing issue, it is a significant national emergency planning issue. It is imperative that resources be allocated for a national emergency planning effort. Perhaps through these means another dimension can be added to the deterrence posture of the West.

NOTES

1. The best historical evidence of construction as a mobilization pacing issue is contained in the findings of the Truman Committee Hearings and

Reports. See in particular:
U.S. Congress, Senate, Special Committee Investigating the National Defense Program, 77th Cong., 1st sess., *Hearings*. Parts 1 and 6, 1941.
U.S. Congress, Senate, Special Committee Investigating the National Defense Program, 77th Cong., 1st sess., *Report*. No. 480, Part 2, 1941.

2. John J. Fialka, "All Kinds of Foul-up Hamper Army Mobilization," *Washington Star*, 3 November 1979.

3. Department of the Army, U.S. Army Corps of Engineers Studies Center, *Corps Mobilization Capabilities, Requirements and Planning*, Washington, D.C., March 1980, p. 49.

4. Paul N. Howard, "President's Message," *Constructor*, Washington, D.C., December 1979, p. 2. See also U.S. Department of Commerce, Construction Review, Vol. 25, No. 3, March 1979, p. 60.

5. U.S. Department of Commerce, *Construction Review*, Vol. 24, No. 8, December 1978, pp. 1-5.

6. LTG John W. Morris, *The Military Engineers*, Vol. 72, No. 465, pp. 4-8.

7. U.S. Congress, House, Committee on Military Affairs, *Hearings before the Committee on Military Affairs*. 77th Cong., 1st sess., 30 September 1941, p. 11. Reaffirmed by C.W. Duncan, Jr., Deputy Secretary of Defense, in a memorandum for the Director, Office of Management and Budget, Washington, D.C., 8 January 1979. For a foreign analysis on this point see G.N. Tack, "The Engineer Task in Future Wars," *Royal Engineer*, Vol. 68, June 1954, pp. 108-123.

8. *Military Peace Establishment Act*, 1 Stat. 132 (1802). *Appropriations for the Military Establishment Act*, 1 Stat. 183 (1824). *Military Peace Establishment Act*, 2 Stat. 206 (1803). It is interesting to note that the authorization and appropriations creating a Corps of Engineers are contained in documents deliberately posturing the Army for peace. The first missions were to survey water and overland routes.

9. *Improvement of the Ohio and Mississippi Rivers Act*, 4 Stat. 32 (1824). This act formalized the role of the Army Corps of Engineers in water resource development. See also W.J. Hull and R.W. Hull, *The Origin and Development of the Waterways Policy of the United States* (Washington, D.C.: National Waterways Conference, Inc., 1967).

10. The dual role of Civil Works is vividly portrayed in the histories of the individual district offices. See for instance:
Department of the Army, Army Corps of Engineers, *History of the Honolulu District*, by Ellen Van Hatlen, Honolulu, 1970.
Department of the Army, Army Corps of Engineers, *Of Men and Rivers*, by Harry B. Mills, Vicksburg, 1978.
Department of the Army, Army Corps of Engineers, *History of the Los Angeles District, U.S. Army Corps of Engineers: 1895-1965*, by Anthony P. Turhollow, Los Angeles, 1975.
Department of the Army, Corps of Engineers, *A History of the Little Rock District, U.S. Army Corps of Engineers, 1881-1979*, by Floyd M. Clay, Washington, D.C., 1979.

11. Recent examples of natural disasters in which the corps played a major role in cleanup operations are: Mt. St. Helens' eruptions, Hurricane Frederick, and the Wichita Falls, Tx., tornados.

12. Reported in *Army Research Development and Acquisition*, Vol. 21, No. 21, March-April 1980, p. 4.

13. Truman Committee, *Hearings*, Part 1, Op. Cit., p. 239.
14. Ibid., Part 7, p. 2018.
15. Lenore Fine, and Jesse A. Remington, *The Corps of Engineers: Construction in the United States*; one in a series on "The United States Army in World War II, The Technical Services," (Washington, D.C.: Office of the Chief of Military History, U.S. Army) 1972, p. 392.
16. Truman Committee, *Hearings*, Part 7, Op. Cit., p. 2036.
17. U.S. Department of Commerce, "Construction Review," Vol. 24, No. 8, December 1978, pp. 1-5.
18. Fine and Remington, Op. Cit., p. 703.
19. Truman Committee, *Hearings*, Part 1, Op. Cit., p. 71.
20. *Corps Mobilization Capabilities, Requirements and Planning*, Op. Cit., pp. 41-58.
21. These figures are derived from the historical relationships shown in Figure 1.
22. 41 Stat. 11.
23. 90 Stat. 1255.
24. Fine and Remington, Op. Cit., p. 562.
25. Truman Committee, *Report*, Op. Cit., pp. 17-21.
26. See Fine and Remington, Op. Cit., for discussions of the operations and effectiveness of WW I Board of Reviews of Construction and the WW II Construction Advisory Committee, Construction Contract Board, and National Advisory Council on Real Estate.
27. U.S. President, Executive Order 12127, *Federal Register*, Vol. 44, No. 65, 3 April 1979, p. 19367. See also U.S. President, Executive Order 12148, *Federal Register*, Vol. 44, No. 143, 24 July 1979, p. 43239.
28. See the Annual Report of the Chief of Engineers for each year 1940 through 1945. Civil Works declined from a high of $262 million in 1940 to a low of $135 million in 1945. New Starts were drastically reduced. These reports can be found in the Office of Chief of Engineers and the Library of Congress.
29. Fine and Remington, Op. Cit., p. 592.
30. U.S. Congress, Senate, Committee on Military Affairs, *Hearings*, Part 4, Washington, D.C., February 1918.
31. Thomason chaired the House committee and Truman chaired the Senate committee.

Section IV

Current Vulnerabilities and Mobilization within the Wider Free World Context

12

Strategic and Critical Materials

Alton D. Slay

From its earliest days and until World War II, the United States basically was a self-sufficient country. It is still self-sufficient in agriculture, but, in terms of many essential nonfuel minerals, the United States is a "have not" nation.

It may surprise the average reader to learn that every person in the United States today requires 37,639 pounds of minerals each year. Almost 18,000 pounds of this staggering total is fuel; another 18,000 pounds falls in the category of nonmetals, like sand, gravel, stone, cement, salt and clays. The remainder is perhaps the most urgently important to defense mobilization—the 1,324 pounds of metal required each year by every man, woman and child in the United States. The United States Gross National Product is now over $2-1/2 trillion in 1981 dollars. To support such a GNP requires on the order of $250 billion—or 10 trillion pounds—of raw materials.

One should note that the United States imported almost 30 billion dollars worth of nonfuel minerals last year. It is a matter of record that the United States is more than 50% dependent on imports for 23 of the 40 most essential nonfuel minerals. Worse yet, the United States is almost totally import dependent for 12 of the most critical of these, and many of them come exclusively from very unstable areas of the world. On the other hand, the Soviet Union is totally independent of foreign sources for all but 5 of these 40 minerals and in none of these 5 does this dependency exceed 50%.

Siberia and Southern Africa contain 99% of the world's manganese ore; 97% of the world's vanadium; 96% of the world's chrome; 87% of the world's diamonds; 69% of the world's gold; 60% of the world's vermiculite; and 50% of the world's fluorspar, iron ore, asbestos, and uranium. Zaire and Zambia alone have 52% of the world's supply of cobalt and currently provide 65% of the world's needs and 90% of our needs.

As a bench mark, OPEC controls only 52% of the world's oil supply. Third World nonfuel mineral cartels, based on the OPEC example, are brewing.

Back in 1939, Congress recognized the danger of constrained mineral resources when it passed the Strategic Materials Act. After World War II, the problem was addressed again by the Strategic and Critical Materials Stockpile Act of 1946, creating a strategic and critical materials stockpile for use in time of war. That stockpile was supposed to cover defense-related purposes only; but there have been sales from the stockpile to balance the budget, to control commodity prices, and to reduce inflation. This has severely hurt the system. Today, the stockpile is characterized by gross imbalances, deficits and overages.

Currently, the stockpile is woefully short in many of these essential minerals. Stockpile shortages exist in 37 critical materials amounting to a total of $11 billion or 61% of the desired inventory of $18 billion. There is also a surplus of about $6 billion in unneeded materials. Until the budget year 1981, no purchases had been made to add to the stockpile since 1960. The 1981 budget contains $100 million for that purpose. Not considering inflation, it will take over a century to bring the stockpile up to established goals if we spend $100 million on the stockpile each year.

The United States could reduce its dependence on foreign sources for raw materials through expansion of domestic sources for cobalt, bauxite, chromium, platinum, zinc, fluorspar, gold, nickel, titanium, and many others. Every pound of productive capacity reduces the stockpile requirement by 3 pounds. It takes up to ten years to bring a mineral deposit into production without any federal constraints to mining. But eighty different federal laws administered by twenty different federal agencies constrain mineral exploration and mining operations in the United States. As a result of these laws, over 75% of the public land in the United States has either been withdrawn or severely restricted from mining and mineral exploration—most of it in the last few years. This is equivalent to an area the size of the entire United States east of the Mississippi River. And most of that land has been withdrawn in the most heavily mineralized areas of the country.

Even when we have adequate supplies of basic materials from friendly sources, there are often bottlenecks in processing capacity. Titanium is one example. In the United States, there are only three companies which process titanium ore and their production falls 15% to 20% short of domestic demand. As another example, there are only three remaining United States suppliers of large forgings.

This shrinking industrial base, coupled with increasing worldwide demand, has resulted in greatly lengthened lead times—by as much as 200%—and greatly escalated costs—a price rise of as much as 300% just in the last two years.

There are many other problems which beset our industry today, but without a dependable raw material base, solutions to these secondary difficulties will be of little help in solving the total national industrial base problem.

Action is needed to encourage expansion of domestic raw and processed critical materials, and/or to build up the national stockpile of critical materials. Development of substitutes for critical materials in short domestic supply should be encouraged by every possible means, and development of manufacturing processes which conserve critical materials should receive similar emphasis.

The dimensions of the strategic materials problem can best be appreciated by investigating the status of United States dependence on four key substances—cobalt, manganese, chromium, and the bauxite/alumina family of minerals.

— Cobalt is critical to defense production, and the United States imports every pound of cobalt it uses. An average of about 1,000 pounds of it is in each jet engine made. Cobalt is used to sinter tungsten carbide for tools and drilling bits. Total U.S. consumption has averaged about 10,000 short tons annually for the last several years, 75% of which was imported from southern African nations, particularly Zaire and Zambia. The national stockpile of cobalt stands at 48% of the current goal.

The identified cobalt resources of the United States exceed 700,000 tons and are mainly located in the midwest and far west, but there has been no domestic mining since 1979. In the United States, two former sources of cobalt production are under active consideration for redevelopment. Noranda Mines, a Canadian firm, anticipates that approximately 2000 metric tons per year could be produced from the Blackbird deposits in Idaho. Auschutz Uranium Corporation has purchased the former Madison Cobalt Mine at Fredericktown, Missouri, and indicates a potential for producing 700MT to 900MT per year. Major concerns by both companies are that cobalt prices could drop below $15 per pound making U.S. deposits uneconomical to develop. Their legitimate concern is that current world prices are being held artificially high by Zaire and Zambia. Another concern relates to environmental restriction.

In 1980, the Federal Emergency Management Agency (FEMA) drafted a proposal to establish a purchase guarantee program under Title III of the Defense Production Act, to guarantee a floor price for cobalt. Unfortunately, the proposal did not survive the budgetary process.

— No adequate substitute currently exists for titanium, a metal needed in large quantity for a wide range of defense-related projects.

Only three domestic producers of titanium sponge currently operate—TIMET, OREMET, and RMI. (Dow HOWMET is experimenting with a new production process but has not yet decided to produce titanium.) The combined capacity of these three producers is about 52 million pounds of sponge per year; planned expansions will increase production to approximately 60 million pounds per year by 1983.

Current domestic demand is about 15% in excess of domestic supply, as it has been for the past several years. In 1980, the United States imported 4,500 short tons of sponge, up 80% over 1979 and up over 200% from 1978. 1982 demand has been projected to be about 68 million pounds, but that projection does not include defense programs such as the MX, CX, a new bomber and the KC-135 re-engine project. If approved, these efforts could boost total demand for titanium sponge to 85 million pounds by Fiscal Year 1984; demand well in excess of 100 million pounds per year may be expected by 1985. As an added consideration, the national stockpile contains only 21,465 short tons of usable sponge versus a goal of 195,000 short tons—a deficit of 89%.

The United States produces very little rutile (the mineral containing titanium dioxide); in 1979, foreign sources provided 100% of the U.S. consumption. In 1980, an Australian firm at Green Cove Springs, Florida, geared up to produce about 25,000 tons of rutile per year, but consumption is running around 330,000 short tons per year, leaving the United States well over 90% import dependent.

Currently, most of our rutile comes from Australia—a reliable and friendly source—but since the source is many thousands of miles away, it depends upon availability of sea transport which could be effectively cut off in some future conflict. Domestic substitutes would seem to be called for.

Among the substitutes for rutile are ilmenite, titaneferous slag and synthetic rutile made from ilmenite. Currently, these materials are used for pigments and welding rod coatings, but environmental and economic problems must be addressed and solved before these substitutes can gain more widespread acceptance.

Other problems include land use conflict along the Atlantic coast where black sand deposits exist, and the manufacture of pigment or titanium tetrachloride (feed for sponge) from ilmenite uses a sulphate process. This process results in 3-1/2 tons of waste per ton of product, compared to only 600 pounds of waste per ton of product from rutile processing which uses a chloride process. There is an obvious environmental concern with sulphates over water pollution. A method exists whereby acid wastes from ilmenite processing can be treated with calcium carbonate and lime to produce a gypsum-like product which can be used in wall board and cement, but it is an expensive operation. Much more work needs to be done to solve these waste problems.

Since 1976, U.S. consumption of titanium metal has doubled; consumption of titanium products will skyrocket starting in 1983. We face a potentially critical shortage of titanium in virtually every form. A prudent alternative might be the creation of incentives for expansion of titanium metal manufacturing. If production is not increased, the 84% lead time increases for titanium forgings which have occurred since 1978 may be dwarfed by future shortages.

Titanium is the most expensive of all processed metals in terms of energy used per pound. 80% of this energy is used to convert raw rutile into sponge, with the remaining energy needed to turn the sponge into ingot—about the same amount of energy required to make steel.

Because of this high energy use and the probable bottleneck problem discussed earlier, stockpiling of processed titanium metal should be considered. Currently, the stockpile has a goal only for sponge. Stockpiling metal would have the very salutary side effects of stockpiling energy as well as providing a much better surge capability for defense related products made of titanium.

Last year, the United States exported 8,800 short tons of new titanium scrap, and recycled 19,000 short tons. A large amount of the recycled metal was used in combination with sponge to make titanium metal. Since titanium sponge and scrap are combined in producing ingot, if demand for sponge surges, the demand for new scrap titanium will climb in direct proportion. Thus, it seems prudent to guard against a bottleneck by reducing the flow of titanium scrap to overseas customers until domestic production reaches adequate levels.

— The United States is 98% dependent on imports for manganese and ferromanganese. The remaining 2% is obtained through recycling. There are no known economically recoverable deposits of manganese in the United States. Over half of the 1,500,000 short tons of manganese and ferromanganese imported last year came from Southern Africa with Gabon alone furnishing 44%. Southern Africa contains 53% of the world's known reserves of manganese ore. The country of South Africa and the Soviet Union account for 90% of the world's known reserves. The national stockpile contains 89% of the established goal for metallurgical manganese ore, and is in excess by 37% of high carbon ferromanganese and by 60% in battery and chemical grade ore.

Manganese is essential for making steel; ferromanganese is the principal form of the mineral used in steel production. Since much of the United States' industrial base depends on steel, a sure supply of manganese is vital. In recent years, the United States has imported no manganese from South Africa which has half of the world's reserves. For political reasons, American imports have come from countries which have only 10% of the world's reserves (Brazil—less than 2%; Australia—6%; and Gabon—less than 3%). This poses no immediate problem, but should emphasize the long term fragility of the supply of manganese. There are two alternatives, with serious political and economic costs. The first alternative is sea bed mining; the second is establishing the nation of South Africa as a principal source of supply. No attempt will be made here to evaluate the second alternative since the political considerations are likely to remain complex. But sea bed mining deserves close attention.

Extensive deposits of manganese oxide rest on large areas of the ocean floor, particularly in the Pacific Ocean between the Tropics of Cancer and Capricorn. Vast deposits of nodules on the ocean floor contain not only manganese, but nickel, copper, and cobalt as well. Estimates vary as to the capital required to start a sea bed mining operation, but it will certainly be a very costly undertaking.

— The United States mines no chromium ore; 91% is imported and the remaining 9% is obtained through recycling of stainless steel scrap. 40% of our chromite ore comes from South Africa, 16% from the Soviet Union, 15% from the Philippines, 10% from Turkey and 19% from elsewhere. Processed ferrochromium comes from South Africa (62%), Yugoslavia (11%), Zimbabwe (9%), Japan (5%), and others (1%).

99% of the world's reserves of chromite—about 36 billion tons—is in South Africa and Zimbabwe. This huge amount is enough to last for centuries. The United States has some deposits in Montana and in beach sands in Oregon, but it is highly doubtful that these deposits will ever be mined without substantial involvement by the federal government due to the poor economics of such a venture as well as rather severe environmental considerations. The stockpile contains just under 55% of the established goal of 4,725,000 short tons of chromite ore. An additional 530,000 tons of non-stockpile grade chromite ore is stockpiled but does not count against the goal.

There are several potential substitutes for chromium but all have drawbacks—principally performance and cost. Nickel, zinc, cadmium, cobalt, molybdenum and vanadium can replace it for uses with steel and iron. Mangesite and zircon have potential as replacement in refractory applications, and titanium can be used in chemical processing equipment. Added research and development funds are needed to find solutions for some of the performance and cost problems associated with these alternatives.

Much more needs to be done to conserve and reclaim chromium. If scrap dealers across the country receive the proper incentives, enough stainless steel scrap could be collected to make a large scale reclamation industry feasible. Also, techniques for surface treatment (surface alloying) of steel for certain applications instead of a total alloy are certainly worth pursuing. Finally, development of economical processes for recovery of chromium from latterites and low grade chromite ores is needed.

— The United States uses from 5 to 6 million short tons of aluminum metal every year, and will need almost 10 million tons per year by 1990. Most of the primary aluminum metal made in this country uses bauxite imported from Jamaica (42%), Guinea (32%), and Surinam (11%). Less than 10% of the bauxite used in the United States is mined domestically. Deposits are also not large—roughly 40 million tons as compared to 23 billion tons of known economically recoverable reserves worldwide. Perhaps as much as 50 billion tons of bauxite exist if subeconomic and undiscovered deposits can be tapped. It is apparent, therefore, that the basic raw material for aluminum will not soon disappear. But one should recall our World War II experience—in 1942, 25% of the ships that left Surinam and British Guiana were sunk by German U-boats—quite regularly within sight of our shores.

A related factor is the extent of Soviet/Cuban influence in the bauxite producing areas of the Caribbean. Also, eleven of the major bauxite exporting countries are members of the "International Bauxite Association" which was established, like OPEC, to control prices and, if necessary, supply as well. The organization has been instrumental in increasing the taxes on bauxite production to the extent that the tax is the largest element of cost to U.S. importers. The leverage associated with the fact that the United States imports such a large amount of bauxite—around 15 million short tons per year—certainly has not escaped notice by that organization nor by the Soviet Union. Therefore, it seems prudent to develop domestic alternatives.

In addition to subeconomic deposits of bauxite in the United States estimated at around 300 million short tons, the United States has potentially large resources for producing alumina from domestically available nonbauxite materials. These materials include Kaolin clays abundantly available in the southeast United States, anorthosite deposits in Wyoming and Utah, and alunite, coal wastes, and oil shales. Research on producing alumina from such materials has been carried on for several years but at a relatively low level of funding. Also hindering the efforts are environmental problems associated with the disposal of some of the residues from production of alumina.

The United States imports 250,000 tons of refractory grade bauxite each year. Refractory bauxite is the rarest and purest of all bauxite ores in natural state. Against a goal of 1,422,000 short tons, only 177,000 tons are currently contained in the stockpile. Today, there is only one source in the western world for refractory bauxite—Guyana—an unreliable supplier at best since governmental nationalization of the industry. The Peoples Republic of China has supplied several hundred thousand tons of the material but it is of a far inferior grade. Aluminous refractories could be manufactured from alumina extracted from Kaolin clays and, perhaps anorthosite, but no major R & D effort has been mounted to develop a production process.

Many other examples of critical problems in our raw and processed minerals industry exist, but the underlying theme remains; these problems are national in scope and will require a serious national commitment. Aggressive implementation of a sound national nonfuels mineral policy is badly needed. The goals set forth in the Mining and Minerals Policy Act of 1970 and expanded by the National Materials and Minerals Policy Act of 1980 are adequate, but little has been done to attain these goals.

More specifically, Congressional oversight should be exercised to ensure that the nation's mineral needs and resources are adequately considered in all actions and decisions of Federal Agencies and Departments. The national stockpile program must be rejuvenated, to support adequate stockpile goals; a long term commitment must be made to expand productive capacity; and we need tax reform to create incentives for capital investment in new industrial plants and equipment. Finally, Congress should increase domestic supply of critical materials whenever possible, through incentives such as use of Title III of the Defense Production Act of 1950.

In 1973, Leonid Brezhnev declared, "Our aim is to gain control of the two great treasure houses on which the West depends—the energy treasure house of the Persian Gulf and the mineral treasure house of Central and Southern Africa." America's dependence on the foreign "mineral treasure house" need not become a strategic vulnerability. A clear and concise statement of a national energy and minerals policy, adequately funded and aggressively implemented, will go far towards correcting this problem. President Brezhnev certainly understood the potential advantages of American inaction, and presumably so does General Secretary Andropov.

13

Oil and Western Security: The Mobilization Dilemma

David A. Deese

Oil and other fossil fuels are fundamental to Western security. Since World War I, nations' success in executing their grand strategies has to an important degree hinged on their access to energy supplies. In the past the United States has muddled through with a long mobilization after the commencement of hostilities. Today, however, a sharp decline in U.S. and Western control over world energy supplies makes energy readiness in advance of conflict absolutely essential. Yet the severe energy vulnerability of the West through at least the 1980s may preclude effective mobilization for military conflicts.

During war, international crises, and key peacetime policy decisions, petroleum has influenced strategy in several distinct ways. It has been an important factor in the formulation of strategy during both peacetime and war. Frequently it has also been one cause of the outbreak of hostilities, and one factor in the process of bringing about peace. Finally, it has been central to the ability of nations to execute strategies, for example, as an essential element of national mobilization. This chapter analyzes energy, especially oil, as a factor in Western mobilization.

The purpose of analyzing the ability of Western nations to mobilize is threefold. Most important is reducing the fears and uncertainties that arise during international crises, especially those involving the world oil market, and thus strengthening the deterrence and prevention of conflict that occurs as a result of miscalculation or error. Second, it is also crucial to reduce the costs of oil supply disruptions during peacetime to the civilian economies of the West. This includes a reduction in the probability that Western oil import vulnerability can become a coercive tool of foreign policy in the hands of the oil exporters or the Soviet Union. Finally, if it becomes necessary, Western nations must stand ready to mobilize and fight a war in the Persian Gulf, Europe, or elsewhere.

Although most war planning in the United States and NATO has for decades assumed rapid escalation to a nuclear exchange, this seems to be changing. At precisely the time in the 1970s that the United States lost the ability to control events in the world oil market, war planning evolved to include major conventional wars. The evolution reflects, in part, vital Western interests in the Persian Gulf and the need to dissuade the Soviet Union from undertaking any activity that could lead to a conventional war between, or even involving, the superpowers in this region. We thus reach a central hypothesis of the analysis: the 1970s brought forth simultaneously both a significant, increasing probability of major conventional warfare (with the attendant demand for the capacity to mobilize and dramatically increase petroleum supplies), and a significant probability that regional instabilities, war, or denial or manipulation by the Soviet Union could make unavailable for months to years part or most of the 40% of Western oil consumption that comes from the Persian Gulf. These possibilities have evolved at a time when the United States has lost the ability not only to fulfill its own wartime needs but also to supply the Allies with petroleum for war. The petroleum import levels and sources in Figure 1 show that in 1980 key Western nations got over one half of their imports from the Persian Gulf, such

Figure 1

NET IMPORTS OF CRUDE OIL AND REFINED PRODUCTS
1ST HALF 1980
(THOUSAND BARRELS/DAY)

IMPORTERS	NET IMPORTS	PERSIAN GULF (PG)	SAUDI ARABIA	IRAN	IRAQ	OTHER PG	TOTAL OPEC	OTHER FREE WORLD	USSR	OTHER COMMUNIST
US	7066	1887	1391	43	43	410	5052	2007	-4	11
CANADA	181	255	203	3	19	30	440	-259	0	0
WEST GERMANY	2705	851	405	215	41	190	1615	839	136	115
FRANCE	2325	1674	771	80	547	276	2134	38	146	7
UK	171	834	369	39	94	332	895	-751	26	1
ITALY	1952	1057	620	25	252	160	1672	108	123	49
OTHER EEC*	3711	848	447	38	19	344	1152	2430	94	35
JAPAN	5027	3215	1387	537	367	924	4039	826	7	155

*EEC – IRELAND + NORWAY = NATO

Source: U.S. Department of Defense

as France at 73%, Japan at 65%, and Italy at 54%. Without large and well-protected stockpiles in the theater, any major war in the Persian Gulf would make full Western mobilization extremely difficult, if not impossible, especially for conflicts longer than six months or a year; it could thus also sharply increase the probability of escalation to a nuclear war.

Western Petroleum Imports and Military Consumption

The focus for this analysis is crude oil and petroleum products rather than all energy supplies. The overwhelming reliance of Western nations on energy imports remains heavily petroleum-based. Petroleum made up 92% of all U.S. energy imports in 1979 and 1980. When combined with natural gas, this constituted 99% of all U.S. energy imports in 1979 and 1980, and 19% to 23% of all U.S. energy consumption in 1979 and 1980.[1] For major West European nations such as West Germany, Italy and France, crude oil and products made up about 85% of all energy imports throughout the mid to late 1970s. Petroleum and natural gas together account for 90% to 100% of all their energy imports.

In France and Italy coal accounted for only 8% to 10% of imports. Most West European nations will, however, be deriving increasing proportions of their energy import needs from natural gas and coal in the 1980s and 1990s. For this reason, it is also important to monitor the sources and levels of nonpetroleum imports, especially natural gas, with respect to their effects on mobilization capabilities. This applies particularly to the possibility of large natural gas exports in the 1980s from the Soviet Union to Western Europe, especially to Italy, West Germany, and France.

Crude oil, and petroleum products in particular, are also central to this analysis because they are much more important to the military services than to the civilian economy. Figure 2 shows that petroleum covered over 67% of energy consumption by the U.S. Department of Defense in the Fiscal Year 1980, as opposed to about 45% for the country overall. This forms a dramatic comparison when placed in the context of Figure 3, the division of Department of Defense petroleum use by military service and operational function. By far the largest component of DOD petroleum use, about 84%, supports ship and aircraft operations. Not only is the Defense Department heavily reliant on oil, but oil also goes largely to support the most vital functions of its mission. Furthermore, the two-thirds of DOD petroleum consumption used for aircraft requires very high-grade products and refining equipment; the general conversion is 2 barrels of crude oil for every barrel of military products. Finally, during mobilization and wartime conditions, support of vital aircraft, ship and ground operations will dramatically increase energy consumption—particularly use of high-grade petroleum products. Thus, it also becomes clear why achieving major peacetime advances in DOD energy conservation is difficult without degrading the operational readiness of both strategic and tactical forces.

Figure 2
DEPARTMENT OF DEFENSE ENERGY CONSUMPTION FY 1980

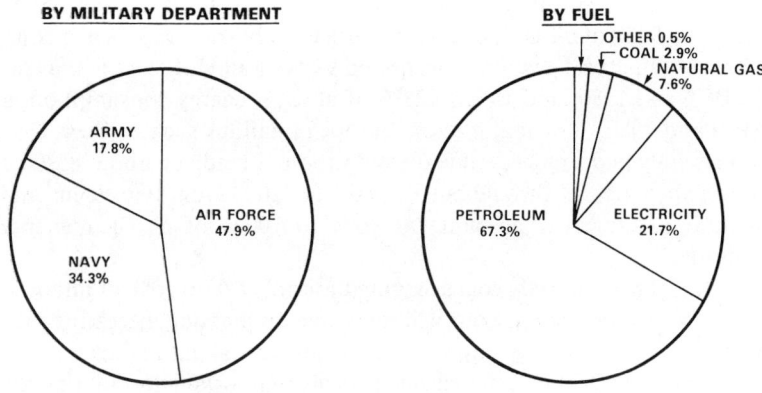

TOTAL ENERGY CONSUMPTION
1.4 QUADRILLION BTU

Source: U.S. Department of Defense

The Department of Defense consumes over 250 million barrels (mb) per year in oil equivalent energy, making it the largest single U.S. energy consumer. This amounts to almost .5 mbd in petroleum or .7 mbd in total energy in oil equivalent. In 1980, over 2% of U.S. energy consumption and 80% of federal sector consumption was in the Department of Defense. By April 1981, DOD use was up to about 2.7% of total U.S. consumption due to reduced overall U.S. energy use. DOD energy costs in fiscal year 1981 exceeded $10 billion, or over 5% of its approximately $200 billion budget. This is a dramatic increase over 1973, at under $2.6 billion, and even 1978, at just over $4 billion. Oil alone for the Defense Department now costs about $7.5 billion.

The Department of Defense relies heavily on energy, especially oil, for the operational readiness of the strategic and tactical forces. In Fiscal Year 1980, oil constituted 68% of DOD energy use and over 78% of its total energy costs. It uses 50% of the gasoline, 85% of the heating

Figure 3

DEPARTMENT OF DEFENSE PETROLEUM CONSUMPTION FY 1980

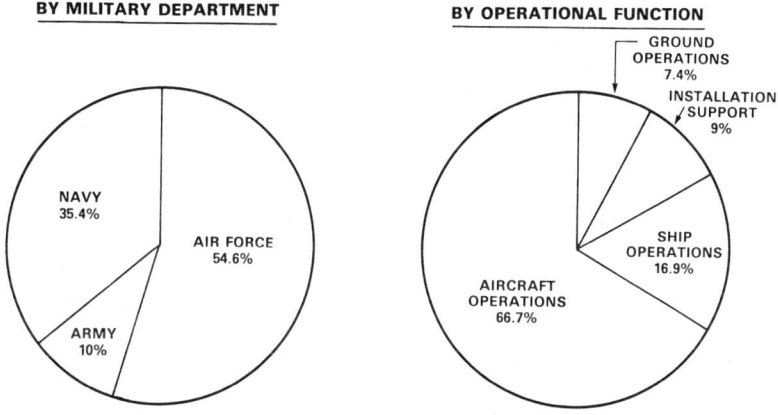

TOTAL
PETROLEUM CONSUMPTION
169.5 MILLION BARRELS

Source: U.S. Department of Defense

oil, and almost 100% of the jet fuel in the federal government. U.S. national, and broader Western, security is thus obviously dependent on assured access to adequate petroleum products at all times, but especially during period of heightened tension or international crisis. Our record to date even in noncrisis periods is not encouraging. We now face decreased readiness and operational effectiveness, especially in NATO, due in part to reductions in petroleum consumption. During the relatively minor oil crises of 1973-1974 and 1979, the Department of Defense, in particular, was hard pressed to maintain even normal operational capabilities due to fuel shortages.

United States, Japanese or NATO petroleum consumption during peace, mobilization and war can be divided into four categories. Figure 4 shows that civilian use is largely "nonessential" during peace, with about .5 mbd of petroleum products going to the approximately 100,000 "defense-related" suppliers such as Lockheed. During peacetime the only military petroleum use comes from the .5 mbd in the "direct" category since indirect use of civilian transportation assets starts only in mobilization or other emergency situations.

In order to determine approximate Western energy demand during mobilization and war, we make two simplifying assumptions. Consumption for petroleum rather than for energy overall is calculated due to data constraints. While relatively little appears to be known in the appropriate Departments of Energy and Defense offices about petroleum use during mobilization and various wartime contingencies, even less appears to be known about other energy sources. We also assume a conventional war of at least one year in duration; this includes either the 1½-war scenario involving the superpowers, or a limited war with Rapid Deployment Joint Task Force participation (RDJTF) and no direct Soviet involvement.

Under the limited or major war contingencies, the rates of increase and actual levels reached for petroleum consumption can only be estimated. During World War II, direct military consumption alone increased from 1% to 33% of all U.S. petroleum production.[2] The United States and the Allies were hindered by serious problems in supplying the required quantities of oil almost throughout the War, with easing of the shortages by 1944.[3] During the 1980s, nonessential civilian demand in the United States may increase as economic growth improves over the poor performance of 1980. Under mobilization the nonessential civilian sector would probably demand more petroleum, but would be unable to obtain even the prior peacetime level since it would become the source for fulfilling increasing military needs. We must also carefully analyze the indirect military effects of curtailing the nonessential civilian sector. If some of the movement of regular or reserve troops around the United States is, for example, assumed to take place on civilian carriers, this would be directly affected by allocation of fuel away from this sector. As will be seen, the DOD relies heavily on immediate access to this oil under the Defense Production Act of 1950. The remaining three sectors would pose rapidly escalating demands for oil under mobilization. As shown in Figure 4, defense-related civilian use by the 100,000 suppliers of military products would increase by at least factors of two to three, peaking at about 1.5 mbd. These numbers are only estimates since even peacetime consumption in this sector is not known exactly. Direct military consumption would scale up in approximately the same proportions, but these numbers are more accurate since we know that consumption was 170 mb, or about .5 mbd, in 1980. Depending on the degree of pre-positioned fuel available, consumption for the RDJTF could be even higher since both airlifts for logistical support and in-flight refueling for large numbers of attack aircraft over long distances consume very large quantities of fuel.

The final category, indirect military consumption, includes all civilian aircraft, especially under agreement with United Airlines, ship charters and trains and trucks that become available for conversion to military use. Conversion can occur at limited levels under authority up

Figure 4

U.S. Petroleum Consumption (mbd)

Nonessential*	Peacetime (1980)	Limited War (1980s)	1½ Wars
Civilian Nonessential*	15.5	~16.0	~18.0
Defense Related (Lockheed)	.5	~1.0	~1.5
Military Direct (Military Services)**	.5	~1.0	1.5
Indirect (Conversion to military use)	0	1.0 ???	
Total	16.5 mbd	19.0 mbd	~21 mbd

*This category is based on 1980 data, which are low in part due to very slow economic growth.

Other NATO direct military petroleum use starts at about 1 mbd in peacetime; nonessential civilian use is about 13 or 14 mbd.

Source: U.S. Department of Defense and estimates by the author.

to the Secretary of Defense; large-scale conversion requires that the President authorize use of the Defense Production Act of 1950. Fuel use for each of these forms of transport must be calculated and provided separately. Given the constant turnover of capital stock in each area of civilian transport and the uncertainties surrounding the rates and the ultimate levels of conversion to military use, the calculation of fuel use for this category is highly uncertain. There are already some indications that it would be difficult to fuel all the required trucks.

The level of conversion accomplished is in part a function of the length of mobilization and war. Longer wars would provide the time required to convert large fleets to military functions, but it is not at all certain that adequate fuel supplies would be available. For present purposes, we assume fuel use of about 1.0 mbd for this category of indirect military consumption.

Western Fuel Planning and Stockpiling

The DOD operates with two normally separate types of petroleum supplies: peacetime operating requirements and war reserves. Peacetime petroleum stocks meet training needs and all other demand for routine operational activities. War reserves are prepositioned to support forward deployed and reinforcing units in a particular theater of operations. They are designed to meet all needs between the outbreak of conflict and the time of resupply, or approximately thirty to sixty days (closer to the lower level for NATO). After this period resupply is assumed from the most secure U.S. source: the Gulf Coast and refining in the Caribbean.

Actual fuel planning and stockpiling is conducted on a regional or theater basis. Each principal theater forms a baseline: war in Korea; a major war in the Middle East; use of the RDJTF in a conflict, especially in the Persian Gulf; war between NATO and the Warsaw Pact (starting a specified number of days after mobilization begins); and a world war. In each case the most demanding scenario is supposedly assumed in calculating fuel needs. This normally excludes, for example, U.S. commercial and military operating stocks, foreign commercial stocks, and petroleum in tankers afloat.

The United States Department of Defense tasks each military service with setting war reserves for each petroleum product in consultation with the unified and specified commands. This process takes place under the annual guidance of the Secretary of Defense and the wartime contingency guidance of the Joint Chiefs of Staff. Each service calculates its required war reserves for every theater of operations at the beginning of the fiscal year. The Defense Fuel Supply Center (DFSC) then receives total fuel needs from the theater commanders. Once DFSC sets the storage locations, it publishes an Inventory Management Plan, which is updated quarterly. The DFSC and the services also calculate peacetime operating fuel needs, which are allocated in accordance with specific accompanying levels of operations and readiness.

Petroleum supply planning in NATO remains the responsibility of each country. Although NATO has set a minimal target for national war reserves, it has not yet really dealt with this problem. There is, for example, no provision for checking to determine national reserve levels. In NATO this effort is, however, aided by the military Central European Pipeline System, or CEPS, which crosses France and spills over into West Germany. While the significance of CEPS is limited since it does not extend into the mid and eastern portions of West Germany, it does connect with twenty-one refineries, a complex system of pipelines, railroad off-loading terminals and other logistical elements in the emergency oil distribution system. Efforts are now focused on trying to begin extensions of CEPS to the east and expansions of its capacity.

Military and defense-related petroleum consumption could be much less troubling for Western mobilization if large stockpiles were available to cushion against the sharp increases in demand that occur during emergencies. Petroleum could be drawn from both civilian and military stocks. If civilian stockpiles were very large and firm arrangements for military contingencies were in place, military needs could be met from civilian supplies while war reserves were held back for longer war requirements.

Unfortunately, civilian stockpiles offer little assistance in this regard. The public sector's Strategic Petroleum Reserve (SPR) is woefully behind schedule, with little over 10% of its intended level. To date, it is unavailable for use by the Department of Defense. By late 1981 the SPR held over 150 mb of crude oil, or about four weeks of U.S. petroleum imports equivalent at then current levels. The current schedule calls for a stabilization of the SPR fill rate at 200 to 256,000 bd, reaching 500 mb in storage by Fiscal Year 1984.

The U.S. SPR program continues to limp along under a number of serious handicaps. Bureaucratic competition simmers over control of the program by the Department of Energy, the Department of State, the Office of Management and Budget, and Department of Defense. Indecision and delay is the norm over the financial and management structures. The Department of Defense is unable to go much beyond strong expressions of concern over the necessity of maintaining continuity in fill rates and meeting the rescheduled storage levels. As long as no national security or defense component of the SPR is defined and no procedures exist for DOD access, planners certainly cannot rely on any crude supplies from these stocks. Since commercial sector stocks fluctuate both with seasonal demand and with conditions in U.S. and international markets, it is also impossible for the Department of Defense to rely on these for war planning. Furthermore, the only direct governmental access to these stocks short of involving the DPA of 1950 resides in a law which expired in September of 1982.[4]

As mentioned above, military petroleum stockpiles divide into operating and war reserve categories. The military services hold only several mb in operating stocks and a slightly higher level of war reserves. The Defense Logistics Agency (DLA) "normally" has over 20 mb in operating stocks and more than twice that amount in war reserves. Its operating stocks, however, fluctuate widely. There were over 10 mb in April 1981. DLA's war reserves have also been drawn down to nearly 10% of the total at times of tightening in the world oil market. Another several mb of storage space is needed for war reserves, but it is not currently available to either the military or the DLA.

Department of Defense planners can therefore count on a total steady-state war reserve of crude oil and petroleum products in the United States of about four months of peacetime direct military consumption, or about sixty days of such use for a limited contingency without Soviet involvement. Once the escalated levels of indirect military and defense-related civilian petroleum consumption are added, however, for a major conflict, those reserves would be depleted much more rapidly.

The Department of Defense has apparently begun to take at least three offsetting measures. Where it is possible to negotiate firm contracts, some reliance can be placed on host nation arrangements to increase stocks and to ease rapidly escalating costs. Tanks can also be leased in host nations and operating theaters to make short-term increases in stocks available. Military construction programs and new NATO infrastructure development provide assistance for the longer term.

Under existing U.S. petroleum requirements and constraints, the ability of the Department of Defense to mobilize effectively and to respond to a limited full war contingency is dubious at best. War reserves would be quickly depleted by consumption of about 1 to 1.4 mbd by direct military functions, perhaps 1 mbd by indirect military needs, and another 1 to 1.5 mbd in defense-related civilian production. At least over the foreseeable future, DOD cannot count on the SPR for any assistance.

Assuming, therefore, that most petroleum products must be taken from "nonessential" civilian sources, the feasibility of mobilization depends on where conflict breaks out. If Persian Gulf supplies are available, it may be feasible theoretically to conduct a major conventional war for at least six months by very strict allocation of supplies to the civilian economy. Since, however, the highest probability of conventional war at least through the 1980s must be assigned to the Persian Gulf, the mobilization problem is completely different.

In a Persian Gulf war, the United States would likely confront a dramatic disruption of the world oil market, and the loss of 15 to 20 mbd to the West, depending on the number of countries involved. These supplies, including about 2 mbd to the United States (see Figure 1), 3 mbd to Japan, and at least another 5 mbd to Western Europe, could easily be interrupted for 6 to 18 months. Even keeping a minimum civilian sector operating, meeting defense-related industrial production demands, and fueling U.S. military forces might consume 17 mbd, or about 7 mbd above U.S. petroleum production, and strain supplies very quickly. This includes no provision for assistance to NATO or Japan, and certainly no capacity to manage any simultaneous contingency beyond the Persian Gulf.

Even if the United States provides no military supplies for NATO or Japan, other international events will intervene. The United States must expect cuts in imports available to it from Mexico, Venezuela, Indonesia and elsewhere as the oil exporters try to allocate supplies to the nations that would be hardest hit by the disruption. The United States must also count on complying with its likely oil sharing obligations under the International Energy Agency's emergency oil sharing system. Under a disruption of 15 to 20 mbd, for example, the United States might have to provide several million barrels a day to Japan and Western Europe.

The Department of Defense also faces stiff competition for its petroleum product purchases in the domestic market. Lengthy contracts and burdensome procedures have made DOD a notoriously weak customer in the U.S. commercial oil market, especially during the crisis in 1979. The Department was unable to compete with corporate customers, and supply shortages led to the drawdown of war reserves at precisely the time when an outbreak of hostilities seemed most likely. If the United States had become involved in even a limited conflict in Iran, it would have been the worst possible time for its fuel supplies. Some progress has been made in simplifying contracts and procurement procedures, but the Pentagon probably remains relatively uncompetitive against private sector customers.

The Department of Defense thus relies heavily on its ability to request that the Secretary of Energy invoke the Defense Production Act of 1950. Its emergency procedures allow priority supply of crude and products to DOD and defense-related contractors. DOE's Economic Regulatory Administration (ERA), which has been under heavy attack for its intervention in the private oil market, must make a formal determination that a grant of priority rating is necessary to meet the defense requirements identified by DOD and that a proposed supplier is capable of delivering the crude or products. In order to elicit a favorable response, DOD must already be experiencing petroleum supply problems. These procedures became even more troublesome after September 30, 1981, when the federal government's ability to allocate source petroleum supplies during an emergency expired with the Emergency Petroleum Allocation Act. Furthermore, the budget for ERA starting in 1982 will be cut dramatically. Under these new conditions, it is not at all clear how oil would be obtained and distributed.

It is assumed that the Pentagon will immediately be able to draw directly on refined products from the commercial petroleum system. Depending on the initial state of the commercial market, this may cause immediate shortages and economic slowdowns elsewhere in the economy. Prior to the creation of DOE, during the 1973-1974 crisis, the Secretary of Commerce invoked the DPA for defense purposes.[5] This was the only time that the DPA was used, and it was completely ineffectual. It took five months to make the system operate; responsibilities were completely lacking among the federal departments and agencies within the Department of Defense. A new final rule of 1980 gives a clearer definition of assigned responsibilities and specific time limits for action. The ability, however, of the ERA to make such a system work in real emergencies, with many urgent requests to fulfill, is highly dubious. At best there would be long delays.

One final Western fuel planning problem is unique to the Persian Gulf. Since U.S. war planning relies heavily on prepositioned war reserves in the theater to support at least the first few weeks of operations, severe constraints arise in the Gulf. The area is vast in size, with little or no basic infrastructure. Water as well as petroleum supply poses a crucial problem. Air defense and command control capabilities to protect and coordinate logistic support in the area are also very limited.

Given these problems, the U.S. government is tailoring its strategy to include fuel prepositioning at Diego Garcia and other ports in the Indian Ocean. The Defense Fuel Supply Center is trying to arrange leases for storage facilities in Kenya and Somalia. One of the seven ships now stationed at Diego García is a tanker. Such arrangements are very limited to date, however, in the amount of petroleum available and the speed and locations of possible delivery. They may also be highly vulnerable to interdiction by Soviet air forces, naval forces, or even mines.

Broader Threats to Western Mobilization in the 1980s and Beyond

After decades of rhetoric and counterproductive actions on petroleum as a national security issue, the United States finally faces a real and present threat to Western security. American control over international economic issues has declined sharply since its peak in the 1950s in parallel with increasing Soviet military force projection capabilities. American dominance of the world oil market, as demonstrated during the Suez crisis of 1956 and 1957 and war in the Middle East in 1967, gave way to producer nation control by the late 1960s and early 1970s. The oil embargo of 1973 and 1974 culminated the first phase of this shift in international economic and political power.

During the next major oil crisis in 1979 the United States lost much of its remaining power to control the prices, allocation and foreign policy dictates of petroleum. The multinational companies' ability to allocate effectively oil supplies during emergencies, as vividly demonstrated in 1973–1974, was sharply curtailed, and Western governments began to lose even this indirect source of leverage. The continuing Iran-Iraq war takes this loss of control one crucial step further. Both superpowers now lack the capability to control even major conflict in the Persian Gulf. Both oil producing nations demonstrated a willingness and ability to destroy every component of each other's oil production, refining and transportation system. Iran has been plummeted from its position as policeman in the Gulf to a catalyst which could set off a broader war in the region at any time.

In order to retain the capacity to mobilize within this broader context, Western nations must define and react to a specific set of threats to each component of the oil supply system. The threats include sabotage, terrorism, political instability in oil producing nations, regional crises and war, conflict involving Soviet proxies, and superpower confrontation. These all pose significant threats to oil fields, collection stations, local refineries and shipping terminals.

For tanker transport routes, especially through choke points, Soviet submarine attack is by far the most important threat, although regional war could cause temporary disruptions. Perhaps the greatest menace to Western mobilization would be threatened, feigned or actual Soviet mining from the air of the Strait of Hormuz. If tanker traffic were unable or unwilling to transit during weeks of mine sweeping in the Strait of Hormuz, deep strains could develop in a Western mobilization effort for conflict anywhere worldwide. As mobilization for conventional war appeared increasingly difficult, the pressures would mount for either West European and Japanese negotiations with the Soviets or escalation to a nuclear confrontation between the superpowers.

Today NATO war planning continues to be skewed toward an intense, short war which would quickly escalate to at least a theater nuclear exchange. This of course is designed to maintain the tightest possible links between a conventional attack by the Warsaw Pact and escalation to a nuclear exchange involving the United States. Under this planning scenario the Allies rely on very limited logistical arrangements, including only a few weeks' supply of petroleum. The Long Term Defense Plan for NATO agreed to in 1979 under pressure from the Carter Administration offers some marginal future steps toward shifting this planning base to a longer war scenario. If enacted by individual governments, the Long Term Defense Plan will gradually help ensure both that fuel is actually stockpiled before conflict breaks out and that petroleum war reserve levels are raised. The Reagan Administration appears to be pushing even harder towards planning for the long conventional war, but NATO remains far from being ready for the required mobilization.

The longer term threat assessment is no less challenging. Western ground, naval and air forces must eventually confront the depletion of world petroleum supplies. Without careful and prescient planning now, the forces may be unable to either gain access to the quantity or quality of required petroleum products or to bear the rapidly escalating costs of all fuel supplies.

Western Responses to the Mobilization Dilemma

Western responses to the mobilization dilemma posed by petroleum vulnerability range from increasing national war reserves to planning for the coordinated use of airlift capabilities within NATO. Only a sampling of policy responses will be offered here since much work remains to be done before we can even fully define this dimension of the mobilization problem. Policy options are illustrated below in a figure

		Foreign Policy	
	Domestic	Unilateral	Bilateral	Multilateral
Short-term	War reserves; Public and private stockpiles; Allocation mechanisms	Prepositioning; Minesweeping; Spare parts/repair	Leased storage tanks; Minesweeping capability	War reserve agreements
Intermediate	New energy sources; Energy efficiency; Refinery upgrading	Strategic petroleum reserves	New storage facilities; Diversification of sources of oil imports	CEPS; International Energy Agency
Long-term	Force design and structure; Oil import reduction; Synthetic fuels industry	Oil import reduction	Joint pricing and production strategy	CEPS; Airlift and Sealift; Defense of oil fields

based on the length of time required for implementation and their domestic or foreign policy nature.

This analysis has stressed shorter term steps such as increasing war reserves and providing realistic estimates of wartime petroleum demand and delivery methods in all key sectors. The Department of Defense must become a more competitive commercial buyer and gain access to publicly guaranteed supplies from naval petroleum reserves or the SPR. Petroleum allocation arrangements domestically and prepositioning internationally are equally important. New tanks storage space can be leased and host nations can help offset costs.

Intermediate- and long-term responses must be started or they will never be available. Over the intermediate term it is possible to change consumption and import patterns. DOD petroleum use should be restricted to the direct mobility demands of the fighting forces. Strategic petroleum reserves can be filled and given a real time function to moderate shortages during a crisis. The International Energy Agency's emergency oil sharing system can be strengthened and brought home to the level of individual Congressmen and citizens' groups. Progress in the CEPS improvement, NATO reserve requirements can be routinely monitored.

A wide variety of steps are possible over the longer term. Western mobilization capacities in the coming decades will be a function of how far future forces can move away from heavy dependence on petroleum supplies. This demands strong research and development support. Engineering and design criteria should already be much more oriented toward greater fuel efficiencies. Refinery upgrading is crucial since military products tend to be of very high quality. U.S. military construction programs and NATO infrastructure development must also greatly improve our capacity for storing and distributing fuel in anticipation of emergencies. Only by phasing in these long-term measures now can we avoid extending our current short and intermediate-term vulnerabilities into the 1990s.

NOTES

1. See U.S. Department of Energy, *Monthly Energy Review*, March 1981.
2. U.S. Cabinet Task Force Report, 1970.
3. *Resources for Freedom*, A Report to the President by the President's Materials Policy Commission, 1952.
4. The Energy Security Act of 1979 also eliminated Defense Department access to the Naval Petroleum Reserve at Elk Hills, California; the NPR in Alaska is also available only for civilian sector consumption.
5. To invoke the DPA for Strategic Minerals, the Secretary of Defense sends a letter to Commerce; for Transportation, a letter must be sent to the Secretary of Transportation.

14

C³—Damaged, Intercepted or Blocked

Lee M. Paschall

Introduction

Planning for, and mobilization of, the nation's telecommunications infrastructure was once a relatively straightforward task as it was almost entirely based upon the Bell System. To illustrate, during the 1962 Cuban Missile Crisis, a single telephone call galvanized the Bell System into the actions required to provide the communications facilities needed to support a possible invasion of Cuba. In one short week the Bell System gathered people and equipment from many different places, removed hundreds of circuits from commercial use and turned them over to the military, installed complete telephone exchanges, and built or extended major radio relay and cable systems in and to Florida. It was a remarkable and reassuring performance and matched earlier efforts in both World Wars. But the changes of the two decades since that event have been equally dramatic and the purpose of this chapter is to examine the importance of command and control, the threats it faces, and today's environment.

The Impact of Evolving Strategies on Command and Control

The critical importance of centralized command and control for decision-making relative to the use of nuclear weapons has become an accepted principle. President Kennedy provided the first unequivocal statement of the policy in March 1961. At that time in history most strategic thinking and war planning was based on the idea of deterring war by the threat of massive retaliation. Our nuclear superiority made such a strategy feasible. Assuming a "no-first-strike" policy meant that our weapons would be launched on warning that an attack on the United

States was underway. The command and control structure required to support such a strategy had to provide *absolutely* reliable and credible warning systems and extremely fast communications links to launch the retaliatory forces. Survivability was of lesser concern.

The decade of the 1960s found the United States preoccupied with the war in Vietnam while the Soviet Union hastened to overcome our lead in nuclear weapons. Gradually it became apparent that massive retaliation meant mutual destruction and the Nixon Administration began the process which led to a "flexible response" nuclear strategy.

A nuclear strategy based on flexible response imposes much more stringent demands on the command and control structure than that required for the launch-on-warning scenario characteristic of massive retaliation. Needed are: highly reliable warning systems, including some level of attack assessment capability; survivability of the command, control and communications systems equal to that of the weapons systems; more extensive communications networks containing an almost invulnerable hardcore "execute and report back" capability; and considerable data processing capacity. The most difficult issues in structuring such a system were how much survivability and how much attack assessment capability was required to assure the National Command Authority that the command and control system could continue to provide the critical information required to allow deliberate selection of an option and to assure controlled execution of that option.

During the 1970s, United States complacency about its technological superiority vanished as the Soviet Union began to equal United States performance in missile accuracy and MIRV capabilities. The flexible response concept was further refined by a desire for more options, concern about command and control of the strategic reserve, ability to ride out an initial (perhaps less than all-out) attack, launch-under-attack scenarios, and the possibility of a prolonged nuclear exchange. All had a major impact on the command and control structure. Growing concern about the survivability of that structure became the principal focus. Systems like the DOD's Automatic Voice Network (AUTOVON) which had been designed to be survivable against a 1960s threat no longer appeared sufficiently robust when the large Soviet warhead population forecast for the 1980s was taken into account. Emphasis on "endurance" and "reconstitution" grew as planners had to contemplate more than one nuclear exchange scenario. The question began to be asked as to whether spending money on reconstitution capabilities might be wiser than trying to harden facilities to the point that they could withstand direct attack or the collateral damage from "near misses." Survivability, endurance and reconstitution of command and control depends almost entirely on the national telecommunications structure which is also in a period of significant change as will be described later in this chapter. Moreover, the threat to command, control and communications is more complex than generally believed.

Threats to Command, Control and Communications

There are three generic classes of attacks that can be mounted, singly or in combination, on command control and communications: physical, electronic and intercept. Soviet published doctrine makes clear their view of the importance of command and control as a target system. They plan physically to attack one-third of an enemy command and control structure, electronically to attack another third, and believe that the remainder will thereby be made relatively ineffective.

PHYSICAL ATTACK

Most physical attack modes are relatively well understood. They include sabotage, direct targeting, and aim point selection against primary targets designed to maximize collateral damage to nearby command and control facilities. Electromagnetic pulse (EMP) is less well understood, but clearly represents a very serious threat. Indirect nuclear effects (e.g., high frequency radio "blackout") can also interrupt radio wave propagation paths for periods ranging from minutes to hours. But it is the EMP threat that poses the greatest uncertainty to the telecommunications planner.

High altitude nuclear detonations have the potential for causing widespread damage to electronic systems. A large nuclear weapon detonated at a height of 500 kilometers above the central United States will generate EMP effects over the entire area of the continental United States. EMP effects are caused by gamma rays which in turn generate large electromagnetic fields. Such fields affect electronic equipment by causing functional or operational disturbances or by causing permanent damage due to burnout of electronic components. Solid state electronics are particularly vulnerable.

Various types of terrestrial communications facilities of the military, Bell System and Western Union have been tested against EMP and some corrective actions taken. But even with EMP-hardened facilities there remains a large area of uncertainty because of the impossibility of modeling the cascading and self-cancelling effects of many low, medium and high altitude nuclear detonations that would characterize a major attack. There is a very high probability, however, that those electronic equipment which have not been hardened against EMP will suffer damage sufficient to require repairs. If a large part of the continental United States is affected by EMP, the repair of damaged electronic equipment would indeed be a very large-scale undertaking. Communications satellites, which cannot be repaired, rely on extensive redundancy in design to achieve acceptable on-orbit life. That redundancy may allow some to survive EMP effects although even those which do survive can be expected to be degraded in varying degrees.

ELECTRONIC ATTACK

An electronic attack on the command and control structure could take three forms: jamming, deception or control seizure. Jamming results when the enemy deliberately interferes with radio or radar signals in such a way as to make them unuseable. Modern electronic warfare uses very esoteric technology both to jam and to counter the jamming. Electronic countermeasures equipment is both expensive and complex. Its success depends in large measure upon available bandwidth. The more radio frequency spectrum that can be used to avoid or to disperse the power of the jammer, the better the result. Microwave radio relay systems are the most difficult to jam successfully as they consist of many radio towers with directional antennas. This will usually require positioning the jammer in the path of the radio beam. Generally, only one link is affected and if the network is richly connected, as in the United States, reroutes would normally be possible. Radio systems with omni-directional antennas (aircraft), earth coverage antennas (satellites) or which use the reflective properties of the ionosphere (high frequency radio) are much easier to jam. Communications satellites are particularly vulnerable unless designed with antennas which provide multiple, very narrow spot beams instead of the conventional earth coverage antennas.

Deception involves an enemy effort to confuse his opponent by intruding into communications links with what appear to be bona fide commands, instructions or reports. Techniques used to counter deception tactics require disciplined adherence to precise procedural safeguards. Deception may be difficult to counter in the initial, confused stages of a war. Electronic techniques are used to counter deception or "spoofing" used against warning and surveillance systems.

Control seizure is another form of electronic attack that could be used with particular effectiveness against communications satellites with unprotected, or with relatively unsophisticated protection of telemetry, tracking and command links. Such an attack could take the form of sending false commands to the satellite, particularly those which could command the satellite into a catastrophic situation. A false command immediately followed by a jamming attack against the telemetry, tracking and command link would be very difficult to cope with. Encryption and some antijamming protection for telemetry, tracking and command links are generally effective countermeasures but must be designed into the system at the outset. No retrofit is possible after the satellite is in orbit.

INTERCEPT

Interception of communications traffic for intelligence collection purposes poses a different kind of threat than those described above. It seeks to exploit rather than deny the use of communications. Modern electronics has made interception relatively easy to accomplish either overtly or covertly. Privacy of telephone conversations over the nation's telephone network is assumed by most people, except for the notorious wiretap. However, most conversations in this country are carried for much of their length over microwave radio systems and are interceptible. Conversations carried on satellite systems are even more vulnerable to intercept. Thus, use of much of the national telecommunications structure without expensive voice encryption devices leads to vulnerabilities of unknown magnitude. Very limited (in terms of extent) secure voice networks do exist both for military and national civilian leadership users. The vulnerability of our national telecommunications structure to intercept is a clear threat in preattack periods. A sophisticated enemy could decide to limit his attack on command and control out of fear that too effective an attack might cause an uncontrolled response. In such a case, interception could also be a serious threat during the transattack period.

Military systems can be built which provide significant protection against most of the threats described above. However, their cost would be enormous and such a military system itself would become a primary target for direct nuclear attack. It is almost impossible to guarantee survival of a command, control and communications facility when directly attacked by nuclear weapons. Therefore, great reliance must be placed on the very extensive commercial telecommunications structure in the United States.

Importance of Commercial Telecommunications Networks to Defense

Well over 90% of the Defense Communications System in the United States is leased from common carriers. The primary suppliers are the Bell System, Western Union, some 200 Independent Telephone Companies and the domestic satellite companies whose market share is growing rapidly. The same is true of the National Communications System, comprised of about 75% defense communications assets and the remainder of networks operated by the major Federal civil departments of government.

Defense communications networks are extensive. They include general purpose networks like AUTOVON (the DOD's direct distance dial network with special military features) leased from Bell System and independent telephone companies, and AUTODIN (the DOD's data and message network) leased from Western Union. The general purpose networks are used for command and control, logistics, operations, personnel and administrative functions. Special purpose networks dedicated to a single function of user are found in great variety.

One network, the Minimum Essential Emergency Communications Network (MEECN) is comprised of the most survivable military communications assets which can be immediately seized in an emergency by the JCS for purposes of sending emergency messages (e.g., an execute attack message). Most of the assets so used are government owned but key elements are leased from common carriers. Moreover, it is essentially a one-way system which greatly diminishes its utility, particularly in a prolonged war scenario.

The most survivable command centers are the airborne command posts supporting the National Command Authority and selected military commands (e.g., SAC). Their endurance is finite and at some point they must locate a surviving airfield and land for servicing. At that time connectivity into the surviving commercial networks becomes imperative.

The enormous extent, geographic dispersion and capabilities of the national telecommunications structure in the United States makes it an almost impossible target to destroy. Parts can be destroyed, parts interrupted by EMP-induced equipment damage, and calling attempts by a distraught population will certainly overload the remainder almost immediately. After an attack there will probably remain enclaves of relatively undamaged telecommunications capabilities. Depending upon the size of the attack and the target systems attacked, such enclaves could either be widely separated but fairly large, or widespread and quite small. The problem, then, is how to organize those residual assets, to reconnect the enclaves and to be able to serve the most urgent national needs. Complicating the problem is that the survival of any preplanned central direction or control center cannot be assured. Another complication emerges when we consider the current national telecommunications structure and the wrenching changes it is undergoing.

Today's Environment

At the midpoint of this century the nation's telecommunications structure was provided by the Bell System, together with about sixteen hundred independent telephone companies serving mainly rural areas, together with Western Union and a handful of international telegraph companies providing domestic and international telegraph services. All were regarded as "natural monopolies" and regulated by the Federal Communications Commission or by the various state regulatory bodies. The Communications Act of 1934 governed the basic structure.

Although generally regarded as natural monopolies where regulation substituted for competition, the antitrust laws also applied—particularly in the case of AT&T. Indeed, immediately after passage of the 1934 Act, the Congress directed the newly established FCC to conduct an investigation of AT&T. The resulting report, issued in 1939, was highly critical of the Bell System. World War II intervened, and the importance of the Bell System to the war effort resulted in no action being taken until 1949 when the Justice Department filed an antitrust suit seeking to break up the Bell System structure. The principal target was Bell's manufacturing arm—Western Electric.

Growing international tension, the resulting Cold War and the build-up of national defense caused the Bell System in its integrated form to be regarded as a major national defense asset. At the request of President Truman, AT&T had taken over management of the Sandia atomic program facilities. Western Electric was also the prime contractor for the NIKE program and, together with Lincoln Laboratories, was working on an extension to the Distant Early Warning radar line. Hence, in 1953 the Secretary of Defense wrote the Attorney General stating that "The Department of Defense wishes to express its serious concern regarding the further prosecution of the antitrust case now pending against Western Electric Co. and the AT&T Company." The Department of Justice prosecutor responded that "The Antitrust Division... was rather cynical about letters from Defense Secretaries seeking postponement or settlement of cases" and continued to press the case. A remarkably similar exchange would take place twenty-eight years later. In 1956 a Consent Decree was negotiated which settled the suit.

Beginning in the early 1950s, the FCC (frequently prodded by the Courts) began to reach a series of decisions leading to increased competition in the expectation of achieving more economic and innovative telecommunications services for the nation. By the end of the 1960s, the bar to interconnection of customer-owned equipment to the Bell network had fallen. Up to that time only the Department of Defense, by using "letters of military necessity," had that privilege.

The FCC opened up the radio spectrum for assignment to private microwave systems in 1959, and approved the first such application by Microwave Communications Inc. (MCI) for common carrier purposes in 1969. The FCC was confronted with forty-six proposals for private line microwave routes by 1971. This led to the Specialized Common Carrier policy decision later that year. Despite objections by the established carriers (AT&T, Western Union and Independents), the FCC allowed new applicants to enter the market in the expectation that they would serve the rapidly growing market for data communications.

Another major erosion of the "unitary" telecommunications structure occurred in 1977 when the Courts reversed an FCC decision refusing

MCI permission to offer EXECUNET service, a form of direct distance dial telephone service. There are now several such systems offered by specialized carriers. For the most part these rely heavily on use of switching and local exchange cable facilities of the Bell System and independent telephone companies in order to reach the customer's location.

The maturing of communications satellite technology led to an FCC decision in 1972 favoring "multiple entry" and competition in providing domestic satellite services. That policy has led to an explosive growth in the domestic satellite arena. In a recent decision the FCC authorized the construction or launch of forty-five such satellites by eight different companies over the next few years, tripling the number of satellites now in orbit. The services to be offered cover the full range of communications services but primarily provide competition with terrestrial intercity transmission routes.

Finally, growing interdependence of computers and telecommunications caused the FCC to examine that relationship with a view towards establishing regulatory boundaries and determining the extent to which common carriers should or should not be allowed to offer data processing services. The first such inquiry (Computer I) resulted in a decision to required "maximum separation," meaning that a common carrier was required to form a completely separate company to offer data processing services. A second inquiry (Computer II) began in 1976 when it became clear to the FCC that the emerging technologies of computers and telecommunications had outdated their earlier policy. The Computer II decision was issued in 1980 and made fundamental changes in the way telecommunications services will be provided. Although a highly complex decision, it basically does five things. It divides telecommunications service into two categories—basic and enhanced. "Basic" is defined as pure transmission of information (a transmission pipeline), while "enhanced" means that the information has been modified or acted upon in some way. Enhanced services will not be regulated by the FCC. Instead, competition will serve as the regulating mechanism. Customer premises equipment will also be deregulated. Structural safeguards are imposed on AT&T, as the "dominant" carrier, requiring that enhanced services and customer premises equipment be offered through a fully separated subsidiary subject to procedural controls to prevent cross-subsidies. Finally, the FCC expressed its view that the 1956 Consent Decree does not preclude AT&T from offering enhanced services. The Justice Department does not agree with that conclusion. Indeed, there are a great number of legal challenges to the Computer II decision pending in the courts at this time. Until the courts dispose of these challenges, Computer II must be regarded as unsettled although actions by the common carriers are underway to comply with it.

Beginning in 1976 a series of legislative proposals were considered by committees of both the House of Representatives and the Senate. Except for one bill sponsored by the telephone industry in 1976, all would have deregulated customer premises equipment and encouraged competition in intercity transmission services. They differed mainly in their treatment of the Bell System organizational structure and its degree of freedom to compete in the various markets. The national security community took an active part in the debate on the draft legislation. It expressed concern that the proposed legislation did not adequately provide for the development and use of technical standards needed to assure interoperability of the nation's telecommunications networks. The national security community also expressed concern about the absence of mandatory service provisions requiring carriers to provide service upon reasonable request by the government. Concern about provisions for the exercise of war powers by the President was also noted. For the most part such concern was satisfied in the final versions of both the Senate and House bills. The end of the 96th Congress caused both bills to expire without floor action. The 97th Congress is expected to once again address the question of revising the Communications Act of 1934.

The impact of all this activity on the national telecommunications infrastructure has been dramatic. The planning uncertainties have become very great. Large users, such as DOD, will find the multivendor world more expensive in terms of management overhead. Acquiring a service "end to end" from a single supplier has long been a policy goal of DOD since it reduced management overhead and greatly simplified network control actions to repair or restore interrupted services. The number of choices now available to the user has grown significantly. There is much greater diversity of telecommunications routes, facilities and equipment, all of which would enhance the survivability of the national telecommunications structure if these separate networks could be organized and interconnected in such a way as to respond to a national emergency. In a competitive environment, and given the structural requirements being levied on AT&T, the centralized network planning and direction once largely performed by AT&T will also erode. It is not clear what will take its place. Some remain convinced that only the Bell System can tie it all together. Others feel the joint industry groups can do so in a cooperative manner with or without (preferably without) government participation. Still others believe that the government must take a much larger role, particularly in light of Presidential Directive 53.[1]

Finally, to conclude our examination of the uncertainties facing the telecommunications industry, brief notice must be taken of the antitrust case initiated by the Department of Justice in 1974 against AT&T. The suit alleged monopolistic practices by AT&T and sought relief by restructuring the Bell System into several competing entities. An intensive effort to reach an out of court settlement failed and trial began in early 1981. In March 1981, Secretary of Defense Weinberger put the DOD's views on record in testimony to the Senate Armed Services Committee and revealed that he had written to the Attorney General urging "very strongly" that the suit be dismissed. The Assistant Attorney General for antitrust activities responded by saying "I don't intend to fold up my tent and go away because the Department of Defense has expressed concern." In June 1982, the Pentagon, reluctantly, agreed not to oppose the formula for settlement of the suit that was proposed by the Justice Department. As finally agreed upon by both parties, AT&T will divest itself of its twenty-two local telephone companies, but retain its long-distance service, Western Electric and Bell Telephone Laboratories, Inc.

Improved Survivability of Common Carrier Networks

Over the past three decades the national security community has been able to influence network planning choices by the established carriers (principally AT&T and WU) so as to enhance the robustness and survivability of their networks. Target avoidance routing and facility protection features are but two examples. These choices add cost to the construction of facilities but are consistent with one of the stated purposes of the Communications Act of 1934 that the nation's telecommunications network should provide for the national defense. More recently, PD 53 has restated that policy more explicitly. The added costs of construction have been indirectly borne by all ratepayers up to this time. The question now is whether the several competing suppliers of telecommunications will be willing unilaterally to incur added cost, thus weakening their competitive posture. Increasingly, the theme is heard that if the national security community wants these added protective features provided, it should pay for them. But the question is how to do so in a way that treats all suppliers equitably and at a reasonable cost to the taxpayer. There appear to be at least five choices available:

— use only those networks most nearly meeting the government's survivability goals, relying on the government's market power (DOD alone spends about one-half billion dollars annually on leased communications equipment and services) to cause potential suppliers to make the added investment;
— direct subsidies to all carriers;
— reliance upon a "chosen instrument" at the expense of competition and the increased diversity that it brings;
— government subsidies to provide increased protection to selected critical facilities; and,
— require that protection features be provided by all carriers in the national interest and hence indirectly subsidized by all users.

It is not clear which one, or combination of more than one of those alternatives might be the best solution. PD 53 appears to rule out the third solution and to encourage the fifth (at least for purposes of achieving interoperability). The Defense Communications Agency has relied upon the "chosen instrument" choice in specific cases (e.g., AUTOVON). Some statements attributed to senior DOD officials in press reports dealing with the AT&T antitrust case seem to imply the "chosen instrument" approach. The Reagan Administration's FY 1981 Supplemental and FY 1982 Budget submissions both contain requests for several million dollars which apparently will be used to provide for hardening of selected critical facilities.

Although the direction is not clear, a number of study efforts are underway. These are made more difficult by the uncertainties present in the current telecommunications environment. But there is little doubt that improving the endurance and survivability of common carrier networks is of major importance to national command and control. During the Carter Administration, the DOD General Counsel, commenting on the proposed revision of the Communications Act, said that the Pentagon "...believes that the nation's telecommunications facilities are national resources that require effective centralized network management and that must be survivable to fully meet the needs of the national defense and security." General Richard H. Ellis, former Commander-in-Chief of the Strategic Air Command, in a November 1980 speech proposed incorporating wartime survivability into the design of commercial satellites as well as including EMP protection in commercial switching centers, microwave relays and other transmission system elements. He concluded by saying "...modernization of our strategic connectivity systems requires the same funding priority as that enjoyed by our newest strategic weapons systems. Without it, the credibility of our entire deterrence policy is suspect." In December 1980, Admiral (Retired) Daniel J. Murphy, then Deputy Undersecretary of Defense of Policy Review, stated that "...we have to attain balanced survivability and endurance—balanced among the forces, weapons and C^3I." Furthermore, "we must also be sensitive to the proper mix of survivable and reconstitutable systems and we must be careful not to place too much emphasis on initial survivability to the exclusion of endurance over a longer term."

Conclusion

Specific policy direction for national command and control has been spelled out in two recent Presidential Directives. PD 53 states that a survivable communications system is a necessary component of our deterrent posture for defense. It further requires that very heavy reliance be placed on the national telecommunications infrastructure supplied by the common carriers. PD 53 recognized that to ensure the credibility of our deterrent posture there is need to improve the survivability of the National Command Authority or his successor who is the only person who can authorize the employment of nuclear weapons. The result has been an upsurge of activity dealing with command, control and communications, and in particular their survivability and endurance which pose difficult choices in themselves. The added complexities inherent in a change in national telecommunications structure make even the issues, questions and options unclear.

NOTE

1. PD 53 is a statement of National Security Telecommunications policy issued on 15 November 1979. It states, among other things, that the nation's telecommunications must provide for:
— connectivity between the National Command Authority and strategic and other appropriate forces to support flexible execution of retaliatory strikes during and after an enemy nuclear attack;
— responsive support for operational control of the armed forces, even during a protracted nuclear conflict;
— support of military mobilization in all circumstances;
— support for the vital functions of worldwide intelligence collection and diplomatic affairs;
— continuity of government during and after a nuclear war or natural disaster; and,
— recovery of the nation during and after a nuclear war or natural disaster.

Section V

Mobilization:
Assets and Liabilities of Interdependence

15

NATO's Nonexistent Industrial Mobilization Capability: Its Impact on America's Ailing Defense Industrial Base

Thomas A. Callaghan, Jr.

Unless the Congress is prepared to vote World War II-scale defense budgets, and a return to Lend-Lease and Military Assistance, America's "ailing defense industrial base"[1] (as it has rightly been characterized), cannot possibly redress the conventional force balance in the Atlantic, in Europe, in the Pacific, and along the energy-mineral lifelines in between; repair the theater nucleus balance in Europe; and restore parity at the intercontinental nuclear level.

The East-West military imbalance has been sixteen or more years in the making. An American defense industrial effort alone cannot restore that balance. But the balance can be restored, without American or Allied economic strain, by a collective and equitable sharing of the financial burdens (and economic benefits) of Western defense by the eighteen industrial democracies to which the United States is allied through the 1949 North Atlantic Treaty with Canada and fourteen European nations; the 1951 Security Treaty with Australia and New Zealand; and the 1960 Treaty of Mutual Cooperation and Security with Japan.

This chapter addresses only the defense industrial deficiencies of the North Atlantic Alliance, but not of Japan, Australia or New Zealand. However, many of the problems are parallel, even if different. For historical, strategic, political, military and other reasons set forth in this chapter, NATO's industrial mobilization capabilities are nonexistent. The fault is partly European, and partly American. A recent Defense Department Report concluded:

> There has long been a view among some in the U.S. military, in the defense industry and in the Congress, that the preservation of the American industrial mobilization base requires that we do everything ourselves.... The U.S. provides less than one-half of the ground and tactical air forces for the defense of Europe. The majority are provided by our European allies.*

* In fact, "the European allies make available about 91% of the Allied ground forces and 75% of the Allied air forces in Europe." See "Twelve Years of Eurogroup—A Contribution to the Alliance," by German Defense Minister (and 1980 Eurogroup Chairman) Hans Apel, *NATO Review*, February 1981, p. 1.

U.S. industrial mobilization capabilities could not possibly make up such deficiencies as Europe may have plus providing for our own needs. Nor could we do it in time.

The U.S. must begin to order its priorities (assuming our allies are willing to join us) towards building a *collective mobilization capability*. This means NATO must have (1) a collective military capability, (2) a collective military-industrial effort to provide that capability, and (3) a collective military preparedness to insure time to mobilize.[2]

NATO today has none of these three. The Europeans have resisted efforts to build a collective conventional warfighting capability, fearful that it would decouple the American nuclear commitment from the defense of Europe. The United States (fearful that the Allies might not be "willing to join us") has been reluctant to press the issue and to insist that deterrence have credible nuclear and conventional dimensions.

There is a profound strategic difference between the United States and its European Allies over the deterrent and defensive roles of NATO's conventional forces in an age of nuclear parity. These differences must be understood, faced, and ultimately resolved by the highest political authorities in the Alliance, namely the Allied Heads of Government, and the Allied Parliaments.

The issue is not NATO (or even American) industrial mobilization, for that is not now a viable option. The issue is what happens if deterrence fails? What happens to American forces in Europe? What are the dangers of intercontinental nuclear war? These are questions and issues the Alliance has never resolved. They are questions and issues that merit the full attention of both branches of the United States Government.

NATO Does Not Have a Collective Military Capability

The North Atlantic Alliance is not what it seems. References to NATO's Integrated Military Command might convey the impression that it is a *collective* force, capable of fighting effectively together. It is not, and it cannot be. It is, instead, a *collection of national forces*, with "only a limited ability to rearm, repair, reinforce, support, supply, or even communicate with one another."[3]

The North Atlantic Treaty was signed, and ratified, while the United States still had a monopoly of atomic weapons. If ever atomic deterrence was sufficient unto itself for the defense of Europe, it was then. But in 1949, the European and American leaders of the Alliance realized that a strong, collective, conventional military capability was needed to deter Soviet aggression.

In his memoirs Dean Acheson tells of presiding at the fourth session of the North Atlantic Council in London in 1950, at which "the basic problems, which NATO has never been able to solve, began to emerge."[4] The North Atlantic Council was considering the recommendation of its Defense Committee that Alliance governments (in Acheson's words) provide a progressive increase in defense forces

> ...based on the creation of *balanced collective forces* rather than balanced national forces. By this was meant a force for the defense of Europe, complete and balanced in its components when viewed as a collectivity, *rather than a collection of national forces* each complete with all the necessary component arms. The latter was beyond the economic means of Europe....[5] (emphasis added)

Council members were asked in the course of the debate, "What would be the fate of an imperiled nation if the collective force did not come to its aid?" There was (predictably) an attempt to gloss over the question. Dean Acheson tells us he intervened to insist that this was a real issue, that it should be understood, faced, and resolved. He agreed the threatened nation would be imperiled if the collective force did not respond. But if the aggressor was the Soviet Union, he said, this nation would be imperiled even if its defense forces were structured on a national, rather than a collective basis. He emphasized that both deterrence and effective defense could *only* be provided by the collective force, which would include all the power of the United States. He asked the North Atlantic Council to recognize that "the sole point at issue was that in raising the forces for the defense of the area, economic necessity required that all duplication of effort be eliminated."[6]

The concept of "balanced collective forces" was approved unanimously by the North Atlantic Council on May 17, 1950. The deputy members of the Council were instructed to remain in continuous session in London "in an attempt to push forward the development of the collective defense."[7]

The momentum thus generated (and spurred by the Korean invasion) continued for the next several years. The Alliance nations agreed on all that was conceptually needed, then and now, for the defense of Europe:
— a forward strategy to resist aggression as far to the east as possible;
— integrated and balanced conventional forces;
— equitable burden-sharing, including (for Europe in those days) balance of payments relief;
— a collective European defense procurement effort; and,
— American economic cooperation in armaments.

In the end, it all came to naught. What went wrong?

For one thing, as Dean Acheson himself acknowledged, "while we

Americans talked of balanced collective forces, our own military planning and budgeting were undertaken aloof and apart from Europe."[8] This problem continues to this day. For another, the Korean War stalemate diminished the fears of a Russian attack. At the same time, dollar deficits, the demand for postwar recovery capital, material shortages, and inflation, all combined to make additional European defense spending politically burdensome.

But two events in 1954, more than anything else, doomed the efforts to raise balanced, collective conventional forces for Europe's defense. One was the defeat of the European Defense Community (EDC) which made it structurally impossible. The other was the doctrine of massive nuclear retaliation, which made it conceptually unnecessary.

The concept of a collective force had not yet been rooted in structures within which it could grow, when the building of the most important structure collapsed. Some aspects of the EDC may have been too ambitious; most were not. If NATO was ever to become more than a subnuclear Potemkin Village, there had to be agreement within Europe (and between Europe and North America) on a single, coherent defense strategy. All NATO nations had to agree they would be fighting the same war together—defending Europe as one geopolitical entity. NATO Europe's thirteen weak nations (fourteen, with the entry of Spain in 1982) would have to heed Benjamin Franklin's advice to another weak thirteen: "We must all hang together, or, most assuredly, we shall all hang separately."

The EDC made "hanging together" possible. There would be common military requirements. A European defense procurement effort, and a continental European defense industrial base, would provide large weapons inventories at reasonable cost. When the *military assistance phase* of American economic cooperation in armaments ended, Europe's defense industry would be prepared to enter into a new *military trade phase* which would insure that standardized weapons were produced on an intercontinental scale. Thus, the burdens and benefits of Allied defense could equitably be shared, and NATO's forces could operate together.

The attainment of these objectives became moot when the United States in 1954 put forth the doctrine of massive nuclear retaliation. This was never a valid, warfighting strategy for the defense of Europe. It was, however, an all too credible budget-fighting scheme. Nuclear deterrence meant that, except for a tripwire, the conventional defense of Europe would be unnecessary.

Massive nuclear retaliation—"more bang for a buck"—meant defense on the cheap. For the United States, the high cost of conventional forces, swollen by the Korean War, could safely be cut back. This made the much lower cost of providing nuclear forces and weapons politically attractive. It also appealed to a Europe that was still recovering from World War II. The United States would now bear the cost of Allied nuclear deterrence. Each European government, and particularly those with colonial commitments, would be free to determine how much it could afford to spend to maintain its own national segment of the tripwire. Politically difficult questions of collective defense could be set aside. There would be peace and prosperity for all NATO nations, under the American nuclear umbrella.

NATO never became the collective force that was originally intended. Duplication of effort was never eliminated. The concept of extended deterrence "gave vogue to the idea that security in Europe lay in the threat to use nuclear arms, and that conventional arms were obsolete."[9] It transformed the Alliance from a mutual security organization to an American military protectorate of Europe, which continues as such to this day.

This may have been a tolerable situation in the 1950s and 1960s, when the United States enjoyed nuclear superiority. As superiority gave way to parity (or less) in the late 1970s and 1980s, the collective weakness of NATO's conventional forces increased the risk of nuclear war. In his 1979 testimony to the Senate Armed Services Committee on the SALT II Treaty, former SACEUR General (and former Secretary of State) Alexander M. Haig, Jr. stated:

> Although a conventional attack would be met in kind, the serious historical imbalance in conventional forces favoring the Warsaw Pact has led to the common expectation among our Allies of *early resort to nuclear weapons*—both tactical and strategic.[10] (emphasis added)

No NATO nation—not the United States, nor Germany, nor any other—can defend Europe against a conventional Warsaw Pact attack. Only a collective conventional capability can do that. Extended deterrence, however, obviated the need for a collective defense. With war deterred, there would be no war to fight. Without the need for a collective military capability, there was no need either for a collective military-industrial effort to provide such a capability.

NATO Does Not Have a Collective Military-Industrial Effort

Extended deterrence destroyed the fabric of collective security. It permitted every NATO government to determine how best to defend itself against the massive five thousand mile Warsaw Pact threat to Europe. There was no need for Allied governments to agree on the magnitude of the threat. Nor was there any need to adopt a common strategy (other than deterrence, and then nuclear escalation) for meeting the threat. As a consequence, NATO's Integrated Military Command today commands almost nothing that is integrated—neither its tactical doctrine, military equipment requirements, weaponry, ammunition, repair parts, nor its war reserve "days of supply" logistics, communications, maintenance nor operational training.

Indeed, NATO's Integrated Military Command is not even an operational headquarters. It is a planning headquarters that would have to make the transition to a command headquarters after mobilization (or war) had begun. Little wonder, then, that the Senate Armed Services Committee concluded last year that "better ways to accomplish the integration of NATO forces must be found."[11] Defense Secretary Harold Brown, in his final report to the Congress on *Rationalization/Standardization Within NATO*, agreed with this conclusion,[12] but explained that:

> Efforts to move in that direction are hindered by the concept of national military requirements. The U.S. is pledged to join in the defense of all of Europe. From a threat point of view, we see the Warsaw Pact forces to be a danger to Europe itself, and not just Norway, or Germany, or Turkey or one or another ally. It would not be logical (or efficient) for the U.S. to have a different military requirement, and different weapons and equipment, to assist separately each of the Alliance's 13 European nations. It is not logical nor efficient for Europe either.[13]

The extent of this inefficiency can be measured by the fact that successive Secretaries of Defense have estimated that NATO and the Warsaw Pact are devoting approximately the same resources to the development, production, training, maintenance, operation, and support of general purpose forces. But these roughly equal resource commitments produce widely disparate results. For the Warsaw Pact they produce a massive, standardized collective force, capable of operating effectively together. For NATO they produce a destandardized and non-interoperable collection of national forces, qualitatively uneven, quantitatively inferior, unable to fight for the same period of time at the same munition expenditure rates, and with only a limited ability to rearm, repair, reinforce, support, supply, or even communicate with one another.

Under the heading "Nuclear Deterrence and Coalition Warfare," the Seventh Annual Report to the Congress on *Rationalization/Standardization Within NATO* dealt at some length with the major political, military and economic problems of the North Atlantic Alliance:

> The long years of U.S. nuclear superiority and the political inertia

inherent in an organization of 15 sovereign states, 14 Defense Ministers and 39 armed forces have made it difficult to concentrate allied and U.S. attention upon coalition warfare objectives.*

The nuclear umbrella placed primary emphasis on the U.S. role as the protector of Europe. Nuclear parity, on the other hand, emphasizes the need for all Allied governments (including the United States) to work together for their common protection: to make the Alliance a collective security structure. When one reflects that coalition warfare—Alliance versus Alliance instead of nation versus nation—is more the norm than the exception in the history of conflict, it is discouraging that Allied governments (our own included) still plan, configure, size, train and equip forces nationally with only marginal correspondence to NATO guidelines...

In his testimony to the Congress early last year, the Commander-in-Chief, U.S. European Command, General Bernard W. Rogers, said that the risks and opportunities we face in the '80s

...must be assessed against the backdrop of a relentless accumulation of Soviet military power over the past 15 years. This military power has accrued, not as a result of some sudden shift in priorities, but rather from a momentum derived from conscious allocation of some 13–15% of the Soviet GNP to their defense budget, with a 4–5% real increase each year.

Of special concern is the effect of these sustained investments on the military-industrial complex of the Soviet Union, which now contains the largest research and development manpower base in the world; receives almost twice the investment funds of any Alliance nation; and outproduces NATO at the rate of two or three to one—or more—in most major weapon systems. It is an industrial base capable of producing vast quantities of high quality operational equipment in a relatively short time. The U.S. cannot match the output of the Warsaw Pact military-industrial base by its resources alone. Nor can any other Allied country. Nor can we or our Allies continue to find comfort in the technological hubris that somehow Allied quality can overcome Warsaw Pact quantity. How many Goliaths can David slay?[14]

Nearly five years ago, Senator Sam Nunn (Democrat, Georgia) made much the same point:

Unfortunately, the price of the West's traditional technological supremacy has been a disinvestment in mass. This is not to deny

* Spain, NATO's sixteenth member, entered the Alliance in 1982.

the importance of technological superiority. It is to say, however, that:
  at some point numbers do count;
  at some point technology fails to offset mass;
  at some point Kipling's "thin red line of heros" gives way.[15]

The collective weakness of Allied conventional forces contrasts starkly with the great economic and industrial strength of NATO. Europe and North America are the two richest, most technologically advanced industrial economies in the world. They have half again as many people as the Warsaw Pact (564 million to 371.3 million), but cannot raise the manpower to defend Europe. They have more than twice the Gross National Product (GNP) as the Warsaw Pact ($3,773 billion to $1,638 billion). Yet the backward economies of the Warsaw Pact are outproducing NATO by two or three to one in most major weapons systems.

The Soviets have great respect for the industrial prowess of the West. One might argue that if the Alliance nations had built a collective military-industrial base sixteen or more years ago, the Soviets would have recognized the hopelessness of trying to beat the NATO nations on the weapons production floor. Unfortunately, NATO's greatest deterrent and defense capability—its collective technological-industrial strength—has not even been put into play.

The consequences of this folly were summarized by Oliver C. Boileau, then President of Boeing Aerospace Company, in an address to a *Financial Times* Conference in 1977:

> The weapons planners in the communistic nations are capitalizing on what we in the free enterprise system proved long ago—that one large production run is cheaper and more efficient than many small ones. They are beating us at our own game![16]

The Report on *Rationalization/Standardization Within NATO* came to the same conclusion, noting that:

> Diseconomies of scale abound, with far too many different and duplicative weapons being developed and produced in smaller than optimum quantities at ever higher unit costs. The legacy of Eli Whitney (standardization) and Henry Ford (mass production) is being more effectively applied by the Soviet Union than by the nations of NATO.[17]

Two years ago, then Under Secretary of Defense for Policy, Robert W. Komer, asked delegates to the Atlantic Treaty Association (ATA) Assembly in Washington:

> How can NATO commanders optimally use national forces whose radios can't use each other's frequencies, whose bombs

don't fit each other's aircraft, whose artillery rounds don't fit each other's tubes, who even have trouble reading each other's map symbols?[18]

Secretary Komer might also have asked: What kind of a collective security organization is it that finds the Americans, the British, the Dutch, the Germans, the Italians, and the Belgians and French working together—seven Allied nations developing six new tactical communications systems? None of these systems can communicate with one another. None of them can communicate with the NATO Integrated (sic) Communications System (NICS). In an Alliance in which each government complains of "resource limitations" preventing adequate defense, each must now spend additional moneys to develop the black boxes that will reduce some of the inability to communicate with one another. Not until 1995 will NATO governments be able to have a common communications system—and then only if all governments agree *now* that there must be a common system.

Like handing on a baton in a relay race, former Secretary of Defense Harold Brown's Report to the Congress provided:

> ...a perspective that should prove helpful to the new Administration and the 97th Congress in continuing the bipartisan efforts to strengthen the collective conventional force capabilities of the North Atlantic Alliance that began in 1974 in the Senate and have been supported and advanced by Presidents Ford and Carter, and Defense Secretaries Schlesinger, Rumsfeld and myself....
>
> If one looks back to 1974 when all this [rationalization/ standardization effort] began, it is clear that great progress has been made. If one looks ahead to the day when NATO's conventional forces are collectively, credibly, and defensively equivalent to those of the Warsaw Pact, then much more needs to be done.[19]

NATO's industrial mobilization capabilities depend upon its current conventional warfighting capabilities, which are very limited. They depend also on NATO's industrial base which is fragmented and practically nonexistent. But an industrial mobilization capability is meaningless unless there is the military preparedness, the military readiness, and the military sustainability to provide time to mobilize.

NATO's Military Preparedness Would Provide No Time to Mobilize

Because NATO has no collective military-industrial effort, every

Allied government determines what weapons it will buy, when, in what quantities, and for what military purposes. Some rich nations are poorly defended, as are all poor nations. The weak endanger the strong to a far greater degree than the strong can protect the weak. Logistic support for what German General Johannes Steinhoff called "a museum of weapons systems" is provided by fourteen national defense ministries for thirty-nine armed forces. No wonder that NATO Secretary General Joseph Luns spoke of "a logistics nightmare that may well prove impossible to support."

The provisioning of forces, and the provisioning of war reserve stocks, is also a national responsibility. Defense ministries (European and North American) buy weapons without adequate ammunition, aircraft without adequate repair parts, missile launchers without adequate numbers of missiles. Shortages of fuel, ammunition and other expendables limit operational training, and severely reduce Allied readiness.

The Report of the Defense Industrial Base Panel of the House Armed Services Committee found that: "...war reserve materiel stocks are at a dangerously low level and can support only the shortest of 'short war' scenarios."[20] Had the Panel addressed the Alliance problem (and not just the American problem) it would have found that the short-war/long-war argument effectively is foreclosed by the long lead times—and gaps of months or years—between war reserve replenishment orders and first production deliveries. It would have found, in other words, that NATO's national forces would one-by-one exhaust their war reserve stocks of ammunition, repair parts, and weapons—and then months and years would go by before the first output of each Ally's industrial mobilization (or procurement) could reach the front. In 1979, another House Armed Services Subcommittee found that:

> NATO's capability to fight a protracted war is almost nonexistent. NATO lacks the capability to fight for thirty days and present plans will not provide such a capability before 1983.
>
> The European shortages of ammunition and replacement stocks are critical; evidence available to the Subcommittee suggests that European forces will begin to run out of equipment and ammunition in a matter of days rather than weeks or months.[21]

The 30-day war reserve capability by 1983 was contained in the NATO Long-Term Defense Program (LTDP) approved at the Washington NATO Summit in 1978. The LTDP was approved at the NATO Summit but improvements did not begin immediately, as President Carter explained on 31 May 1978:

> ...I want to mention the one remaining unresolved aspect of the Long-Term Defense Program. Although the program calls

for new and unprecedented Alliance cooperation, *no procedures have yet been devised for ensuring that it is carried out.* We must avoid bold programs heartily endorsed—then largely ignored. The Report before us directs the Secretary General to present *for national review* what changes are essential for vigorous follow-through.[22] (emphasis added)

The above paragraph should be read most carefully by anyone in the Reagan Administration planning a needed NATO industrial mobilization capability, for it provides an insight into the Byzantine difficulties of implementing decisions within the Alliance, even after they have already been approved at a NATO Summit by fourteen Heads of Government.

Two years after the NATO Summit, it was acknowledged that:

...the LTDP, NATO's new force goals, the integrated air defense program, the AWACS program, NICS Stage II, various arms cooperation proposals, and last but not least the LRTNF [Long-Range Theater Nuclear Force] agreement... all these elaborate projects exist today mostly on paper.[23]

By February 1980, the Senate Armed Services Committee was told that the nations had "accepted approximately 60 percent of the measures as national force proposals for the 1981-86 Force Goal Cycle... [but] progress is slow in provision of war reserve stocks of ammunition."[24] Thus, the planned 30-day war reserves by 1983 had already slipped by at least two years. The following colloquy between Representative Norman D. Dicks (Democrat, Washington) and General Bernard W. Rogers is instructive:

MR. DICKS:	One of the factors involved in the ammunition equation is that fact [that] many of our Allies have even fewer stocks than we do.
GENERAL ROGERS:	That is correct.
MR. DICKS:	What efforts are you making to improve the overall Alliance posture in that respect?
GENERAL ROGERS:	Cajole, plead, prod. That is just about the extent of it.[25]

These are the problems that led Representative Newt Gingrich (Republican, Georgia) to comment that "any serious examination of NATO's condition after 30 days of war would terrify our publics. The time to be prepared is before the fight, not after the defeat."[26]

At the beginning of this chapter, it was argued that unless the Congress is prepared to vote World War II-scale defense budgets, and a return to Lend-Lease and Military Assistance, America's "ailing defense industrial base" cannot possibly redress the conventional force balance worldwide. Yet there is nothing in the ongoing industrial base discussions to indicate that either the Administration or the Congress are considering the other alternative of working with our Allies to build a productive and efficient defense industrial base in Western Europe, and in the Western Pacific, to complement the North American industrial base. This effort would require great political skill, dedication and leadership by the President and the Congress.

But it would be easier for the United States than the impossible task of trying to defend the Western World unilaterally. In his testimony to the Congress last year, CINCEUR (SACEUR) General Rogers noted that the Warsaw Pact's current capabilities have largely diminished any advantages NATO might expect to gain after mobilization:

> Twenty years ago, we could rely on Western ability to mobilize, deploy and transport supplies and forces in the quantities and to the places where needed in a timely manner. Today, we are increasingly deprived of that margin of safety. The Soviets have methodically isolated and addressed those forces, weaknesses and vulnerabilities which previously enabled the West to counterbalance traditional Soviet strengths without matching them. As a result of that concentrated effort, no single facet of the Soviet military effort is today susceptible to unilateral Western exploitation.[27]

Nor is it susceptible to unilateral American industrial action, except at the intercontinental nuclear level. The United States can (by its resources alone) maintain the intercontinental nuclear balance. It can contribute substantially to redressing the European theater nuclear balance, but only with European approval, and European infrastructure and other financial support.

But the United States cannot (by its resources alone) maintain the conventional force balance in the North Atlantic Treaty area. In Europe, the United States provides 10% of the ground forces, 25% of the tactical air forces. On the Central Front, both *before* and *after* mobilization, the United States would provide approximately 25% of the ground and tactical air forces.

In 1978, the Congressional Budget Office published a series of four papers entitled, *U.S. Air and Ground Conventional Forces for NATO*, in which it emphasized that:

> The strength of NATO defense depends less on the capabilities of the U.S. forces than it does on the capabilities of the remaining three-quarters of ground and air forces which are provided by Western European Allies. How well these Allied forces are armed largely determines not only the strength of NATO, but also the effectiveness of further improvements in U.S. forces.

Most Western European forces are not as well provided as U.S. forces with critical weapons, equipment, and supplies. Compared with those of the United States, Allied forces appear to be less able to counter improved Soviet ground and air forces or to sustain combat in the fact of a very intense Warsaw Pact attack. Although Western European governments have procurement plans to strengthen their capabilities, it does not seem likely that these improvements will remove the basic discrepancies between U.S. and Allied forces. Such discrepancies present a major problem for NATO defense; they also present the most difficult kind of problem for expenditures on U.S. NATO forces to correct.[28]

Thus the time that may be available to mobilize either American forces, or American and Allied forces to fight a war in Europe does not depend upon the strength or weakness of American forces alone, or on the productive capability of the American industrial base. Rather, it depends upon the willingness and readiness of our European Allies to join the United States in developing a collective capability to fight a conventional war in Europe.

Extended Deterrence Must Be Superseded by Reinforced Deterrence

It would be wrong to draw the conclusion that our European Allies are simply unwilling to shoulder their fair share of the common defense. The issues are far more fundamental. The question that continues to perplex most members of the Congress, and to frustrate both civilian and military officials in the Executive Branch, was well phrased by Chairman Joseph P. Addabbo (Democrat, New York) of the House Defense Appropriations Subcommittee:

> Why does it seem that our NATO partners do not carry their fair share of our mutual defense costs when it appears that they have much more to lose than we do in any NATO-Warsaw Pact conflict short of an all out nuclear war?[29]

The answer lies in the phrase, "short of an all out nuclear war." Americans think in terms of defending Europe, short of an all out nuclear war. Europeans think in terms of deterring an attack on Europe, by threatening all out nuclear war. Many Europeans fear that if NATO's conventional forces are collectively strong enough to defend Europe from a Warsaw Pact attack, without resort to nuclear weapons, it would decouple the American intercontinental, theater and battlefield nuclear commitment to extended deterrence. They understandably fear that for the third time this century, European cities would be destroyed, and

Europe's peoples slaughtered or made homeless, in a devastating conventional war of attrition.

Many Americans fear that with nuclear parity, the United States may find itself precipitated into a nuclear war because of the unnecessary weakness of Allied conventional forces. Understandably, they fear that U.S. cities may be destroyed, and millions of Americans incinerated in a nuclear exchange to protect European cities from conventional destruction.

The mischief set loose by the doctrine of extended nuclear deterrence (instead of collective conventional defense) has now come home to roost. In his address to the NATO Thirtieth Anniversary Conference in Brussels in 1979, Henry A. Kissinger declared:

> ...it is time that we decide what role exactly we want for our ground forces on the continent. These forces were deployed in the 1950s when American strategic superiority was so great that we could defend Europe by the threat of general nuclear war. And they were deployed in Europe, as I have often said, as a means of ensuring the automaticity of our response. Our forces were in Europe as hostages. Everybody had a vested interest in not making the forces too large. We wound up with the paradox that they were much too large for what was needed for a tripwire yet not large enough for a sustained conventional defense.[30]

Dr. Kissinger probably touched a raw nerve in Europe when he also said:

> ...to be tactless—the secret dream of every European was, of course, to avoid a nuclear war but, secondly, if there had to be a nuclear war, to have it conducted over their heads by the strategic forces of the United States and the Soviet Union.[31]

At the same conference, Brigadier Kenneth Hunt, former Assistant Director of the International Institute of Strategic Studies in London, and currently Director of the British Atlantic Committee, explained that:

> ...if conventional forces were too strong, they would, in the eyes of many Europeans, weaken deterrence, since they would tend to weaken the nuclear link between a European battlefield and the United States. Such a defense would run the risk of inviting a protracted conventional conflict in Europe, with all the destruction that would surely follow.[32]

The doctrine of extended deterrence has fostered the view in Europe that the credibility of the nuclear deterrent depends upon the noncredibility of the conventional defense of Europe. This concept of coupling the American intercontinental nuclear forces to the inability to defend

Europe extends also to the Theater Nuclear Force (TNF) modernization. Even after the deployment of Pershing II's and cruise missiles in Europe, the theater nuclear balance will still heavily favor the Soviet Union. But Americans report discussions with German leaders who favor this inequality to insure escalation to U.S. intercontinental nuclear forces.

The North Atlantic Alliance thus faces a testing time for which it is ill-equipped to cope. The habits and attitudes of European leaders were formed in an era when Europe could find shelter under the American nuclear umbrella. The Alliance may well founder in this its fourth decade because it cannot resolve European and American differences over burden-sharing, NATO readiness and weapons standardization. These are but symptoms of much deeper divisions. The real root of Allied discord is a fundamental strategic disagreement as to whether deterrence can still rest on inadequate defense.

The issue is not, as the Europeans have seen it, the coupling of nuclear forces to conventional forces. The issue is coupling American strength to European weakness, and then having to suffer the consequences. Coupling American strength to European strength will always have popular and political support in the United States. But strength to weakness will lead to decoupling, even of conventional forces.

It is time that NATO recognizes that extended deterrence has been made obsolete by nuclear parity. It must now be superseded by the concept of "Reinforced Deterrence:" credible, collective conventional parity, *reinforced* by theater nuclear parity and intercontinental nuclear parity. This is a credible defensive posture that is entirely within the economic and industrial capabilities of Europe and North America.

To paraphrase a statement made famous in our earlier history, we and our Allies must agree on: billions for defense, but not one more cent for a tripwire!

NOTES

1. *The Ailing Defense Industrial Base: Unready for Crisis*, Report of the Defense Industrial Base Panel of the House Armed Services Committee, 31 December 1980, Committee Print, Report No. 29 (Washington, D.C.: U.S. Government Printing Office, 1980).
2. *Rationalization/Standardization Within NATO*, Seventh Annual Report to the Congress, January 1981, by Secretary of Defense Harold Brown, p. 14.
3. Ibid., p. 12.
4. Dean Acheson, *Present at the Creation* (New York: W.W. Norton, 1969), p. 397.
5. Ibid., p. 398.
6. Ibid.
7. Ibid., p. 399.
8. Ibid.

9. Ibid., p. 398.
10. Alexander M. Haig, Jr., Prepared Statement, Senate Armed Services Committee, July, 1979, mimeograph. p. 1.
11. Senate Armed Services Committee, *Report on Department of Defense Authorization Act for FY 1981*, Report No. 96-826 (Washington, D.C., 10 June 1980), p. 19.
12. *Rationalization/Standardization*, Op. Cit., p. 7. This year's Report to the Congress included (in the words of the Secretary of Defense) "a seven-year look at where we have been, where we are, and what yet needs to be done." The Secretary said this seven-year overview would "be mindful of the Senate Armed Services Committee's conclusion, with which I agree, that 'better ways to accomplish the integration of NATO forces must be found.'"
13. Ibid., p. 12.
14. Ibid., pp. 11-13.
15. *Senator Sam Nunn, Gearing Up To Deter Combat in Europe: The Long and Short Of It*, An Address to the New York Militia Association, Reprinted in the *Congressional Record*, 13 September 1976, p. S-15661.
16. Oliver C. Boileau, Financial Times, International Aerospace Conference, Paris, 1977, mimeograph.
17. *Rationalization/Standardization*, Op. Cit., p. 13.
18. Robert W. Komer, Remarks to the Atlantic Treaty Association (ATA) Assembly, Washington, D.C., 12 October, 1979, Department of Defense News Release No. 501-79, p. 4.
19. *Rationalization/Standardization*, Op. Cit., pp. 7 and 9.
20. *Ailing Defense Industrial Base*, Op. Cit., p. 18.
21. House Armed Services Special Subcommittee Report on *NATO Standardization, Interoperability and Readiness*, H.A.S.C. No. 95-101 (Washington, D.C.: U.S. Government Printing Office), p. 2.
22. Statement by the President on *NATO Long Term Defense Policy*, The White House, 31 May 1978, mimeograph, p. 2.
23. Robert W. Komer, 17th International Wehrkunde Conference, Munich, Federal Republic of Germany, 9 February 1980, Department of Defense News Release No. 46-80, p. 4.
24. Written answer provided for the record by the Defense Department. Senate Armed Services Committee, *Hearings on FY 1981 Defense Authorization Act*, (Washington, D.C.: U.S. Government Printing Office, 1980) pp. 389-90.
25. House Defense Appropriations Subcommittee, *Hearings on Department of Defense Appropriations for Fiscal Year 1981* (Washington, D.C.: U.S. Government Printing Office, 1980), Part 4, p. 55.
26. "War in Europe," A Letter to the Editor, *The Economist*, 13 June 1981, p. 4.
27. Prepared Statement for the Armed Services Committees, and the Defense Appropriations Subcommittees; see for example, House Defense Appropriations Subcommittee Hearings, Op. Cit., p. 6.
28. *U.S. Air and Ground Conventional Forces for NATO: Overview*, Congressional Budget Office (Washington, D.C.: U.S. Government Printing Office, 1978), p. ix.
29. House Defense Appropriations Subcommittee Hearings, Op. Cit., p. 20.
30. Henry A. Kissinger, "The Future of NATO" in *NATO The Next Thirty Years*, edited by Kenneth A. Myers (Boulder, Co.: Westview Press, 1980), p. 9-10.
31. Ibid., pp. 8-9.

32. Kenneth Hunt, "Alternative Conventional Force Postures" in *NATO The Next Thirty Years*, Ibid., p. 134.

Note: For a fuller discussion of the consequences of NATO's failure to develop a collective defense industrial effort, see author's paper entitled *The Structural Disarmament of the West—Our Most Critical Defense Industrial Challenge*, presented at the 1981 Senior Conference, 4-6 June, United States Military Academy, West Point, New York. Copies available from the Center for Strategic and International Studies, 1800 K Street, N.W., Suite 400, Washington, D.C. 20006.

16

The Alliance Framework: East Asia

Leonard Unger

In East Asia the United States is allied or more loosely associated with a number of nations which lie along the western rim of the Pacific Ocean, from Japan in the north to Australia and New Zealand in the south. In the cases of Japan and South Korea, the Philippines, Thailand and the ANZUS partners (Australia and New Zealand) there are formal alliances with America in the form of mutual security treaties and other explicit ties. While the obligations in these treaties are not as automatic as in the case of NATO, the expectation is that any military action involving the United States and the Soviet Union in the Western Pacific area would involve them to some degree or possibly totally. In a situation where the danger of war hung heavy over the region or the world as a whole, the concern and sense of potential involvement would be strong.

Other East Asian nations lie outside this framework. Among those is Burma, which could be expected to seek in every way possible to keep itself divorced from any assocation of a military or security nature with any nation in or outside the region. Indonesia is politically associated with its ASEAN partners, two of which (Thailand and the Philippines) have explicit security pacts with the United States, and two of which (Malaysia and Singapore) have a loose but important security relationship with Australia, New Zealand and the United Kingdom. Taiwan (The Republic of China) was once part of the security chain extending from Japan to Southeast Asia, linked to the United States by a Mutual Security Treaty. Normalization with the People's Republic of China brought this to an end—at the close of 1979, one year after the Treaty was denounced—and no such formal relationship now obtains. The United States has committed itself to a peaceful solution of the Taiwan question, however, and to provide Taiwan with necessary defensive weapons. It is likely that in case of a contest between the superpowers, Taiwan would be aligned with the United States and those nations allied or associated with it. Taiwan's facilities and productive capacities moreover, would probably be at the disposal of the United States and its allies, if this were considered necessary or advisable and could be managed in such a fashion as to avoid a critical impasse with the People's Republic of China. Two nations in the Western Pacific, in addition to the Soviet Union itself, could be expected to join the Soviet Union outright in case of trouble, or if not, at least to assume a hostile posture toward any of the other East Asian nations which were cooperating with the United States. These two are North Korea and Vietnam.

In anything like the present situation it would seem that the People's Republic of China might well be involved in the event of a military confrontation between the United States and the Soviet Union. There might develop circumstances, however, in which China would remain neutral and any indications of a reduction in Sino-Soviet tensions should be monitored carefully. China's involvement on the American side, should this take place, would have to be anticipated as a net drain of resources; it will be many years before the PRC even approaches having the infrastructure and industrial output adequate to support its forces which would be confronting the Soviet Union. This is not to say that China would easily or rapidly succumb to a Soviet attack, assuming it were something short of a massive nuclear or chemical weapons assault. But its resistance would be widely dispersed and successful only over a long period; this would require considerable external supply and support.

Against the background of these relationships, formal and otherwise, we will examine, country by country, what reactions it would be reasonable to expect in response to the development of a confrontation between the United States and the Soviet Union and how this would bear on the availability of the resources and facilities pertinent to any conflict which might break out. Before turning to that highly speculative process, however, let us take stock of the assets and liabilities, country by country, of our allies and friendly associates in the East Asian region. This will entail an inventory, albeit in very general terms, of their resources, industries, labor skills, transport and storage facilities, repair and maintenance capacities as well as their armed forces.

Inventory of Assets Pertinent to Mobilization

JAPAN

Books have been written, especially recently, on Japan's productive capacities. Attention has been drawn by some to the facilities and services which could make a major contribution, if Japan were prepared to have them utilized, to the defense of the Free World. This pertains especially to crises in the West Pacific-East Asian area, but also could relate to Southeast Asia (witness the Vietnam War), the Indian Ocean area and, conceivably, even Europe and the Mediterranean. Japan has military forces which, while small and essentially defensive, are modern and very well trained and equipped. Japan states that its fundamental policy is to possess a defense capability of an appropriate scale and to maintain the credibility of the security arrangements with the United States. In response to various Soviet moves, especially the invasion of Afghanistan, deployments into the Soviet-held Kurile Islands, and the Soviet presence at Danang and Cam Ranh Bay, there has been an acceleration of equipping and preparation, and a greater willingness to discuss with the United States and other friendly nations the kinds of contingencies that may arise and what role the Japanese armed forces might play.

Japan is the world's leading shipbuilder today and even so there is unused capacity—all could be put to service for naval and transport needs. The level of technology in this industry is as high as anywhere in the world and includes experience in constructing nuclear-powered vessels.

Japan's aircraft industry likewise ranks with the world's largest. The production of military aircraft, with which Japan has already had considerable experience (the F-4 and 104, and coproduction of the F-15, and manufacture of the F-1s, as well as the most advanced commercial aircraft) represents another field in which Japan's support in a military crisis could be most significant. This is also true in many sectors of industry, including the electronics field where there is great adaptability to new tasks and extensive productive capacity. Japan produces tanks, and tractor production, including diesel tractors, could readily be adapted to expand this capability. Ordnance capacity for artillery, guns, missiles and smaller rockets is large. With the supply by the United States of necessary parts, aircraft and space vehicles could be readily converted to military use, and made compatible with U.S. equipment. Japan is, today, confident of its capacity to develop equipment comparable with the best available elsewhere. In fact, Japan (and to a lesser extent Korea and Taiwan) today produces many of the components which go into United States equipment critical to defense; this raises a potential difficulty if the availability of such items should come into question in a crisis.

Japan also represents an immense logistics base which, if available in time of emergency, could provide for U.S. and Allied forces repair, storage, loading and unloading, transport and other facilities of the most modern sort. There are the drydocks at Sasebo, Yokosuka and Yokohama; logistics bases such as at Sagamihara; container ports; and roll-on, roll-off facilities. A reflection, albeit on a relatively small scale, of what Japan could undertake is the proposal currently under discussion that Japan assume the noncombat task of resupplying the Allied forces in the Indian Ocean area. This proposal reflects, on the one hand, a recognition of Japan's reluctance to become involved in military deployments far from its home islands (in part because of the strict "defensive" rationale for its military preparedness and interpretations of Article 9 of the Constitution) and, on the other hand, the absolutely vital importance to Japan of the sea lanes to the Middle East whence comes the major share of Japan's energy supplies.

Current reports from Tokyo refer to serious discussions in Japan today on "the possible revision of the American-imposed 1946 Constitution" that in principle forbids armed forces (and by extension, therefore, the development of nuclear weapons), large expenditures for arms, and conscription for what is now a "self defense force." This trend of thinking suggests that the capacities and facilities referred to above will, if anything, be expanded and improved; Japan today, in fact, has more destroyers and aircraft in the Pacific than does the United States. Similarly, prohibitions and inhibitions which for many years have limited Japan's functioning in the military field are being relaxed, and some may be entirely removed. Decisions have been taken for joint U.S.-Japanese exercises and training, logistic studies concerning supply, transport, maintenance, and facilities. These developments, combined with a growing willingness on Japan's part to discuss contingencies and emergency planning (including "situations in the Far East outside of Japan"), suggest that the assets which Japan could bring to mobilization might be, if anything, more substantial than they even appear to be today. That, of course, leaves open the question of the circumstances under which Japanese support could be counted on.

Specific attention is called to Japan's role in connection with any military emergency involving Korea. Japan must play a positive role in case of trouble, since it provides a base structure for air, naval and logistic forces which are essential to support the U.S. and South Korean forces in Korea; similarly it is from Japan that there emanates the intelligence and logistical support for those forces in South Korea. In due course, Japan may also be expected to be an important source of weapons and defense-related equipment for forces in Korea.

SOUTH KOREA

South Korea is both a significant asset and a potential liability in terms of mobilization to meet emergencies in East Asia. It is a liability in that Korea is itself a continuing, unresolved issue between the United States and the Communist powers, one which led to armed conflict in the early 1950s and which has threatened periodically to do so again in the years since then. It is hard to imagine a crisis situation developing in East Asia, in which the United States was involved, in which the involvement of the Republic of Korea would not also be a probability. Therefore

Korea needs to be seen not only for the considerable input it could provide in terms of industry, facilities and the like, but also as generating major requirements for the support of military operations which might take place there. This is a problem particularly because of the considerable strength of the North Korean forces.

But let us look at Korea in the same sense that we just assessed Japan and its potential contribution to mobilization for possible conflict. As for the Korean armed forces themselves, they are the largest military force in East Asia outside the Communist countries. In many other respects what the Republic of Korea could contribute is a great deal more limited than what could be expected from Japan, particularly in the industrial field; this is true both in quantity and in the state of the art. Nevertheless, Korea is, in many respects, the second largest economy in noncommunist East Asia. In fact, in shipbuilding, in which the Korean product is deemed by some to be as good as Japan's, Korea has demonstrated its capacity to compete successfully with the Japanese product.

Korea has a growing experience in military aircraft production, based primarily on its F-5 coproduction arrangements with Northrop, similar to a scheme begun earlier in Taiwan. Production is also under way in Korea of howitzers, 105mm guns, M-16 tanks (including the rehabilitation of M-48's), and other weapons. In the nonmilitary field there is the large Hyundai complex with a variety of pertinent products including earth-moving machinery. The electronics industry is likewise extensively developed, with many potential and actual military applications.

In the logistics realm Korea also has significant assets. Port facilities at Pusan are modern and large scale, and there are many overhaul and maintenance facilities where experience with U.S. weapons is extensive. Korea is also the site today of a significant U.S. Air Force repair and overhaul facility which has certain equipment and some skilled labor which earlier operated in Taiwan at Tainan. Experience there with the F-5 and the F-4 has been extensive.

Except for some of the newer industrial complexes in Korea in such locations as Ulsan—the Hyundai complex, for example—there is a major concentration in the Seoul area. This lies just thirty miles from the Demilitarized Zone and the boundary line of North Korea, where the North is deployed in force in an offensive posture. Dependence on production from industries in that region obviously entails special risks not faced elsewhere. Another complication with regard to Korea is the Japanese position. While past reservations and inhibitions have been reduced, there remains a question as to the degree to which Japan would seek to circumscribe its support or the support by U.S. forces based in Japan in case of the outbreak of hostilities in Korea.

Viewed another way, South Korea can supply only part of the requirements of its own ground forces. It produces some artillery and smaller weapons; it has moved into tank rebuilding and production and can handle the maintenance of its missile systems. Light manned armored vehicles can be produced and there is increasing ammunition production capacity. There is a limited capacity to support naval forces, but Korea depends on external sources for virtually all really sophisticated equipment, e.g., fire control and electronic equipment. The building of frigates is getting under way, but again, the weapons and other sophisticated gear are imported. Ammunition supplies come heavily from the United States.

Assessment of Korea's role would not be complete without reference to the presence of the U.S. Air and Ground forces there and the utilization by the U.S. Navy of extensive facilities in Korean ports. This assures a readiness and the existence of support facilities which means that many of the steps which otherwise would be required in case of emergency can be omitted and forces can move into action on the shortest notice. It also means that a close relationship has been established with the Korean military forces which again assures instant collaboration in an emergency situation, with respective roles and missions already well understood.

TAIWAN

Following the conclusion in 1954 of a Mutual Security Treaty with the Republic of China there developed a close cooperative relationship with the United States which persisted until the derecognition of that government at the end of 1978 and the termination of that Treaty one year later. Early in the period the military cooperation was heavily focused on the situation in the Taiwan Straits and the recurring incidents involving the forces of the People's Republic of China. More recently the American military presence was concerned with other tasks, most notably the Vietnam War. Ports and naval facilities on Taiwan provided an important base for the operations of the U.S. Seventh Fleet, and several major, fully equipped airfields were the points of departure for American B-52 missions and other air operations in support of those missions and in other activities. Certain facilities supplemented information available from other sources concerning situations in sensitive and critical areas.

Chinese-American cooperation on Taiwan in the military field extended also to storage and repair facilities. Industries in Taiwan, manned by a highly skilled labor force, provided some of the requirements of U.S. forces operating in the East Asian arena. The geographic location of Taiwan provided a valuable position along the key sea lane to China, Korea and Japan from the Strait of Malacca and the Indian Ocean and Persian Gulf.

Taiwan's industry has steadily expanded this capacity to produce arms, equipment, vehicles, ships, aircraft and other products which could contribute to a mobilization effort in East Asia. Coproduction of the F-5E and F-5F is well under way and it is expected that coproduction in a similar mode of a follow-on aircraft may be begun before too long. The capacity of Taiwan's shipbuilding facilities in Kaohsiung and Keelung is dramatically demonstrated by the 500,000 ton tankers which have been turned out; such facilities (including the adjacent China Steel plant) could be readily adapted to repairing and constructing naval vessels if this were required. A small but growing automobile industry probably in due course could, in a time of emergency, be converted to military vehicles. The vast electronics industry of Taiwan, now occupied primarily with T.V. and similar products, could be converted to military requirements. A key aircraft repair and maintenance facility at Tainan continues in operation even though it no longer services the U.S. military aircraft which it was originally set up to undertake as its central function. Thus Taiwan continues to perform many indispensable functions and in the event of an emergency could, in all likelihood, provide a considerable measure of support for a military effort involving the United States and its East Asian allies.

THE PHILIPPINES

Under the SEATO (Southeast Asia Collective Defense) Treaty, signed in 1954, the United States, the Philippines and, among others, one other Southeast Asian nation, Thailand, agreed that an attack upon one of the parties would be recognized as dangerous to the peace and safety of the others. In such an event, each member agreed to "act to meet the common danger in accordance with its constitutional processes." (This restated in essence the security undertakings already in force between the Philippines and the United States as set forth in the bilateral Mutual Security Treaty signed in 1951. The Philippine-U.S. Bases Agreement, signed in 1947, and recently updated, provides for the use by the United States of military facilities in the Philippines, most notably Clark Field and Subic Bay).

The base rights enjoyed by the United States in the Philippines are among the most significant in East Asia. Those bases constitute a virtually indispensable position for the projection of power across the South China Sea and Southeast Asia, and through the Indian Ocean where runs the long logistical sea lane from the Middle East to Japan. Thus the Philippine bases constitute one of the most significant sets of assets in the Alliance framework and the United States has devoted substantial sums in aid of the Philippines in an effort to support the promotion of economic and social development in that nation, as well as for the continual improvement of the military facilities themselves, together with various kinds of support activities.

Repeatedly, and most notably during the Vietnam War, the United States has depended on the Philippine bases and, in the process, has continually improved the facilities there to adapt them to new weapons systems. Thus the quite significant assets for mobilization in the Philippines are primarily those under direct U.S. administration and management. Nevertheless in the last analysis those facilities are available at the pleasure of the Government of the Philippines; moreover many of the key facilities employ the labor of citizens of the Philippines and if these employees were not available the functioning of the facilities would be substantially jeopardized and some probably put out of action. Aircraft and shipbuilding (for example, Kawasaki on Subic Bay), repair and overhaul and a variety of communication and listening installations provide support to the central facilities represented by the major airfield (Clark) and the naval base (Subic).

Aside from these major U.S.-operated facilities, the Philippines produces commodities and provides services useful in any mobilization situation. In due course it is expected that this will include a light diesel engine factory as part of an ASEAN program. Probably none of these, however, is unique or highly significant in terms of volume. Fortunately the location of the Philippines makes it less vulnerable, militarily, and therefore it presents less of a defense burden for the United States. Volatile politics inside the country repeatedly present to the world a picture of instability and uncertain future. Thus far the connection with the United States, a central factor in Philippine foreign policy, has not been seriously challenged, but a critical period may lie just ahead and we may see developments having strong implications for future U.S.-Philippine military cooperation.

THE OTHER ASEAN COUNTRIES

The loose association of nations called ASEAN (Association of Southeast Asian Nations) brings together Thailand, Malaysia, Singapore, Indonesia and the Philippines. The special U.S. relationship with the last named has already been discussed; the other ASEAN nation linked with the United States in an explicit security agreement is Thailand. Like the Philippines, it is one of signatories of the SEATO Treaty, and it is only the SEATO Treaty which has linked Thailand with the United States in a formal sense. Under it there developed a close U.S.-Thai relationship in the political, economic and security realms and the United States has provided Thailand with assistance including a considerable amount of equipment and training for Thailand's armed forces. At various times, and most notably during the Vietnam War, Thailand has granted U.S. forces, primarily air and naval, the use of bases on Thai soil; in the 1970s approximately 50,000 U.S. military personnel were stationed in Thailand. In that period the air and naval facilities required for U.S. use were considerably expanded and equipped with modern facilities and some of those bases continue to be used by Thai forces and are in a reasonably ready state; others would require major rehabilitation to be put back into full service. Finally, Thailand does produce substantial agricultural surpluses, notably rice and rubber, and valuable minerals such as tin, tungsten and rare metals. Thailand otherwise could not be expected to play a significant role in a mobilization effort. Its industry and other facilities, while rapidly developing today, would not be major contributors to meet defense needs.

Another ASEAN member, Singapore, because of its location beside the Strait of Malacca, has a possible role in a mobilization situation of considerable importance. Through the Strait go vital commodities for the nations of East Asia, most notably Japan which receives more than 90% of its oil from tankers transiting these waters. Singapore's position, and that of the ASEAN nations in general, has also become more important as the Soviet Union has established naval and air positions, at Cam Ranh Bay and Danang in Vietnam.

The importance of Singapore, however, extends beyond its location and includes its considerable ship repair facilities, refineries, container terminals and generally very modern and well-equipped ports and industry. These assets, which include shipbuilding, offshore oil exploration enterprises, aircraft maintenance, and electronics manufacture, could obviously play a significant role in any mobilization effort in East Asia. In Southeast Asia there is no other reservoir of skills, albeit on a small scale, to match those of Singapore.

Malaysia, yet another ASEAN member, is linked with Singapore, Australia, New Zealand and the United Kingdom, in a five-power arrangement which is rather loose. It nevertheless recognizes an interest in cooperation to sustain the friendly countries of generally like-minded political and economic orientation in the region. There are joint military exercises and some continuing small-scale missions in Southeast Asia for Australian and New Zealand forces. This provides a further link and general commitment which could have some significance in a mobilization situation.

The ASEAN countries are on record as favoring ASEAN as a Zone of Peace, Freedom and Neutrality (ZOPFAN). Malaysia and Indonesia, of the ASEAN members, appear to be those most devoted to this concept. What the concept means, or could mean in differing circumstances is, however, not very clear. It is also pertinent to note that while Thailand, Singapore and probably the Philippines, tend to see Vietnam (and the Soviet Union behind it) as Southeast Asia's central security problem, Malaysia and Indonesia continue to express doubts about the long-term intentions of the People's Republic of China. In any event, neither Malaysia nor Indonesia would be expected to play significant roles in a mobilization situation, with two important exceptions: they both adjoin the Strait of Malacca and Indonesia controls the only nearby alternative routes to the Strait; and they both produce critically necessary commodities, most notably oil and gas.

AUSTRALIA AND NEW ZEALAND

These two nations are not, strictly speaking, a part of East Asia. Nevertheless, Australia, and to a lesser extent New Zealand, has in recent years seen itself as more and more affected by developments in that region. World War II brought home sharply what East Asia means in security terms and that region has become steadily more and more a factor in the economic life of Australia and New Zealand. It is hard to imagine either nation regarding with equanimity the development of any serious security threat to Japan or the other nations of the region; in fact, the participation of both nations in the Korean and Vietnam conflicts, despite misgivings particularly in the latter case, attests to their interest in East Asia, and also to their commitment to ANZUS. They see it as their link with the United States and they assume a common concern with the United States about East Asia, its peace and security.

In any mobilization situation Australia, in particular, could be expected to play a significant role. Its manufactures in some fields could be of importance but, more pertinently, Australia stands out as a supplier of both raw materials and food, particularly minerals. It also provides sites, increasingly, for secure naval bases and various kinds of special installations situated far from the probable scene of action, but making a considerable contribution to preparedness and, if need be, to operations. It should not be forgotten that Australia is an Indian Ocean as well as a Pacific power, and it can be expected to provide significant base facilities to support the greatly increased Allied deployment in that area.

National Reactions to a Soviet-American Crisis

We have discussed what the countries of East Asia could bring to a mobilization effort in resources, facilities, productive capacities and pertinent experience. That is an essential part of the picture in seeking to assess what the United States could count on in the way of assistance and support in a developing crisis with the Soviet Union. But what is available is only a part of the story. What will be the assessment of the East Asian countries as to where their most important interests lie in case of a developing crisis between the superpowers? How will they assess relative strengths and determination? What will be their expectations about the use of nuclear weapons and how could that influence decisions? While those nations which have been discussed above can all be identified as friendly to the United States, in greater or lesser degrees, they may have quite different views as to the likely outcome of a test of strength between the superpowers. They may feel that, at least until the picture is clearer, it would be wiser to avoid commitment. And that could, and usually would, mean avoiding commitment of the kinds of assets and facilities discussed above.

Several countries seem so clearly to have their fate intimately tied up with the United States that their remaining apart from a developing conflict seems unrealistic—South Korea is a case in point. Others are so committed ideologically and traditionally, as well as by treaty terms, that their commitment to a course paralleling that of the United States seems probable. Australia would be a case in point, particularly if Western Europe and other Commonwealth members were also involved. The Philippines, for historical reasons as well as because of its heavy involvement in any case via the two major bases, seems likely to accept commitment. In the case of Japan there is the Security Treaty and the position of the Liberal Democratic Party, both of which suggest the strong likelihood of Japan's playing an active role; but there are also powerful currents resisting Japan's involvement except in case of direct attack. This applies with even more force to the other countries of the region, in spite of their fairly strong identification with the Free World.

Let us turn to the treaty language and see what is provided for in the various pacts that were concluded, primarily in the 1950s, between the United States and individual East Asian nations, or in some cases in collective frameworks involving more than two countries.

In the first such pact, that of ANZUS (Australia, New Zealand and the United States), which entered into force in April 1952, the pattern was set which has held true, mutatis mutandis, in the other Pacific-East Asian pacts concluded subsequently. There are provisions calling for "self-help and mutual aid" in order to "maintain and develop individual and collective capacity to resist armed attack." In each case there is a provision calling for consultation whenever the political independence or security (and, except for Korea, the territorial integrity) of either party is "threatened by external armed attack" in the Pacific, or, in the case of Japan, only "in the territories under the administration of Japan." Each treaty asserts that an armed attack in the Pacific area (or the SEATO area, in the case of that treaty) on any or all of the parties is dangerous to the peace and safety of the other(s) and there is agreement to act to meet the common danger in accordance with the constitutional processes of each. The automaticity of the North Atlantic Treaty is not found in any of these treaties; i.e., an attack on any one member is not regarded as an attack on all, but is regarded as being "dangerous to the peace and safety" of the others.

Each treaty has it special features reflecting the peculiar conditions relating to the countries involved. For example, the U.S.-Korean Treaty is so worded as to reflect the special *de facto* situation of a divided Korea, with half of the country under the jurisdiction of another government. The U.S.-Japanese Security Treaty speaks of the "Far East" instead of the "Pacific." In the ANZUS Treaty there is the declaration of a sense of unity so that "no potential aggressor could be under the illusion that any of them (i.e., the parties) stands alone in the Pacific Area." Finally it should be borne in mind that there are overlaps, in that Australia and New Zealand are covered by the ANZUS Treaty, and the Philippines by the bilateral Treaty, as well as all three by the SEATO Treaty. The SEATO Treaty incidentally relates only to *Communist* attack.

Perhaps most germane is the provision cited above, contained in all these pacts, especially calling for self-help and mutual aid to maintain and develop the individual and collective capacity to resist armed attack. Here is a policy undertaking to cooperate not only in a direct military mode in case of armed attack, but also to cooperate in preparing to meet military contingencies. This would seem to include not only organizing and training armed forces but developing appropriate facilities, including the mobilization and logistical bases required to support the military effort which might be undertaken pursuant to the terms of the treaties. Indeed such cooperation has been invoked, albeit sometimes without formal reference to those treaty provisions, in cases such as the Korean War and the Vietnam War.

There has never developed in the East Asian area, between the United States and its various partners in the security realm, anything approaching the extensive and specific logistical planning and preparation which has been carried on among the NATO countries. Such study and planning for contingencies and how to meet them as has taken place has been usually on a bilateral basis (to some extent trilateral in the case of ANZUS), and it has been much less specific and comprehensive. The modest planning that took place on the military side in SEATO has long since been terminated and it becomes increasingly irrelevant as time passes. Given the continuing presence of U.S. forces in Korea, contingency planning has been in order and it includes such considerations as supply, support, repair, and infrastructure. In this one special case, as long as U.S. forces are present, it can be assumed that the assets of the Republic of Korea would be completely committed to any military action which might take place. There is a movement toward increasing consultation on such matters in Japan, but much remains to be done and there is always question of what decision Japan would make to commit its resources and facilities in case of crisis.

Finally, let us undertake a highly speculative assessment, country by country, of the extent to which, and under what conditions, the contributions of that country would be available to a common defense effort in case of a military contest involving the United States and the Soviet Union in the Pacific.

There are certain questions that countries in East Asia would ask themselves if they perceived a deteriorating international situation in which armed conflict between the United States and the Soviet Union appeared to be a likely possibility. Their posture, with reference to their own separation from or involvement in the confrontation that might ensue, would depend on the answers to those questions. This discussion does not attempt to deal with the contingency of an all-out nuclear war, a situation in which the mobilization considerations under study would have little relevance, and in which it should probably be assumed that the East Asian Allies, and not the least among them Japan, would seek to dissociate themselves from the crisis.

Today the most likely U.S.-U.S.S.R. confrontation would appear to center on the Middle East and particularly its oil producing areas. Such a conflict, with the serious risk of cutting off petroleum exports, would deeply affect the economies and security of Japan, Korea, Taiwan, Southeast Asia and the ANZUS countries. If it were clear that the United States intended to resist Soviet efforts to take control of those Middle Eastern petroleum producing areas, and was prepared politically, psychologically and materially to undertake this task, it could be expected that the U.S. Allies in East Asia would support such an effort in the various ways discussed above, even though it seems unlikely they would be direct belligerents unless they were drawn directly into the conflict by Soviet action. Thus the bases and other facilities, and the productive capacity would be expected to be available to support, as necessary, the direct U.S. military effort.

A Soviet attack on the People's Republic of China which would involve the United States in an effort to support the Chinese defense of their country, would probably be accompanied by the, at least passive, involvement of U.S. Allies. They could be expected to accept U.S. use of bases and other facilities on their territories as long as their direct involvement could be avoided. Similarly, action on the part of the United States to support South Korea in resisting incursions or total invasion from the North would probably be supported by Allies in East Asia to the extent, at least, of their permitting use of their facilities and industrial capacity in support of the defense of South Korea. This would probably also hold true in case of a direct Soviet attack on Japan. Finally, to complete the list of military actions which today seem within the realm of possibility, if Vietnam (with at least some Soviet support) were to become involved militarily with Thailand over Laos and/or Cambodia, and the United States were to move in support of Thailand, it would again seem likely that the facilities and other support of America's East

Asian allies would be forthcoming, although, in this case also, their direct military involvement would seem unlikely.

The foregoing estimates are obviously highly speculative and abbreviated; they leave a great deal unsaid. Nevertheless, they must be put together with all that preceded them to formulate whatever answer it is possible to make at this time to the question: in East Asia, what are the assets and liabilities of interdependence between the United States and its Allies and friends in that region as they bear on the mobilization of resources to meet military contingencies?

Section VI

Priorities for United States Mobilization

Mobilization Preparedness: Lessons from the Recent Past

William K. Brehm*

Introduction

This arsenal of democracy, this strongest of all industrial nations, continues to view with shuddering abhorrence the world of conflict in which it finds itself. It still wishes it could continue to dream about colored bathtubs, longer wheel bases, and quicker-freezing cubes. It would like to run the war, but with automatic overdrive and finger-tip control.

Fortune, Volume XXIV, Number 2, August 1941

Then, as now, the nation struggled with its priorities, and with the basic question of how much emphasis to place on military preparedness in peacetime. However that may be answered, the United States still depends on mobilization to assemble the total resources needed to meet a major military emergency.

As long ago as 1924, the Army Industrial College was training senior officers for industrial mobilization. Well before Pearl Harbor, in the face of a rising threat, detailed plans were prepared for industrial expansion and military manpower mobilization. Following World War II, mobilization preparedness continued to be an important factor. A major portion of the World War II industrial capability was placed in standby. The nation maintained a reserve of industrial plants and machine tools, and supported the production and stockpiling of critical materials. The military conscription apparatus was kept operable and, except for a brief period, actually used to augment voluntary enlistments.

During the past fifteen years, however, certain trends have changed

---

* The author headed a term of former government civilian and military executives that evaluated Exercises NIFTY NUGGET in 1978 and PROUD SPIRIT/REX-80 BRAVO in 1980. These exercises explored the effectiveness of U.S. rapid mobilization and deployment planning and execution capabilities.

The present chapter identifies the major policy-level issues facing the government as it sets forth to improve rapid mobilization and deployment preparedness, and also notes the trends that led to the country's current preparedness posture.

the U.S. mobilization equation dramatically, generally to the detriment of the deterrent value of United States conventional military forces. While interest in United States military preparedness has flagged, the threat has increased in size and complexity, and in the face of that threat the difficulties inherent in maintaining a credible mobilization preparedness posture have become much greater.

The Trends

THE SOVIET BUILDUP.

The increase in Soviet conventional warfighting capability over the past fifteen to twenty years is nothing short of astonishing. It is clearly deliberate and purposive, and hard to justify as purely defensive, especially in view of the enormous price the Soviet people are paying in terms of retarded living standards. The first indications were increases in Soviet active duty strength and accelerated production of military equipment. We then said that the United States could overcome any quantity deficiencies we might face with superior quality. Now the Soviet emphasis is on both increased quantity *and* quality. The United States has run out of safe rationalizations. While rationalizations have the virtue of low cost, they no longer explain how the United States and its Allies in their present posture expect to counter growing Soviet advantages in active force size, capability, and mobility; in ready reserve forces; and in high peacetime military materiel production rates.

The Soviet leaders also are much more practiced today at lulling the United States and its Allies into complacency by interspersing peace offerings among their various military adventures (the Afghanistan invasion; the military maneuvers around Poland). According to the press, recent initiatives have included suggestions for renewed SALT negotiations, proposed discussions about limiting military activities in space, and overtures to limit nuclear weapons quantities in Western Europe. The tactic by now should be transparent, even to the naive. But it is energetically pursued by the Soviet leaders, nonetheless, because they know that over time it can have an eroding effect on United States popular resolve to put additional resources into America's military program.

The sustained Soviet buildup has not engendered a clear-cut crisis situation for the United States. Because the United States tends to be a crisis-oriented problem solver, it has had difficulty reacting to the buildup other than to grumble occasionally. Moreover, the Soviet periodic peace offensives have also muddied the waters in the sense that we seem to find it hard both to negotiate in good faith and to maintain our strong military posture upon which the free world depends.

One cannot say precisely when the force balance tips between two superpowers because there is no way to measure such things well. One can only look at trends, and trends are less likely to cause sharp changes in United States national priorities, particularly in the early stages when corrective action would not only be easier to effect but would also produce more effective results.

As early as 1976 former Secretary of Defense Donald H. Rumsfeld identified the adverse United States/Soviet trends for the Congress. He described the deteriorating situation repeatedly in formal testimony as well as in classified briefings suitably substantiated by intelligence information.

The military also sought ways to underscore the adverse trends. A series of extended mobilization exercises designed to reveal requirements and deficiencies in conventional force capabilities was begun in 1976 with the Army's MOBEX-76. These exercises, which also included NIFTY NUGGET in 1978 and PROUD SPIRIT in 1980, did much to sensitize government leaders to the problems and, largely through press reports, raised public awareness of them as well. However, at least until very recently, the Soviet conventional buildup has gone largely unchallenged as far as meaningful United States action is concerned.

THE UNITED STATES BUILD-DOWN.

To possess an effective conventional deterrent the United States must be able to deploy large-scale military forces rapidly. We are fortunate that to defend American freedom does not now involve direct defense of U.S. soil, but the price we must pay for that is the expense and difficulty of having to be able to move quickly, to operate, and to sustain a suitably large force over intercontinental distances. In recent years, the cost has been driven higher by inflation and by the increased Soviet threat. We have been unwilling to pay the higher price.

The idea of maintaining a large standing force to facilitate a rapid military response dates back to the early 1950s, a product of the Cold War and our NATO commitment. We realized then that to rely in peacetime on only a cadre of active military forces would not be sufficient, and so we retained a sizable active force after the Korean War. A decade later, with the advent of efficient jet cargo aircraft and the prepositioning of equipment, rapid deployment of those forces became a realistic possibility. Indeed, during the period 1961–64, United States conventional forces were actually expanded and strengthened, and "Mobility Forces" became an official Defense program category. Equipment prepositioning in Europe for some of the United States Army forces that would deploy there was undertaken, and the giant C-5 cargo transport was ordered. These moves, proposed and directed by the Kennedy Administration, were intended not only to strengthen our NATO-oriented forces, but also to move us away from exclusive focus on the NATO commitment, thus recognizing that American interests elsewhere in the world could be threatened as well.

But the war in Vietnam halted this effort. Though forces were increased temporarily in overall strength, the ultimate result of the Vietnam war was to produce deep cuts in United States conventional capability. The war consumed resources without replacement, and forced postponement of such critical tasks as ship construction and maintenance. The war's aftermath of antimilitary feeling combined with the appetite of the Great Society programs forced massive reductions in the active forces, to the point where by 1973 they were smaller than in 1961 before the Kennedy buildup—this in spite of the fact that the Soviet Union had grown stronger, both in conventional forces and in strategic nuclear forces. NATO defense again became the dominant justification for the United States active forces. Even the size of our NATO commitment was repeatedly criticized as too large by some Congressional leaders.

However, even cutting United States force levels did not generate the funding needed to support the forces that remained. Readiness suffered as maintenance, modernization, and procurement of basic supplies and ammunition were stretched out. Two contributing phenomena were higher levels of inflation that raised the cost of procurement and operations, and increased manpower costs resulting from adoption in the late 1960s of the principle of private sector pay comparability for federal civilian and military personnel. Direct manpower costs rose from roughly 40% of the Defense budget in 1964 to roughly 60% in 1974. (The conversion from the draft to the volunteer force added some costs as well, but the increases there were small compared with the impact of adopting pay comparability.)

Thus at the time when the Soviet Union was making remarkable improvements in both strength and capability, the United States was retrenching. Indeed, the United States was mortgaging the future, with a substantial balloon payment in the offing—as is now evident and manifest in the proposed large increases in defense spending.

RESPONSE TIME.

It is hard to appreciate fully the importance of rapid response capability for United States conventional forces, or the impact such a requirement places on United States force posture and crisis management. The Soviet leaders have shown both the ability and the will to move quickly and decisively. The available strategic warning of such moves is shrinking as the readiness of Soviet forces continues to improve and their mobility is increased. The notion that the next war, if it comes, must be preceded by years of rising tension and unambiguous military preparations is faulty. The outcome of the next war could well be settled by the forces in being at its outbreak. While this is not a new thought, its implications have not been fully appreciated or properly reflected in either the United States force posture or its crisis management preparations. And even though such a conflict conceivably could also be protracted—thus theoretically affording the United States the opportunity to bring its vaunted industrial capability to bear in some sort of decisive way—the price paid in the meantime could be enormous, and the world balance of power changed irrevocably in a direction unfavorable to the United States. United States military response times in the future must be measured in days and weeks, not months and years. The implications in terms of peacetime preparations are dramatic.

MANPOWER.

With short warning times, the character of the United States military manpower readiness and mobilization program changes significantly. Basically, the trained manpower assets needed in the early stages of an intense conflict must be on hand at the outset. Today there are severe shortages, particularly in reserve manpower. Yet, even the Defense Department has been slow to take corrective action, for it has been unwilling or unable to apply the resources needed to develop a balanced manpower program.

In the Congress and elsewhere, patriotic nostalgia has interfered with logic for some who see a return to the peacetime draft as the solution to all of our manpower problems. While it is important to have the draft machinery well oiled to assure manpower availability for an extended war (or to strengthen military forces in an extended crisis), the draft is of virtually no consequence in the early stages of a fast-breaking, short-warning conflict—the most logical Soviet tactic and the one for which Soviet forces are designed. Such a war will be fought by people already trained when the fighting starts. Thus, there is no purely military need today to have the draft prior to a crisis; rather it should be *ready* to operate, as an adjunct to mobilization. This point is stressed here because the tendency for debate to focus on the peacetime draft issue diverts attention from the corrective manpower actions that are really needed.

A peacetime draft for the active forces also would do nothing to stop the continuing heavy outflow of skilled mid-career personnel; nor would it help fill undermanned units in the Selected Reserve, or expand the pool of trained manpower in the Individual Ready Reserve (IRR), where the massive quantitative shortfalls (about 250,000) really lie. Of course a draft could be instituted for the Selected Reserve or the IRR, or both; or indirectly for them by having a draft for the active forces and allowing deferments for reserve duty, a path we followed with mixed success during the 1960s. In fact, there are much better ways of meeting reserve manpower needs, even though the gap to be closed is large.

The peacetime draft issue should be treated as a socio-economic matter, and the issue (an important one) honestly debated on socio-economic grounds. The resolution of that issue may well be a return to the draft sometime in the next few years, but if so, the justification will transcend purely military requirements. Indeed, it would have to be found within the context of a national service program (though not necessarily a universal one).

In the meantime, the government must take the steps necessary to guarantee that the shortfall in the required pool of trained and experienced reservists is eliminated, and that incentives are established that will keep skilled managers and technicians on active duty.

Civilian manpower requirements under today's potential emergency mobilization conditions are less well understood and appreciated than military manpower needs. If, for example, total mobilization were required, both the public and the private sector work forces would have to expand quickly. Substantial relocations would be necessary. But there are no summaries available of skill requirements for various scenarios, much less plans to meet them. Nor do we understand the consequences of the inevitable three-way competition among the manpower requirements of the military Services, defense production, and the consumer economy.

Another complicating trend in the manpower program relates to training. The preparation both of civilian and military specialists now takes far longer than it did ten or fifteen years ago, to say nothing of the period during World War II. Weapons and support systems are more sophisticated and thus more difficult to produce, operate, and repair—activities that all require skilled personnel. The competition for trained manpower assets in any sort of mobilization will be keen, suggesting that some means of rapid identification of skilled personnel is essential at the very least.

MATERIEL.

Trends in materiel requirements and readiness parallel those in manpower. The need for a full set of equipment on hand for all active and reserve units is far more important today than ever before, as is the need for the supplies and replacements to sustain them, some prepositioned overseas. The United States cannot plan to equip existing units or build stockpiles *after* the emergency begins; war can break out too quickly for that. Yet today there are significant shortages in unit equipment, supplies, and reserve stocks. The procurement program has been undernourished for several years, and the pain of recovery is substantial, as the projected Reagan defense budgets are beginning to show. And there are other problems as well—less visible perhaps, but just as important.

The industrial mobilization base, so carefully nurtured in earlier years, has been allowed to atrophy. Standby capacity is obsolete or in disrepair. Certain strategic raw materials are in short supply. Dependence on foreign sources has grown, both for raw materials and for production components, and the degree of such dependence and its implications are not even fully understood.

We cannot know in advance whether a future conflict would be swift and decisive, or whether it might be drawn out into another war of attrition. Some say the latter is not possible, either because modern conventional weapons are too destructive for a conflict involving the major powers to endure for long, or because a losing side would resort to nuclear weapons in desperation.

The fact is, however, that we cannot predict what such a war would be like. We have to protect our options and thus we must consider the relevance of industrial mobilization capability to our deterrent posture. Not to be strong in this aspect in fact could be destabilizing. Moreover, the United States could become involved in a protracted crisis during which the ability to expand production quickly could help materially to resolve the crisis without conflict.

Yet industrial response times are becoming very lengthy, both because of the high technology of today's weapons, and because industry has been given few incentives to preserve or construct surge production or rapid base expansion capability. Today the reorder lead time for jet engines has grown to forty months or more. Ship construction time is now measured in many years. In the last two years the lead time for acquiring certain critical aircraft landing gear components has nearly doubled. These trends all are in the wrong direction.

Overall, today we have in one sense the worst of all worlds, with shortages in unit equipment and stockpiles, lengthening production reorder lead times, and dimming prospects for early and unambiguous strategic warning that would give us time to react. That is not to say that we are destitute, but we have much to do. We may already have received our strategic warning.

MANAGEMENT.

The United States has never mobilized on short notice. It has no historical precedents upon which to draw, much less any current experience. Ironically, the potential for rapid crisis development, and thus the need for capable crisis management, has never been greater. Yet, of all the ingredients that make up military preparedness, management readiness is at once the most important and the least attended to. The United

States must consider carefully how to improve its ability to plan for and manage a transition from peace to war. A transition that promises to be swift and sure not only gives real meaning to standing military forces, but adds immeasurably to their deterrent value.

The recent mobilization and deployment exercises—NIFTY NUGGET and REX-78 in 1978, PROUD SPIRIT and REX-80 BRAVO in November 1980—show that we are not prepared to mobilize quickly. The United States possesses neither the government organization, the procedures, nor the manpower and industrial programs to manage effectively a short-warning, rapid deployment of large-scale forces. Yet national military strategy, military planning, and public expectations assume that we do. Improvements have occurred since the earlier exercises, but much remains to be done at each management tier: the Joint Chiefs of Staff for military operational matters; the Office of the Secretary of Defense for plans and crisis management preparations; the Executive Branch for interagency planning and coordination. Fortunately the corrective action is not costly, but it does require time and careful management attention to detail.

Summary

In brief, we face the following situation:
1. The Soviet Union, for reasons best understood by its leaders, seems bent on building an overwhelming conventional force capability with the attributes of high readiness, great striking power, and long-range projection. It also exhibits the will to use it.
2. Had the United States continued the trend to strengthen its forces begun in 1961 it could well be ahead of the U.S.S.R. today in virtually every aspect of force strength and readiness. The trend was not sustained for a variety of reasons, most notably the Vietnam War and its aftermath.
3. American forces are now smaller and in some ways less flexible than in 1961 when the United States had absolute nuclear superiority, and its conventional force capability was much less important as a deterrent.
4. America's military manpower program is barely adequate for the active forces (and the situation may worsen if some means is not found to stem the outflow of career personnel). This program is unacceptable in the case of the reserve plans, particularly the Army Individual Ready Reserve.
5. Our civilian manpower mobilization programs do not exist.
6. Materiel stocks are inadequate in terms of meeting the first-line needs of active and reserve units. Supplies and replacement stocks have long been neglected, generally being casualties in the budget review process.

7. Our ability to surge production and to expand the production base is seriously limited.
8. We are not equipped to manage a major mobilization and deployment; we lack plans, procedures, and trained and committed executives.

The mood of the country now seems to be to effect cures for these ills. The world situation and United States' credibility demand that we do so. We seem to be moving in the right direction, but the battle for resources is only now being joined in the Congress. It is too bad that it costs so much to catch up, but that is the price for years of indifference and neglect. In any case, the priorities have not yet been established by those august bodies that have the Constitutional responsibility for raising our Armed Forces.

Two points are worth making, in conclusion:

First, while the cost of fixing the force structure, manpower, and materiel programs is high, to fix the management problems costs almost nothing. What the latter requires is a set of modified agendas for government executives, and a commitment on their part to the notion that a strong military posture is not only sensible but worth working for. Agendas can only be changed by direction from above, however, and thus the new Administration—and the leadership in Congress—must press hard to see that the necessary homework gets done.

Second, as noted earlier, the United States is a crisis-oriented nation. It generally waits until the problem is severe, then gathers its strength and ideas, and moves out. We perhaps are in that process now, as far as national defense is concerned. But the solution to the military preparedness problem will take a long time, and a good deal of national treasure, year after year after year. We must realize that the Soviet leaders may try to avoid presenting us with sharply-defined, high-threshold events that would spur us on or rekindle our interest should it flag. They will also ply us with various "peace" initiatives. Other resource demands, and perhaps other problems in our society, will appear or even erupt to distract us.

The question is: Can the national interest be sustained? Will the consensus we appear to have now hold together?

Let us hope that the United States public interest in a strong and balanced defense program can be sustained, that we can continue to foster enough uncertainty abou the outcome of any conflict or threat of conflict to deter a sensible adversary, and that common sense will prevail on all sides.

Government and Industry: Some Priorities for Mobilization

E. F. Andrews

American industry depends on foreign sources for a growing number of vital minerals, without whose assured and long-term supply we cannot function in the industrial sense. Denied these critical materials, United States industry could provide neither for our overall economic well-being nor for the common defense. The explosion in technological development during and after World War II produced unprecedented advances in the quality of American life, wondrously transformed older industries, and brought forth new industries unimagined only decades ago. But that explosion also ended America's historic self-sufficiency. As technological development accelerated, the minerals predicament was enormously complicated by vast worldwide political changes. These included "decolonization" by the old Western imperial powers and the emergence of Third World nations. It so happened that Providence chose to endow a number of the Third World nations, particularly those in southern Africa, with minerals on which the United States is heavily dependent. However salutary certain global political changes may be in the historical annals of self-determination, they have reduced the reliability of overseas mineral sources. This has presented the private sector with a new set of problems that it cannot solve in the environment of the policies and practices of the past.

Chromium presents a good example of why a new policy is needed. The United States has virtually no domestic sources of chromium. At a time when domestic consumption of chromium was rising, Congress enacted environmental legislation that virtually mandated an increase in the consumption of chrome to make pollution control equipment, including converters for automobiles. After this Congressionally mandated increase in the consumption of chrome, the Executive Branch placed an embargo on the importation of chromium from what was then our largest supplier, Rhodesia, and we applied stricter environmental enforcement standards to the antiquated ferrochrome industry, reducing its productive capabilities. While these measures were being taken, the United States allowed unlimited export of stainless steel scrap, each ton of which contained four hundred pounds of chrome. The obvious lack of a coordinated approach on this issue pointed up the need for a coherent, cohesive materials policy.

The United States should develop a two-part national materials policy—for those commodities we have and for those we have not. This is by no means a call for a national economic planning activity. History has proved that permitting the free market to work remains the best method of resolving our problems. However, since we are operating ever increasingly in a global *political* marketplace which tends to override the *economic* marketplace, consideration must be given to policies that will help prevent abrupt and noneconomic interruptions such as have occurred in the recent past.

Efforts to develop an integrated minerals policy must guard against two extremes of mental attitude. First, blind faith in technological solutions must be avoided. Misplaced confidence in technological solutions is not to be blamed on research and development. Many remarkable developments have altered our dependence on certain minerals; consider how laser and satellite communications have reduced the use of copper wire. There will surely be technological developments at some unforeseen time that will lessen or perhaps eliminate the present dependence on one or more strategic minerals, but *time* is the heart of the problem. What presses for immediate attention and coordinated action is the midterm future to the end of this century. In the next century it may become possible to extract minerals from mines located on the moon. But what can be done to mine the earth to obtain access to its minerals in the next fifteen years?

At the opposite pole from blind faith in technology is abject despair that basic resources will be consumed before effective policies can be devised. Of course, all resources are finite. If somehow we consume or destroy until there is no place to stand on this planet, then we could conclude that raw materials are gone. It seems unlikely that any serious natural constraints on the existence of raw materials will be encountered, at least in the next twenty-five to fifty years and possible twenty-five decades. If some sources of raw materials run out, man will merely reach deeper into the bowels of the earth for less yielding ores. As the cost to extract these materials increases, the price to the consumer will also rise. As the price rises, consumers will be forced to find substitutes and, by the time the supply is exhausted, the need for the product will also be gone. The system will gradually adjust itself if permitted to do so.

Avoiding, then, either extreme—the one of blind trust in instant technology, the other of resource-despair—let us examine the status of four basic minerals: chrome, cobalt, manganese, and platinum. These minerals, selected from a longer list, surely qualify as "strategic" and the reliability of their supply is less than reassuring. The hallmark of strategic minerals is their pervasive use throughout a modern industrial economy. Without these four minerals it would be impossible to build a jet engine or an automobile, run a train, build an oil refinery or a power plant. These minerals are needed to process food, run a sanitary restaurant and hospital operating room, build computers, and clean up the air and water. Without manganese, for example, the United States simply could not make steel.

These four minerals mentioned, together with others which are imported, are vital to national defense—for what defense could there be without planes and tanks and missiles? But they also play important roles in basic industry, the quality of life, and the employment of the work force. With regard to jobs and national output, Chancellor Helmut Schmidt of the Federal Republic of Germany has said that if West Germany's chrome supply were interrupted for a year, 2.5 million people would be unemployed and the GNP would fall by 25%. A similar situation in America would be a "crisis" by the most conservative definition of that term.

What can government and business do to alleviate mineral dependence or at least render it less dangerous? One thing we can and must do is stop commissioning studies that come to nothing. Studies are needed upon which government and business are determined to act. A solid start in that constructive direction was made by the Congress in the National Materials and Minerals Policy Research and Development Act of 1980, which declares that "...it is the continuing policy of the United States to promote an adequate and stable supply of materials necessary to maintain *national security, economic well-being and industrial production* with appropriate attention to a long-term balance between resource production, energy use, a healthy environment, natural resources conservation, and social needs."[1] Economic well-being and industrial production are regarded as indispensable to national security. Against the background of this promising start, some general comments and recommendations on certain aspects of a future program may be made.

First, a coordinating agency operating immediately under the President is needed, such as a National Nonfuel Minerals Board (NNMB), which should have full authority to cut across departmental jurisdictions in the interest of designing and carrying out a total and consistent minerals policy. As part of the Executive Office of the President, the NNMB would coordinate and integrate programs, tasks and analyses among the various agencies relating to the security of strategic minerals supplies. It would also recommend actions for the President, Congress and other Executive agencies. It would add no new bureau or department, but in minerals policy would combine the current functions of the Departments of State, Treasury, Defense, Commerce, Interior, Transportation, Labor and Energy.

Second, to facilitate *private sector advice*, a President's Resource Advisory Board (PRAB) should be established. This Board would be patterned after the former "President's Foreign Intelligence Advisory Board," with limited term membership of distinguished experts from relevant fields, from the mining, minerals production, and end user industries; together with the fields of labor, environmental studies, regulation impact, investment banking and geopolitical/national security affairs.

Third, a thorough inventory of our nation's reserves and resources in strategic and other minerals, to develop a reliable data base, would be another valuable step. Specifically, this inventory would include every resource that may be available in America's public lands. The Federal Government owns about one-third of the U.S. land area, mostly in the West and Alaska. In 1968, the amount of this land withdrawn from mining and exploration totalled 17%. Eight years later, the figure was almost 70%. As an Interior Department official noted at the time, the withdrawal for conservationist purposes, "is being done too often without detailed knowledge of the existing mineral potential of these lands."[2] Americans have a right to know what resources have been locked away, are being locked away, and why!

Fourth, as a complement to this domestic inventory, the international capabilities of the U.S. Bureau of Mines should be improved. The data base provided by the Bureau in this country—in the areas where it may freely operate—is the best in the world. But the minerals problem is worldwide in scope, and the data base should be as worldwide in scope as international political conditions allow. The new public law recognizes this need by directing the Secretary of the Interior to initiate prompt actions to improve the Bureau's capacity overseas. A decided improvement could be effected by stationing twenty to thirty Bureau experts in a few select countries.

The fifth needed measure is the reassessment of our present defense stockpile—amounting, at today's current inflated prices, to about $12 billion—combined with new policies for managing the stockpile. The reassessment should encompass such considerations as quantity, quality, and a mix of stockpiled minerals. The effects of time and weather on the quality of cobalt and other minerals that were laid down twenty-five years ago must be evaluated. For example, the reduction of ferrochrome productive capacity in the United States may dictate a change in chrome stockpile needs. Careful study and resolution of these issues can help bring about a viable stockpile that is adequate in light of current realities. Maintaining the stockpile will require a new program for buying and selling relatively small quantities each year to preserve the quality of stockpile materials and to make sure that markets are not dislocated. In turn, this will make necessary very close cooperation between government and business based on trust which does not now exist.

Further, Congress should establish parameters for certain limited economic uses of the stockpile. This statement must not be taken as implying there should be an economic stockpile, distinct from the established one for defense, but rather, that in the case of certain imported stockpile items which are essential to national well-being, Congress should allow for carefully circumscribed conditions under which they can be drawn on for economic purposes. Economic use of the stockpile could have value in providing the time needed for the United States to implement such long-term solutions as substitution, conservation, and the development of alternate sources. The United States must consider this alternative, and it should explore the possible use of tax incentives to encourage private stockpiling. The present policy of using the strategic stockpile as a de facto economic stockpile, subject only to the vaguest guidance and controls, is unwise and should be discouraged.

Congress should set forth in legislation the conditions under which items would be taken out of the stockpile. Stockpile withdrawals for price stabilization purposes are an unwise intrusion in the free market; however, certain other conditions for withdrawal should be clarified so that all concerned would know when a withdrawal time was near. Management of the stockpile under these conditions is a difficult problem. How can economic use of the stockpile be designed and operated so that it will not be misused for the financial advantage of special interest groups? How can it be insulated adequately from the political process to prevent its misuse, yet sufficiently responsive to the public needs for which it was established? How can it be sufficiently insulated from the political process that it may act in the public interest, and yet remain responsive to Congressional scrutiny?

Even under ideal conditions, stockpiling is not, and cannot be, a long-term solution to our import-dependence on strategic minerals. It can only serve as a buffer in case of crisis, such as war, or disruption at a source of overseas supply. In short, stockpiling is a limited hedge against risk in a highly disturbed world.

The sixth vital ingredient in a national minerals policy is promotion of a vigorous, comprehensive, and coordinated program of materials research and development, as stipulated in the new legislation to which reference has already been made. At the same time, tax policies towards the mining and metallurgical industries must be overhauled. Ironically, these policies have been a disincentive both to research and to the capital formation needed to develop the fruits of research.

But even with new attention to research and development, policy-makers must avoid fantasies of a quick technological fix. Substitution—the use of a new or modified substance for another—can readily become a voodoo incantation to exorcise the demons of mineral dependence. But realistic substitutes for strategic minerals must perform as well as, and cost no more than, the mineral for which it substitutes. One considered estimate indicates that a substitute for chrome would take ten years to develop and might cost as much as $1 billion; meanwhile, there is more than a thousand-year supply of chrome in southern Africa that might well be sold for about fifty cents a pound.

These comments should not be taken as deprecating purposeful research and development across the spectrum of materials and minerals, but rather as putting the problem of dependence in focus. The one key element of that problem is diplomatic and requires that the United States reconsider the balance struck in recent years between the requirements of national security and the position of human rights issues in American foreign policy. An editorial in the now defunct *Washington Star* put the issue well:

> ...While the Kremlin has been trying to advance its interests via build-ups of well-positioned bases and client states in such areas as Africa, the United States has concentrated on human rights and hopes of coming out 'on the right side of history' by forbearing to press material or geopolitical interests against revolutionary regimes.
>
> There is still time for us to protect ourselves in the area of strategic materials. But it will take a rethinking of priorities in the way we define allies and adversaries abroad as well as in domestic stockpiling policies.[3]

The problem is not sufficiency or strategic minerals but rather the peculiar nature of their geographic distribution. Given that distinction, disruption of some supply is a very real possibility, and the power to disrupt is—in this matter—the power to deny.

The phenomenon of selective indignation which has characterized much of U.S. diplomacy towards mineral-rich areas of southern Africa must be guarded against. At one time the United States embargoed the importation of chrome from Rhodesia while at the same time buying chrome from the Soviet Union. What is the answer to this inconsistency and, more specifically, to the need for looking after security interests no less than moral ones? At least, the United States should ascribe to the principle that conducting trade with another nation carries no implication of approval or disapproval of that nation's internal policies.

Further, efforts are needed in international organizations and with individual Third World countries to shore up contract law and equity in financial and commercial transactions. The advantages of such law and equity are common to all parties concerned, but to realize these advantages will take persistence and a stockpile of patience.

Can the growing needs of the "multinational corporation," so necessary to the private enterprise system and its material supply problems, be reconciled with the forces of nationalism in newly developing nations? The problem of access to future supply is compounded by the fact that demand for minerals and metals is rising at a faster rate now in many of those very states than it is in the developed countries. As a result, such states are beginning to compete to obtain an increasing share of world supply. The less-developed countries are promoting more aggressively their own industrialization and, therefore, are increasingly sensitive to what they view as "exploitation."

Many of those countries lack the technology to discover, extract and market their resources. They also mistrust and fear business corporations that possess the capital and the technical and management skills needed. American business and government must address jointly this problem because the governments and businesses of other industrial nations have already cleared this hurdle.

In this day of "instant communication" and fast transportation, Americans must learn to tell their story better. Industry has found a use and a market for the Third World's raw materials and it has the technology to develop them. In most cases, industry possesses the capital to provide the infrastructures and plant facilities. It can furnish the skilled manpower, and it can make available job opportunities to local citizens. All of this leads to a better life than those local citizens otherwise might expect if left to their present technical, financial, and management capabilities. But how to provide all this and still protect the multinational corporation's investments—which really represent the savings of millions of people and the pension funding for other millions, here and abroad—is a serious problem yet to be solved.

The relationship between government and business in America must change from an adversary relationship to a cooperative one. This may well be the most serious deficiency of the United States, when compared to other industrial nations. A political, economic, and legal climate must be created that encourages investment, exploration, and development of domestic resources and facilities. Legislators must consider the impact of proposed measures on the supply of strategic materials, keeping in mind that laws which appear desirable in the short run may be too costly in jobs, inflation, and consumer interruptions, or even risk national security interests. Government and business must work together again as they once did in this country—and still do in most of the industrialized world. While some branches of the government have always maintained the best of relations with industry, the time has come for a truly cooperative effort, for failure in this area carries the gravest implications for national security and for our economic well-being.

NOTES

1. Public Law 96-479 (H.R. 2743); October 21, 1980, 94 Stat. 2305. Under Section 3.
2. Statement by Thomas V. Falkie, Director of the Interior Department Bureau of Mines, to a meeting of the American Mining Congress in 1976. In Editorial Research Reports, Special Report of May 28, 1976, page 391.
3. *Washington Star*, September 2, 1980.

An Agenda for U.S. Mobilization Policy

Robert L. Pfaltzgraff, Jr.

At least since World War I, the capacity for industrial mobilization and "surge production" in times of national crisis has been considered an American "long suit." However, as the United States embarks upon programs designed to strengthen defense capabilities in the 1980s, critical deficiencies can be detected in the industrial infrastructure needed to produce modern weapons systems. There is no single cause for this decline in American mobilization potential, and, to a large extent, current constraints on our productive capacities are unique to this era, without parallel in modern American history. Indeed, the present context differs sharply from the past as a result of numerous factors, addressed in this volume, two of which are given special attention because of their ominous implications: greatly lengthened lead times in the development, acquisition and deployment of weapons systems, and sharply narrowed warning time of impending attack. The security dilemmas posed by both factors, especially in the realm of mobilization, have become more acute with the elimination of advantages historically conferred upon the United States by our geographic location far from the immediate scene of conflict and battle.

Lessons of the Past

This is not to suggest that the lessons of the past are totally irrelevant to today's predicament. Even under circumstances seemingly more simple than those of the late twentieth century, the United States historically has confronted formidable problems in developing and maintaining an adequate defense mobilization base and has usually fallen short of its defense needs at the outset of a war. For example, during the colonial era, as Harry Ennis suggests, the American capability for the manufacture of gunpowder had been allowed to atrophy between the French and Indian War and our War of Independence, a factor which had profound effects upon the viability and "staying power" of Continental Army units. During the Civil War, the initial failure of Union and Confederate industrial bases to keep pace with the demands of war virtually assured the prolongation of the conflict. Both examples seem to illustrate the need for timely investments in production capabilities before war breaks out, but they also point to an American penchant for ignoring this critical rule of defense preparedness.

It should be remembered that in two World Wars, the industrial machine of the United States eventually produced vast amounts of armaments not only for American use, but also for our European allies. In both cases, however, the American armaments production infrastructure had been strengthened by the purchases of European allies, especially Britain, and by lend-lease preceding our entry into World War II, and thus the United States had begun to mobilize well before its actual entry into war. In the Korean conflict, according to John McLaurin, the American industrial mobilization base was once again strengthened, but because of lead-time factors, vast amounts of armaments were produced too late to be of use in the war itself. As a result of the Vietnam conflict, the overriding importance of maintaining public support for major defense efforts, whatever the availability of men and materiel, was brought to the foreground.

Given these lessons of the past, there is rising concern today over the obsolescence or inadequacy of a mobilization base that once again has atrophied in spite of the importance of American defense industries in producing weapons systems for the U.S. military and for arms transfer abroad. Indeed, in light of more recent experiences, namely those provided by mobilization exercises such as NIFTY NUGGET in 1978 and PROUD SPIRIT in 1980, it has become increasingly clear, as William Brehm asserts, that we lack the plans, organizations, procedures, and communications to manage a rapid mobilization, although such exercises have resulted in the beginning of an awareness of the formidable problems confronting us.

Alternative Conflict Scenarios

Of principal importance is the need for the United States to have available the industrial infrastructure deemed necessary to meet existing and planned increases in defense capabilities. Yet, according to Norman Friedman, the answer to the question of how much will be enough is exceedingly difficult because, even it we knew what kind of war we will eventually have to fight, the lessons of the past, especially from the October 1973 Arab-Israeli War, suggest the far more rapid expenditure of materiel than anticipated. What then, it must be asked, is the requirement in weapons and in manpower, keeping in mind that the loss of the former has tended to be greater than the latter in a hypothetical conflict, as in a 30-, 60-, or 90-day war on the NATO Central Front, and that it apparently takes less time to train manpower than to produce new weapons systems.

In an effort to answer the question posed above, a substantial portion of this book is devoted to a consideration of alternative scenarios for future conflict. Several writers have maintained that ultimately the adequacy of the overall defense mobilization base of the United States is related inextricably to the validity of assumptions about the kind of war our forces might be called upon to fight. If the defense mobilization base needs hypothesized for a long war differ greatly from those of a short-war scenario, and if we cannot be certain whether we will fight one or the other type of conflict, the optimal solution would appear to lie in the development of military strategies and forces, together with a defense mobilization base, sufficiently broad and flexible to accommodate both. Those who prepare only for short wars may be condemned to fighting long wars in which they will be defeated. Substantially different mobilization priorities and needs arise in the so-called twilight conflict, in which we have already found ourselves for long periods, contrasted with conventional or nuclear war.

The type and length of the hypothesized conflict have profound implications not only for the composition of military forces, but also for the defense mobilization infrastructure to be developed, maintained and augmented, as well as for the timing of such actions. Using Britain in the months before the outbreak of World War II as a principal example, Colin Gray suggests that democracies have elected to rearm not at the moment war broke out, but instead when they crossed a particular threshold of belief that war was imminent. In the present context, that may be reinterpreted to mean that rearmament has been stepped up as a means of enhancing the prospects for maintaining strategic nuclear deterrence when to do otherwise might tilt the balance to an adversary and encourage miscalculation. Hence the renewed interest in, and need for, an adequate defense mobilization infrastructure in the United States in the 1980s and the availability of a variety of military options, including the means to fight conventional wars. Indeed, in an era of putative nuclear parity, the importance of conventional forces to deterrence may increase substantially. But left unanswered was the question of which type of conflict is most likely, and for which kind of war should our defense mobilization infrastructure be prepared.

If any consensus emerges on this issue, it lies in the assumption that we confront the need for an industrial infrastructure that will support both an R & D capability and a productive capacity adequate to maintain and to strengthen our strategic nuclear forces and, simultaneously, to sustain forces at other levels of conflict—namely, conventional land and maritime capabilities. If we hypothesize that nuclear war fought for total objectives will terminate rapidly when fatality exchange ratios clearly favor one adversary or the other, then there will be little time—and some would say need—for the formation of additional forces or for the augmentation of industrial infrastructure.

In contrast, it would be wiser to assume that future wars may be protracted, especially if varying levels of nonnuclear weapons are used. In that case, the central question, as Edward Rapp suggests, concerns the minimum upgrading needed now to support requirements in future mobilization efforts, since we will never be prepared to fight a protracted conflict if we do not reduce lead times. Time is said to be our most constrained resource. We must approach mobilization using wartime, not peacetime, rules.

Lamented is the fact that no one seems to be in charge of "discontinuity thought" which would serve to ease the transition from peacetime "business as usual" attitudes to wartime planning. In this regard, nuclear war may not necessarily be a short war, nor can such a conflict be clearly distinguished from a war that is both protracted and fought with conventional *and* nuclear weapons. Presidential Directive 59 holds the implication that a nuclear war will not necessarily be a short war. Because of the magnitude of the threat and the diminution of our margin of safety, the problems of mobilization, both in industrial infrastructure and personnel, appear far more profound now than they were in the past.

Surge Potential and Mobilization: A U.S.-Soviet Comparison

To answer questions about the length of war and the level of combat this volume has examined the concept of surge potential, and addressed what was another principal theme: the relationship deemed to be optimal between the readiness level of existing forces and the infrastructure needed rapidly to augment both weapons systems and personnel to adequate levels in time of war. Here we confront an inherent dilemma in the approach taken by the United States and its allies, operative in both contemporary and historic context. In peacetime the United States and its allies have been reluctant, or unwilling, to finance large programs of new weapons. Therefore, they usually plan long production times at moderate output levels and thus limit the size of production facilities. If this raises unit costs, it also works against the development of the surge capability that would be needed in wartime. Potentially it leaves the nation neither with the weapons systems that may be needed nor with the industrial infrastructure for rapid surge capability, unless other facilities can be rapidly converted to wartime use. To produce large amounts of weapons in peacetime, however, is to incur obsolescence unless governments are prepared, as they seldom are, to replace such weapons as quickly as they become obsolescent.

Although this volume addresses principally the American defense mobilization infrastructure, Michael Checinski focuses specifically on Soviet mobilization capability. Numerous differences in approach to defense readiness and mobilization are noted between the Soviet Union and the United States, especially with respect to surge capacity. The Soviet approach provides for the improvement of existing military equipment even while new models and types of armaments are being developed and deployed. In the West, by contrast, emphasis is usually placed on the creation of new, or almost new, models. The Soviet approach is said to facilitate the mass production and accumulation of large stockpiles of weapons, a potentially significant advantage in an era of rapid combat attrition rates. The deficiency of this approach lies in the possibility that large amounts of Soviet armaments could be rendered obsolete in a relatively short period of time, especially if the United States were able to develop the equivalent of a "knight's move" in the field of military technology.

Another difference between the American and Soviet defense mobilization infrastructures lies in the ongoing efforts of the Soviet Union to provide a war-survival and postattack recovery capability by building certain defense production facilities underground, by locating outside cities some defense infrastructure to which personnel could be evacuated to continue production during or immediately after an attack, and by stockpiling large reserves of strategic materials and semimanufactured goods. In the state-controlled Soviet economy, the civilian sectors have been subordinate to, and designed to function in support of, the military sector. In fact, it is noted that the Soviet conception of military strategy is the theory and the practice of preparing both the country and its military forces for war, as well as the planning and conduct of war. Thus, in the Soviet Union, mobilization cannot be separated from military strategy.

In a brief discussion of Soviet manpower policy, the importance of ready reserves to provide sustained warfighting capability is noted. The Soviet Union may be contrasted with the United States in that the principal task confronting the Soviets at the outset of war would be manpower mobilization, since the defense production infrastructure and stockpiles of materiel already exist, and the Soviet Union is mobilized for war to an extent without parallel in the United States or Western Europe.

The importance of mobilization as part of Soviet strategy leads William Wadbrook to the question of whether the Soviet Union's posture of permanent semimobilization reflects its respect for our putative mobilization potential, together with a determination to deny the United States the opportunity to maximize that potential. In World War II the attack on Pearl Harbor provided the United States with a fortuitous disaster which, in retrospect, was ideally suited to mobilization for the war effort that ensued. In the present context, given this lesson of World War II, why should an adversary with to galvanize the United States to a vast mobilization effort—the very sector in which he has the greatest reason to fear our ultimate capabilities? An enemy would have every incentive to avoid sounding an alarm which would spur the United States to prodigious efforts to surpass him, especially in light of the immense sacrifices he has made to achieve his present and prospective military status. Viewed from this perspective, might not an American move to repair its mobilization base, so as to redress current asymmetries in the U.S.-Soviet balance, trigger some preemptive move by the Soviet Union in order to exploit its military advantages while the opportunity still exists?

With these points in mind, it may be noted that American mobilization moves may carry some near-term risk of destabilization. It might be agreed, however, that such risks would be outweighed in the mid- and long-term by efforts to revitalize the deterrent potential that is inherent in the American industrial base, but now lie fallow. In question, moreover, is the contemporary relevance of the Pearl Harbor example with respect to surge production, given the present dilemmas of defense posed by narrowing warning time and surprise attack in a high technology military environment, and the attendant problems of trading territory (or space) for mobilization time. Also, in the 1980s the United States confronts the need to mobilize resources not only for contingencies in which our vital interests are clearly at stake, but also for those less obvious contingencies which hold potential for escalation to affect vital interests, and for which the need to mobilize may not seem pressing to the general public. This observation, in turn, produces the suggestion that, to an extent not adequately understood, mobilization potential, at least in democracies, is linked to such complex variables as our value structure, particularly to national will and morale, and to social, political and economic institutions—in short, to the public consensus that can be nurtured and utilized in support of mobilization needs.

The Manpower Problem

In contrast to the Soviet Union, the United States would face the need for vast mobilization efforts both in industry and in manpower. The mobilization base of the United States should encompass the personnel available to meet existing needs and for surge potential. In an examination of recent trends in the manpower dimension of American mobilization, H.R. Ludden suggests that lead times of as many as one hundred days would be needed to bring newly trained manpower into the Army after the beginning of mobilization. The reinstitution of selective service registration was said to represent a significant improvement in reducing the lead time in personnel mobilization. However, the increasing sophistication of weapons systems has placed a premium upon skilled personnel, many of whom are civilians and contractor personnel who would not necessarily be available under combat conditions unless present legal arrangements were to be changed.

Closely related to these concerns is the personnel retention problem that has placed in doubt the ability of the United States to maintain existing capabilities in some instances, not to speak of the augmentation of forces in the programs contemplated for the years just ahead. For example, in order to maintain combat effectiveness, it is said that the Air Force needs to retain 60% of its fighter pilots, yet retention rates in recent years have fallen to 25%. Equally disturbing is the fact that the U.S. Navy now confronts a shortfall of 20,000 key petty officers, of which some 14,000 are needed for the fleet at sea. These gaps in the availability of quality personnel are compounded by the fact that the United States cannot hope to retain people markedly better in aptitude than those who originally enlist; in recent years, a large proportion of new recruits—32% in 1980—has been classified in the lowest category of mental capacity (Category IV), which is equivalent to a fifth grade reading comprehension.

In the event of war, some form of emergency compulsory service undoubtedly could be reinstituted, and large numbers of skilled personnel could be enlisted from the private sector. Nevertheless, each of the services still would face shortages of the pretrained manpower which is indispensable to the maintenance of an adequate "holding force" during the crucially important early phase of a conflict. Curtis Tarr points to a demographic trend in the next decade that will make even more difficult the recruitment of qualified personnel in the United States, with its aging population. This trend, unfortunately, coincides with the substantial buildup now planned in U.S. defense forces, in which a premium will be placed upon the recruitment and retention of personnel possessing needed skills to operate sophisticated weapons systems. Such considerations lead more than one writer to suggest the need either for changes in the all-volunteer Army or for some form of peacetime conscription. In particular, it is thought that increased pay, together with a return to the GI Bill benefits, could help stem the tide of current losses. However, money alone, it is cautioned, will not solve the problem of quality recruitment and retention; at least one writer projects that it would take, in any case, several years of remedial action to redress the negative cumulative effect on the manpower base of personnel losses over the last few years.

Legal Constraints on Defense Mobilization

Among the problems confronting the United States in strengthening its defense mobilization capabilities are those resulting from the legal structure: that is to say, the authority granted to the government to engage in mobilization planning and the obstacles that impede near-term procurement in peacetime and the development of an adequate surge capability. Of central importance is the legal relationship between government and industry. This includes the existence of investment disincentives resulting from disadvantageous Department of Defense depreciation and cost reimbursement policies. Leon Reed points to the deleterious effects of federal regulations that impede investment in new industrial processes and technology, which in turn lengthen lead times and limit surge capability. Needed capital formation in defense-related industry is hampered by government cost reimbursement policies that have tended to ignore investment costs. It is suggested that cost projections have been based on historic (allowable) costs, and target profit rates have been based on such cost projections. Hence, contractors have had little incentive to reduce costs, especially if cost-reduction measures would involve restrictions on allowable costs (labor), increases in unallowable costs (investment), and overall reductions in incurred costs (and thus profits).

Other investment disincentives result from Department of Defense depreciation policy, which requires that depreciation for contract costing be based on the historical useful life or the estimated economic useful life of a piece of equipment. This is said to be the lowest depreciation rate prescribed by any government. Its effect is to limit severely the rate at which contractors can be reimbursed for new investments. In government-owned production facilities, the problem of plant and machinery obsolescence is even greater as a result of contradictory policies. While seeking to maintain, under direct governmental control, an "essential nucleus" to meet current and emergency needs, Congress has mandated that privately owned facilities be used to the greatest extent possible. As a result, needed modernization of government-owned facilities has been deferred to such an extent that this sector represents a rapidly aging capability. This is true especially in the machine tools industry, which represents a critical—and often overlooked—bottleneck in the American mobilization base.

Finally, as in government-industry relations more broadly, the defense sector has become subject to a large amount of socioeconomic legislation, compliance requirements, and punitive enforcement provisions, whose effect is to divert time and effort to reporting and reviewing procedures and plans. In this respect, the extent of government regulation is unprecedented. It is said to exceed even that during the Vietnam War period, not to speak of World War II and the Korean War, and possibly to render irrelevant past experience in assessing the adequacy of our mobilization infrastructure for the future. To the extent that the Reagan Administration can eliminate or streamline regulatory "red tape," mobilization potential will be enhanced.

Raw Materials Supply

Another major deficiency lies in raw materials supply, especially at levels adequate to meet the needs of presently planned defense increases or to respond to even greater surge needs in defense programs. In his analysis of American import dependence in the nonfuel minerals sector, E. F. Andrews suggests the need for policies that will help prevent interruptions in supply, since we live in a world in which increasingly a global political marketplace has replaced and overshadowed a global economic marketplace. In the long term, time and technology provide the opportunity to create potential substitutes for many, if not all, critical minerals, which are often drawn from politically unstable countries or regions, but this will not solve the formidable mobilization problems posed by shortfalls in nonfuel minerals in the years just ahead. At the present time, according to Alton Slay, the United States remains totally dependent upon imports for as many as twelve nonfuel minerals and heavily import dependent for twenty-three of forty critical nonfuel minerals. Many of these commodities are as indispensable to the defense sector as they are to the peacetime civilian economy.

Our national stockpile is said to be grossly deficient because it is below established goals in as many as thirty-seven critical minerals. Before they can be used, moreover, these stocks must often be upgraded to processed or semifinished form, which takes time and is energy intensive. By expanding domestic sources, it would be possible to reduce import dependence on such minerals as cobalt, bauxite, chromium, platinum, zinc, fluorspar, nickel and titanium. But the lead time for bringing new mineral deposits into production is as long as a decade even in the absence of federal regulations, which currently include eighty different pieces of legislation related to mineral production administered by as many as twenty separate federal agencies. Furthermore, in addition to uncertainties about continued access to such minerals at levels sufficient to meet potential surge needs, our domestic minerals processing capacity is considered to be inadequate.

In this volume, then, concern is expressed about the need for a nonfuel minerals policy that is linked to the broader issue of the adequacy of our defense mobilization infrastructure. This includes national stockpiling policies with sufficient reserves of strategic minerals. It is also noted that analogies can be drawn between nonfuel minerals and oil, with the experience of the last decade in the supply of oil providing insights into the future potential cartelization of nonfuel minerals and politically induced interruptions or disruptions in supply. In planning mobilization or surge production contingencies, therefore, one would be foolhardy to assume the continued flow of minerals from abroad at normal peacetime rates.

Similarly, it is noted that, for the foreseeable future, our defense industry, together with our armed forces, will remain so heavily dependent on the immediate availability of oil and other fossil fuels that the present energy vulnerability of the West raises serious doubts about our ability to mobilize for long or even short military conflicts. According to David Deese, several simultaneous changes in the international security environment have produced a series of ominous potential threats to U.S. energy security. The decline in the efficacy of extended nuclear guarantees as a result of changes in the superpower strategic nuclear balance has enhanced the importance of conventional forces, which are heavily dependent on large supplies of energy, at a time when the sources of energy themselves are highly vulnerable to interruption. In fact, the most likely scenario for conflict in the near term probably would be focused on the control of Persian Gulf oilfields. In the other contingency most widely discussed, a Soviet-Warsaw Pact attack against Western Europe, it must be assumed that the oilfields in the Persian Gulf, as well as tanker shipping, would be the object of attack. These trends, in turn, coincide with inadequate policies to strengthen the American Strategic Petroleum Reserve, which is said to be little more than 10% of its intended level—or roughly the equivalent of three to four weeks of U.S. petroleum imports at current rates of consumption.

Key Support Services: Communications, Air Transport and Facilities Construction

The defense mobilization infrastructure also encompasses command, control and communications (C^3) capabilities, most of which are provided by the private sector. In fact, the surge capability inherent in our private telecommunications system would be indispensable in the event of a crisis: as Lee Paschall notes, the great diversity of telecommunications routes, facilities and equipment provides a potentially survivable national command structure. However, the growth of private carrier networks over the last generation has eroded the once dominant position of the American Telephone and Telegraph Company (AT&T), with uncertain consequences for the national telecommunications infrastructure that would be needed in various wartime contingencies. From the 1950s until the present, AT&T has faced antitrust suits which have been opposed by Secretaries of Defense from the Eisenhower Administration to the Reagan Administration.

Here, as in other issue areas, we confront the choice between the needs of defense and other national values. What has been termed the multivendor private sector communications system that has emerged in recent years may prove more expensive than the "end to end" services of a single supplier of communications to the Department of Defense. In the communications environment of the 1980s, the question is asked, who would undertake the planning provided by the previous single supplier? Finding an answer to such a question is said to constitute an urgent priority, for our communications infrastructure has grown vulnerable to physical attack, to electronic disruption, and to interception at precisely the time when strategies of flexible response, and more recently the countervailing strategy, have placed unprecedented demands upon it.

Analogous to the private sector contribution to our national communications system in wartime is the potential afforded by the Civil Reserve Air Fleet (CRAF) possessed by privately owned commercial airlines. The civil aircraft fleet of the United States and those of its allies provide an indispensable surge capacity in the rapid movement of military personnel in conflict zones. Ralph Novak, however, poses fundamental questions about the adequacy of the Civil Reserve Air Fleet, which is a voluntary program with participating airlines but which faces numerous deficiencies. These include disparities between numbers of aircraft and the availability of pilots to fly them in a mobilization contingency, since most airline pilots do not belong to reserve components. Uncertainties over the cargo capacity of CRAF, especially in regard to "oversized" military equipment, might also pose problems. The relative lack of integration of the civil air fleets of the United States and its allies into the defense mobilization infrastructure is contrasted with the record of Aeroflot, the national airline of the Soviet Union, which is headed by an Air Force general officer and regularly participates in military exercises with Soviet military units. It is noted that similar inadequacies may arise in the American land and maritime transport sectors, especially given the uncertain future of AMTRAK, the potential for severe port congestion in times of rapid mobilization, and the overall erosion of the American merchant marine fleet.

Attention is also focused on the ability of the United States to marshal quickly its facilities construction capabilities, which has been a key pacing issue in obtaining both manpower and production expansion in the past. We have grossly underestimated facility requirements and construction costs in previous mobilizations, and we have consistently undervalued the role of the construction industry in overall mobilization planning. Changes in military technology that reduce warning time and place in doubt the safety of the American industrial home base simply increase the need for prior planning and updated doctrines with respect to construction support of mobilization. It is possible, of course, that the next war will be short and unaffected by construction potential, but, as noted so often in this volume, we cannot count on that eventuality, or make it the centerpiece of defense planning. And without a detailed M-day construction program to support mobilization plans, the strategies of forward basing, ready reserves and rapid deployment may be seriously compromised, no matter what scenario for future conflict is hypothesized.

The Potential Contribution of Allies

The available defense mobilization infrastructure extends beyond the United States to allies to whose security we are committed. Two European allies, Britain and France, maintain extensive arms industries which enjoy huge export markets. NATO standardization and interoperability are linked to the broader importance of the idea of a transatlantic market and a "two-way street" in arms procurement, although the United States has sold far more weapons systems to the allies than it has purchased from them. As a result of shifts in comparative advantage, however, the United States has become heavily dependent on imports of electronics and other component technologies vitally important to its defense mobilization capabilities. The growing Japanese share of the American automobile market illustrates the potential impact of this change on mobilization planning, for the automobile industry would have the task of producing the land combat vehicles needed for a mobilization surge. As Japan has become the world's leading builder of ships, similar intra-alliance dependencies may exist with respect to the mobilization of maritime power.

There is an even greater defense mobilization base that, in theory at least, is implicit in the notion of technology transfer and the development of indigenous arms industries in a large number of countries, many of them in the Third World. It has been suggested that agreements between the United States and several advanced developing countries might lead eventually to the licensing or coproduction of sophisticated weapons systems and components, and that this diffusion of defense production capabilities might result in effective reserves of military equipment for conflict-ridden areas. Such agreements, however, lie more in a hypothetical future than in the present; in any event, it is noted, such systems are generally more expensive for medium-sized powers to produce than are imports of the same systems from such countries as the United

States, and the volume of such production is said to be miniscule by comparison with major arms suppliers.

On a related theme, it is possible to assess the advantages and disadvantages that accrue to states from reliance on overseas markets to strengthen and broaden their domestic weapons base as well as the respective gains and losses to states which rely on imports. The question may be posed whether smaller and less complex weapons systems, produced in large numbers in medium-sized powers, as well as in the United States, under various forms of coproduction agreements, might increase the stockpiles that could be prepositioned in or near potential conflict zones or rapidly produced in times of war. As an alternative approach to coproduction of weapons systems, it is conceivable that the United States should avoid integrated production in favor of dual coproduction, which provides for the maintenance of separate—and therefore more secure—production bases within each partner nation. And with those smaller allied or friendly powers who do not have the capacity for full dual coproduction, we should encourage offset production of weapons systems, as we did in the NATO F-16 deal. In offset production, portions of a major weapons system—rather than the system as a whole—may be produced in a smaller ally, so as to hold down the costs of "buying American" and to encourage standardization. As a result, the United States might well become dependent on the return flow of essential components, but it could always maintain a duplicative, if temporarily unused, domestic production base, just in case this flowback from abroad were interrupted or found to be inadequate.

In an assessment of overall NATO needs, Thomas Callaghan calls for a NATO defense mobilization capability, the requirement for which has become more pressing as the potential for a Warsaw Pact attack that might include conventional forces has grown because of the eroding deterrent effect of the American strategic nuclear guarantee under conditions of perceived nuclear parity. In addition, several states in the Western Pacific hold important potential as part of an extended industrial mobilization infrastructure. As in the case of Western Europe, the United States has entered into coproduction agreements with Japan and the Republic of Korea for certain defense systems, such as aircraft, tanks and guns. Other coproduction agreements exist with Taiwan. The United States enjoys access to huge weapons overhaul and maintenance facilities, not only in Northeast Asia but also in the Philippines, as Leonard Unger points out in a survey of such infrastructure in the region that might be available to the United States in time of need. It is also suggested that more attention be paid to the potential contribution of Australia, especially with respect to the provision of raw material supplies.

Among allies, then, the defense mobilization infrastructure consists essentially of three components: (1) the bases and other defense facilities directly or indirectly available to the United States under existing agreements; (2) the production capabilities for weapons systems that now are devoted to such purposes, either under licensing agreements with the United States or as part of an indigenous arms industry, especially in the case of Britain and France; and (3) the surge potential that could be made available by the conversion of such industries as electronics, automobiles and shipbuilding to wartime production.

Policy Implications and Recommendations

This volume provides not only an opportunity for an extended critique of the existing mobilization infrastructure of the United States and its allies, but also the occasion for proposals designed to remedy perceived deficiencies. In general, these proposals fall into two broad conceptual categories: those of a short-term nature whose purpose is to improve the readiness of existing capabilities, and those of a longer-term nature intended to increase surge capability. Broadly speaking, the priority attached to the first or second category is a function of varying assumptions made about the nature, level and duration of potential conflict. For example, the longer the hypothesized conflict and the greater the warning time, the greater the need to emphasize surge capability. The shorter the conflict and the warning time hypothesized, the greater the need to stress readiness—although it is suggested that both approaches are necessary to the development of an adequate and balanced U.S. defense mobilization infrastructure.

Several policy implications and recommendations emerge from the chapters in this volume:

(1) A national centralized mobilization authority should be reestablished, perhaps at the National Security Council (NSC) level. However, on M-day, the Executive Branch must be prepared to decentralize contracting authority, in particular by expanding dollar thresholds. This became necessary in World War II in order to handle the magnitude of contract work. It is necessary to set policy controls and broadly expanded levels of authority now so that mobilization planning can proceed using M-day rules, not peacetime rules.

(2) Cost plus a fixed fee (CPFF) contracts, used in 1917 and again in the 1940 initial mobilization phase, are controversial yet necessary because they allow construction to begin before plans and specifications are made final, and provide guarantees to the contractor that he will not face prohibitive losses as a result of rapidly rising and unpredictable labor and material costs. The decision to use CPFF under certain conditions where rapid construction is essential should be made in peacetime to ensure adequate surge capabilities during mobilization.

(3) The impact of environmental protection on mobilization should be reconsidered, and such regulations should be modified as necessary in light of agreed mobilization priorities and needs. The need for such a review seems obvious, since the effect of environmental protection requirements on defense mobilization was not generally known when they were first enacted.

(4) Plans and procedures should be available to halt work on non-essential projects on M-day so that such resources can be directed immediately to wartime production. An organization for review of such projects could have membership from the Federal Emergency Management Agency (FEMA), the Army, Navy, Air Force, and the Maritime Commission.

(5) With respect to key sectors of the defense industrial base, Congressional oversight is too diffuse, and should be given a more central focus. Civil works, for example, falls within the purview of the Public Works Committee, military construction within the Armed Services Committee, the contract construction industry within the Small Business and Commerce Committees. No single Committee is charged with addressing the issue of mobilization infrastructure as a whole, although the Preparedness Subcommittee of the Senate Armed Services Committee, together with the Defense Industrial Base Panel of the House Armed Services Committee, provide an important Congressional forum for the systematic review of the adequacy of the defense mobilization base in many of the dimensions considered in this volume. Given the importance of mobilization infrastructure, a broader effort should be made to review existing legislation, and to propose new legislation, from an integrated perspective. Such a perspective is now lacking.

(6) The maintenance of a national communications structure is indispensable to our national security, and should be accorded a high priority in defense preparedness planning. However, since as much as 90% of our communications facilities is provided by the private sector, decisions related to communications services and technologies may be taken without due consideration of their impact on national security concerns. For this reason, the federal government should provide incentives to encourage potential suppliers to make needed investment in communications facilities to meet specified Department of Defense needs.

(7) The Civil Reserve Air Fleet (CRAF), which included some 430 aircraft in 1980, should be expanded to include all commercial aircraft of the DC-9/Boeing 737 size and larger. An effort should be made to recruit airline pilots, especially the large number with previous Air Force service, into peacetime reserve units.

(8) Measures must be taken to improve the availability of trained military manpower in the 1980s. The option exists, and is supported by

An Agenda for U.S. Mobilization Policy

some, to return to some form of peacetime draft. Another proposal calls for lengthening the period of active service in the individual ready reserve, together with a more imaginative use of reserve forces in general. Such measures, however, are unlikely to solve the formidable problems of personnel retention now confronting the armed services, especially in competing with the civilian economy for persons with skills in high demand. In order to avoid further shortages in quality personnel, military pay and educational benefits should be significantly increased.

(9) The United States should work with its allies, both in Western Europe and in the Western Pacific, to build a defense-industrial base that will complement that of the United States.

10) We must effect a reconciliation between our national military strategy, which is based on the assumed need for rapid deployment of forces, and the requisite governmental organization, manpower and industrial defense programs, which are said to be inadequate. Otherwise, we will be preparing a mobilization base that has little relevance to national strategy.

(11) In order to correct deficiencies in our nonfuel minerals policy, we should consider formation of a National Nonfuel Minerals Board with full authority to cut across departmental jurisdictions to design and manage a consistent and comprehensive minerals policy. In order to encourage private sector advice, a President's Resource Advisory Board (PRAB), patterned after the President's Foreign Intelligence Advisory Board, should be constituted, with its membership consisting of distinguished experts. Tax reform should be used to provide incentives to capital investment in new industrial plant and equipment in order to strengthen our nonfuel minerals processing industry. In this regard, greater consideration should be given to the powers of the President under Title III of the Defense Production Act of 1950.

(12) A thorough inventory of reserves and resources in strategic and other minerals should be conducted in order to provide a reliable data base. This includes a survey of mineral potential in lands owned by the government in the western states and in Alaska.

(13) Our present minerals defense stockpile should be reassessed. In order to save time and money, certain items should be stored in their most useful processed form. The possible use of tax incentives should be explored to encourage private stockpiling, and efforts should be made to improve the coordination between private and public stockpile programs. However, the present policy of using the strategic stockpile as a *de facto* economic stockpile, without firm guidance and controls, is unwise and should be discouraged.

(14) Through legislative, regulatory, budgetary or programmatic means, steps should be taken to encourage expansion of domestic production of critical minerals. In order to facilitate surge protection, it

might be wise to prestock key mining equipment, especially those items that have long production lead times and are in short supply.

(15) Efforts should be made to encourage development of substitutes for critical minerals in short domestic supply, and encouragement should be given to the development of manufacturing processes that conserve critical minerals. Exports of minerals such as titanium, whose demand is expected to rise rapidly in the United States after 1982, should be limited. Where appropriate and necessary, as in the case of chromium, the United States should embark on a program designed to recover such minerals. Incentives should be given to the scrap reclamation industry, especially with respect to specialty steels.

(16) The Strategic Petroleum Reserve of the United States should be increased, at least in keeping with established goals which have yet to be met. At the same time, the International Energy Agency's emergency oil-sharing system should be strengthened and plans for its execution made more credible. U.S. military construction programs and NATO infrastructure development should be designed to improve greatly our capacity for storing and distributing fuel in times of emergency. Explicit provisions also should be made to ensure Department of Defense (DOD) access to the Strategic Petroleum Reserve as a fuel source of last resort, complementing DOD's own smaller war stocks.

(17) The present industrial mobilization infrastructure should be preserved and strengthened by continued modernization efforts as well as by the maintenance of built-in, inactive manufacturing capability in key production sectors. Toward that end, mobilization planning should be more directly linked to the current production of defense materiel by expanded use of "surge contracting" techniques, which carry a contractual responsibility for the producer to provide a preset level of expanded production in time of mobilization. In combination with the prestocking of certain long lead time components, surge contracting could greatly accelerate production of weapons and related defense articles.

(18) Several additional steps should be taken to reduce lengthy lead times in defense contracting and production:

(a) In peacetime, contractors should be selected as "planned producers;" i.e., industrial firms which have indicated a willingness to produce a specific military item when mobilization begins, based on surge and/or mobilization production schedules.

(b) Planned contractors, selected in accordance with clearly defined qualifications and stated criteria, should be given preferential treatment in governmental contracts. In peacetime, such firms would have planned with the government and agreed to accelerate production during a crisis.

(c) In order to strengthen industrial capacity to respond to accelerated production needs, multiyear contracting should replace one-year contracts.

The adequacy of our defense mobilization infrastructure is related to other issues that have been of concern to a larger number of Americans. These include declining levels of productivity, the need for greater capital investment in existing industry, and the conduct of research and development leading to new products and increased productivity to meet human needs, whether they be in the civilian or military sectors. If it is clear that each of the seemingly discrete elements of our defense mobilization infrastructure is linked, it should be equally clear that there are fundamental linkages between the defense infrastructure and the broader civilian economy. Unless issues of productivity, capital investment, the training of adequate human resources, the supply of critically important fuel and nonfuel minerals, the conduct of research and development, and the dampening of the corrosive effects of inflation can be managed, we will have neither the defense mobilization infrastructure nor the strong civilian economy upon which our national security and well-being are so vitally dependent in the late twentieth century.

INDEX

Acheson, Dean, 220-1
Addabbo, Joseph P., 231
Afghanistan, 100, 150, 238, 254
Africa, 150, 183, 262
Alexander, Clifford, 83
American Telephone and Telegraph Company (AT&T), 279-80
AMTRAK, 280
Andrews, E.F., 278
ANZUS, 236, 245-8
Armstrong, Bill, 85
Association of Southeast Asian Nations (ASEAN), 243-4
Australia, 184-5, 219, 236, 244-7, 282. *See also* ANZUS

Baruch, Bernard, 132
Beard, Robin, 83
Belgium, 227
"Blitzkrieg" in Europe, 16, 29
Boileau, Oliver C., 226
Brazil, 17, 185
Brehm, William, 271
Brezhnev, Leonid, 29, 188
British Guiana, 187
Brown, Harold, 224, 227
Burma, 236

Callaghan, Thomas, 282
Cambodia, 248
Cato, Marcus, 24
Canada, 117, 183, 219
Caribbean, 187, 196
Carter, Jimmy, 201, 214, 227, 228-9
Central Africa, 188
Central America, 17
Central European Pipeline System, 196, 203
Checinski, Michael, 274
Cold War, 210, 255
Cuba, 187, 204
Czechoslovakia, 100

Danzig, Richard, 121
Deese, David, 279
Dicks, Norman D., 229
Diego Garcia, 200

Eastern Europe, 17
Efimov, N.A., 145
Egypt, 155
Ellis, Richard H., 214
Ennis, Harry, 270
Europe, 189, 219-23, 228, 230-3, 238, 246, 254, 274, 279, 282, 285
European Defense Community, 222

Far East, 99
Federal Republic of Germany, 93, 98, 191, 196, 223-4, 227, 233, 264
First World War, 55, 64, 95-7, 99, 101, 132, 144, 160, 164, 172, 189, 204
Ford, Gerald, 227
Ford, Henry, 226
Fortune, 253
France, 55, 99, 101, 191, 196, 227, 283
Franklin, Benjamin, 222
Friedman, Norman, 18
Frunze, Mikhail, 144, 146

Gabon, 185
Gansler, Jacques, 25, 63
Gates, Thomas, 80
geopolitics, 18
Germany, 24, 33, 64, 95, 101, 150, 191. *See also* Federal Republic of Germany
Gingrich, Newt, 229
Gray, Colin, 272
Great Britain, 29, 33, 55, 85, 88-9, 99, 101, 103, 113, 227, 232, 244, 272, 283
Grechko, A.A., 149
Guinea, 187

Haig, Alexander M., 223
Hayward, T.B., 81
Healey, Denis, 88-9
Hillman, Sidney, 158
Hunt, Kenneth, 232

Ilke, Fred, 120
Indonesia, 198, 236, 245
International Bauxite Association, 187
International Energy Agency, 199, 203
Iran, 199-200

Iraq, 200
Italy, 191, 227

Jamaica, 187
Japan, 29, 186, 191, 193, 198-9, 201, 219, 236-44, 246-7, 281-2
Jones, David, 81

Kaplan, Fred M., 154
Kennedy, John F., 204, 255-6
Kennedy, Robert, 155
Kenya, 200
Khmelnitskaya, Elizaveta, 147
Kissinger, Henry, 20, 232
Komer, Robert W., 226-7
Korea, 64, 160, 164, 171, 246, 248; Korean Veterans, 136; Korean War, 93, 107, 113, 132, 136, 138-40, 196, 221-2, 247, 255, 271, 278; North Korea, 237, 240; South Korea, 236, 238-41, 245-7, 282
Krueger, Paul, 130

Laos, 248
Laqueur, Walter, 20
Latin America, 17
Lew, Allen, Jr., 81
Ludden, H.R., 276
Luns, Joseph, 228-9

Malaysia, 236, 244
Mark, Hans, 113
McLaurin, John, 271
Mexico, 17, 198
Meyer, Edward C., 81, 87, 162
Middle East
  oil embargo of 1973-4, 200; Suez Crisis of 1956 and 1957, 200; War of 1973, 92, 94, 120, 155; U.S.-U.S.S.R. conflict, 248
MOBEX 76, 255
Multinational firms, 18, 19, 26, 200
Murphy, Daniel J., 214
Mutual Assured Destruction, 27-8

Netherlands, The, 227
New Zealand, 219, 236, 244-5, 247. *See also* ANZUS
NIFTY NUGGET 1978, 255, 260, 271
Nixon, Richard, 80
Nonmilitary resources, 14-15
North Atlantic Alliance, 219
North Atlantic Council, 220-1
North Atlantic Treaty Organization (NATO), 66, 71, 93-4, 96, 98, 103-5, 143, 150, 154, 155, 158, 189, 193, 196, 198, 201, 203, 219-36, 246, 255-6, 272, 281-2, 286; NATO Long Term Defense Program, 228
Norway, 224

Novak, Ralph, 280
Nunn, Sam, 83, 225

OPEC, 182, 187
Open market economy, 53-4

Paschall, Lee, 279
Patterson, Robert P., 166
Pearl Harbor, 253, 275
People's Republic of China, 187, 236, 244, 248; Sino-Soviet tensions, 237
Persian Gulf, 103, 150, 188-91, 196, 198, 200, 241, 279
Philippines, The, 186, 236, 242-4, 246-7, 282
Poland, 100-1, 254; Polish military, 151-2; Polish civil defense, 153
PROUD SPIRIT 1980, 255, 260, 271

Rapp, Edward, 273
Reagan, Ronald, 201, 214, 229
Reed, Leon, 277
Republic of China, 236-8, 240-2, 248, 282
REX-78, 260
REX-80 BRAVO, 260
Rhodesia, 262, 267
Rogers, Bernard W., 225, 229-30
Rome, 25
Rumsfeld, Donald H., 227, 255

Sabine, George, 26
SALT II Treaty, 223, 254
Schlesinger, James, 227
Schmidt, Helmut, 264
Second World War, 55-6, 84, 92, 94, 95-7, 99-101, 103, 113-14, 132, 136, 138-9, 144, 147-8, 158, 160, 162, 163-4, 168, 171-2, 181-2, 187, 194, 204, 210, 219, 223, 245, 253, 258, 262, 271, 272, 275, 278, 283
Singapore, 236
Slay, Alton, 25, 278
Sokolovskiy, V.D., 151, 154
Somalia, 200
South Africa, 181, 185-6, 188, 267
Southeast Asia, 88, 236-249
South East Asia Collective Defense Treaty (SEATO), 242-3, 246-7
Soviet Union: Aeroflot, 107; and civil defense, 153; and East Asia, 236-7, 245-9; First Five Year Plan, 145, 148; Frunze Military Academy, 146; Gosplan, 145-6; Kurile Islands, 238; Kuznetz Basin, 151; and mineral reserves, 185-6; Ministry of Defense, 152; and Nazi aggression, 144; and nuclear balance, 233; and the neutron bomb, 150; Obkoms, 146; R & D

Index

institutes, 152; Raikoms, 146; Russian attack, 222; Sino-Soviet tensions, 237; Soviet buildup, 254–5; Soviet Civil War, 144–5; Soviet-Cuban influence in the Caribbean, 187; Soviet growth, 18; Soviet ideology, 102; Soviet leaders, 94, 96–7, 102, 150, 256, 261; Soviet Military Encyclopedia, 143, 151; Soviet military force, 200, 230; Soviet military threat, 97–8, 225; Soviet mining of the Strait of Hormuz, 201; Soviet naval/air positions in Vietnam, 244; Soviet proxies, 201; Soviet Revolution, 144; Soviet warhead population forecast for the 1980s, 205

Spain, 56, 222

Soviet mining of the Strait of Hormuz, 201; Soviet naval/air positions in Vietnam, 244; Soviet proxies, 201; Soviet Revolution, 144; Soviet warhead population forecast for the 1980s, 205

Spain, 56, 222

Stalin, J.V., 146–7, 150

Steinhoff, Johannes, 228

Strait of Hormuz, 201

Strait of Malacca, 241, 244, 245

Surinam, 187

Tarr, Curtis, 276

Thailand, 236, 242–4, 248

Third World, 267–8, 281

Thomason, R. Ewing, 162–3, 173

Truman, Harry S., 162–3, 166

Tupolev, A.N., 152

Turkey, 186, 224

Unger, Leonard, 282

United States:
Administration, 22; Alaska, 160, 265, 285; America's airlines, 104–6, 108–9; American Civil War, 101, 167; American Defense Preparedness Association, 112; American Expeditionary Forces (AEF), 55; American military planners, 104; American Revolution, 55; Armed Forces' Examining and Entrance Station, 73; Armed Forces Qualification Test, 82–3; Arsenal of Democracy, 94; Bureau of Mines, 265; civil defense, 154–5; Communications Act of 1934, 209, 213; Congress, 106–7, 129, 137, 139, 159–60, 162, 166–8, 172–4, 182, 212, 224–5, 230, 255–7, 261, 264, 266, 277; Contract Construction Industry, 159–60; Corps of Engineers, 160–1, 163–4, 171–2, 174; Cost Accounting Standard (CAS), 135, 138; Defense budget, 256; Defense Communications Agency, 214; Defense Fuel Supply Center, 196, 200; Defense Industrial Reserve Act, 136; Defense Logistics Agency, 197; Defense Manpower Policy No. 7 (DMP-7), 138; Defense Materials Systems, 132–3; Defense Production Act of 1950, 129–30, 135–6, 140, 183, 188, 194–5, 199, 285–6; Defense Science Board, 112, 131, 136; delayed entry program, 75; Department of Commerce, 265; Department of Defense, 64–5, 69, 75, 78, 80–9, 105–7, 114, 117, 122, 191–9, 203, 205, 210, 213–4, 219, 257, 260, 265, 277, 280, 284, 286; Department of Energy, 194, 197, 199, 265; Department of the Interior, 265; Department of Justice, 210, 212–3; Department of Labor, 265; Department of State, 197, 265; Department of Transportation, 265; Department of the Treasury, 135; Economic Regulatory Administration, 199; Eisenhower Administration, 280; elite groups, 19; Emergency Petroleum Allocation Act, 199; Executive Office of the President, 130; experience in Korea, 107, 160; Federal Aviation Administration, 107; Federal Emergency Management Agency, 129–30, 171, 174, 284; Field and Forage Act of 1861, 168; Five Year Defense Plan, 159, 172; Florida, 184, 204; GI Bill, 68, 85–6; General Accounting Office, 112, 116, 123–4, 135; General Services Administration, 130; Government, 63; Great Society, 256; Hawaii, 160; House Armed Service Committee, 83, 112, 228; House Defense Appropriations Subcommittee, 231; Idaho, 183; ideals, 23; Inactive National Guard, 74; Individual Ready Reserve, 67, 69–70, 72, 74–5, 86, 257, 260; industrial base, 112, 116, 127, 134; Industrial College of the Armed Forces, 62, 119, 253; industrial preparedness measures, 119; Industrial Preparedness Plan Program, 112, 114, 116–17, 120–1, 122–4, 140; Joint Chiefs of Staff, 78, 81, 260; Kennedy buildup, 256; Long Term Defense Plan, 201; middle class, 19–20; Military Airlift Command, 104, 106, 108–9; Military Enlistment Processing Command (MEPCOM), 73; "military-industrial complex," 122; Minimum Essential Emergency Communications Network, 209; Mining and Minerals Policy Act of 1970, 188;

Missouri, 183; Montana, 186; Mutual Security Treaty with Thailand of 1951, 242; National Command Authority, 209, 215; National Communications System, 208; National Defense Stockpile, 130; National Materials and Minerals Policy Act of 1980, 188; National Nonfuel Minerals Board, 264, 285; National Security Act of 1947, 129–30; National Security Council, 62, 283; National Security Resources Board, 129; National Security Telecommunications policy, 215; Navy Civil Engineer Corp, 163; Nixon Administration, 205; Office of Defense Mobilization, 138; Office of Industrial Mobilization, 132; Office of Management and Budget, 197; Office of Emergency Preparedness, 62, 130; Oregon, 186; President, 129, 131, 168, 264; President's authority, 66, 105, 128, 195; Presidential Directive No. 59, 273; President's Foreign Intelligence Advisory Board, 265; Public Works Committee, 173; Rapid Deployment Force, 103, 194, 196; Reagan Administration, 64–5, 280; Rivers and Harbors Act, 160; Roosevelt Administration, 113; Selective Services System (SSS), 73, 257; Senate, 139, 172, 212; Senate Armed Services Committee, 223, 229, 284; Services of the Selected Reserve, 66, 257; Small Business and Commerce Committee, 173; Society of American Military Engineers, 175; Strategic Air Command, 109–10; Strategic and Critical Materials Stockpile Act of 1946, 182; Strategic Materials Act, 182; Strategic Petroleum Reserve, 197–8, 203, 279; U.S.-Japanese Security Treaty, 247; U.S.-Korean Treaty, 247; Utah, 187; in Vietnam, 24; War of 1812, 160; War Production Board, 172; Washington, D.C., 23; weakness of conventional forces, 232; World War II, 55; Wyoming, 187

Vegetius, Flavius Renatus, 54
Venezuela, 198
Ventsov, S.I., 145
Vietnam, 24, 164, 237, 244–5, 248, 256; Vietnam War, 62, 80, 82, 99–100, 117, 122, 139–40, 237, 243, 247, 260, 278
Vishnev, S.M., 148–9

Wadbrook, William, 274
Warsaw Pact, 27, 66, 71, 143, 154–5, 196, 201, 223–6, 227, 230–1, 279, 282
Washington's (George) army, 55
Washington Star, 267
Westmoreland, William C., 81
Whitney, Eli, 226
World War I. *See* First World War
World War II. *See* Second World War

Yugoslavia, 186

Zaire, 181, 183
Zambia, 181, 183
Zimbabwe, 186
Zone of Peace, Freedom and Neutrality (ZOPFAN), 244